ADVISORY PLUS!

Standards-Based Sessions
with Character Education, Learning Styles,
and Assessment Components

By Imogene Forte
and Sandra Schurr

Incentive Publications, Inc.
Nashville, Tennessee

Illustrated by Marta Drayton
Cover by Kristy Jones
Edited by Patience Camplair

ISBN 978-0-86530-622-6
Library of Congress Control Number 2004102586

2   3   4   5   6   7   8   9   10   11   10   09   08

PRINTED IN THE UNITED STATES OF AMERICA
www.incentivepublications.com

TABLE OF CONTENTS

✳

September

THEME: SCHOOL   VALUE: RESPONSIBILITY

October

THEME: SELF-CONCEPT AND RELATIONSHIPS   VALUE: RESPECT

NOVEMBER

DECEMBER

January

February

MARCH

APRIL

MAY

APPENDIX

HOW TO USE THIS BOOK

Educators today are called upon to teach far more than basic skills. In addition to the curriculum demands associated with content-based instruction, teachers are also expected to help students develop character and explore opportunities and demands present in their daily lives in order to form a basis for good decision making. Research has shown that a positive learning community, attention to individual student needs, and the employment of student-centered, active learning strategies results in a higher level of student success. *Advisory Plus!* has been written to present instructional strategies and student activities in a clear and concise manner to meet the demands placed on teachers and students in today's schools. The ready-to-use format will aid students in achieving academic and social success, but more importantly, in the development of attitudes and learning styles. The activities and projects will aid the development of traits and attitudes leading to positive self-concept and of foundations of character that will serve them well throughout life.

Each module outlines a monthly theme and value that fits into a yearlong advisory program.

Included for each month is:

- a Big Idea for students to ponder
- Writing Prompts and Discussion Starters to encourage higher level thinking
- a Calendar of monthly activities to keep teachers organized
- Teacher Guidelines that make the activities ready-to-use
- Reproducible Student Activity Pages to facilitate active student involvement
- and a Rubric Assessment to serve as a review and/or evaluation

The central theme and value for each month is:

SEPTEMBER: Theme—School; Value—Responsibility

OCTOBER: Theme—Self-Concept and Relationships; Value—Respect

NOVEMBER: Theme—Communication; Value—Honesty

DECEMBER: Theme—Community; Value—Generosity

JANUARY: Theme—Global Awareness; Value—Knowledge

FEBRUARY: Theme—Heroes and Heroines; Value—Courage

MARCH: Theme—Environment; Value—Stewardship

APRIL: Theme—Books and Media; Value—Humor

MAY: Theme—Future; Value—Vision

HOW TO USE THIS BOOK

Sample Student Activities Include:

- Responsible Goal Setting
- Five Ways to Look at a Concept or Big Idea
- Welcoming Responsible Parents as School Partners
- Building Responsible Relationships
- Identifying the "Self" in Self-Concept
- Respect and Relationships
- A Special, One-Of-A-Kind Person
- Showing Respect for Independence
- Communication Barriers and Blunders
- Dealing with Honesty in Difficult Situations
- Actions Sometimes Speak Louder Than Words
- Generosity Begins at Home
- People Who Are Generous with Their Time, Talent, or Treasure
- Social Services that Satisfy
- Cultural Explorations
- Knowledge Means Many Things to Many People
- Awarding the "Quest for Knowledge" Honor
- Questioning Real-Life Issues as Afforded by School Work
- A Hero Is More Than a Sub Sandwich!
- American Women Who Became Heroes Under Duress
- Tell About a Time When You Felt Like a Hero
- Literary Heroes and Heroines
- Stewardship: What Does It Mean?
- Conservation and Recycling
- Participating in an Environmental Stewardship Campaign
- Role-playing an Ecology Council for Your Class
- How Do You Feel About Reading?
- Let's Measure Your Humor Quotient!
- Introducing the Elements of Literature
- Smuggling More Humor Into the Classroom
- Censorship in the Media
- Learning to Write a Media Review
- Free to Be You and Me
- Envisioning a Perfect Community for Life in the Future
- Consumerism and Careers of the Future

©2004 Incentive Publications, Inc.
Nashville, TN

HOW TO USE THIS BOOK

Primarily, this book is designed to give teachers a classroom-ready resource to help students entrusted to their care become secure, self-confident individuals by enabling them to acquire and use the values, goals, and attributes reflective of positive character development. These activities may be added to the curriculum in a number of ways, such as:

- a component of before- or after-school special programs.

- an "extra" within normal classroom lessons.

- an element of team-teaching.

- the basis of a school-wide advisory program.

- use in a homeschool environment.

Therefore, teachers will find that with very little effort, they may integrate an advisory program into their existing lesson plans. The activities included in *Advisory Plus!* will provide students with the ability to make good decisions, be better students, make friends, and consider a world larger than the one with which they may be familiar.

MODULE ONE
SEPTEMBER
✳

THEME: SCHOOL   VALUE: RESPONSIBILITY

If a generally accepted tenet of the school's responsibility to the student is to provide every opportunity possible for every student to become the very best that he or she can be, what then is the responsibility of the student to the school?

- **HOW ARE YOU SMART?—PURPOSE:** To review the eight multiple intelligences and correlate them with appropriate student products and performances based on the individual characteristics of each intelligence

- **RESPONSIBLE GOAL SETTING—PURPOSE:** To establish a set of short-term goals for the current school year

- **WHO IS RESPONSIBLE FOR YOUR BEHAVIOR?— PURPOSE:** To determine who is responsible for one's own behavior

- **SILENCE BREEDS VIOLENCE—PURPOSE:** To examine the issue of violence in schools both at home and elsewhere

- **BUILDING RESPONSIBLE RELATIONSHIPS—PURPOSE:** To explore how personal relationships at home and school are formed and how they can be nurtured over time

- **WHAT AN ORCHESTRA CAN TEACH US ABOUT RESPONSIBILITY— PURPOSE:** To use the orchestra as a metaphor for teaching harmony and responsibility for others

- **HOW ORGANIZED ARE YOU ANYWAY?—PURPOSE:** To help students self-assess their organizational skills

- **THE "ME I AM LEARNING TO BE" FOLDER—PURPOSE:** To create a box of artifacts that best describe the student's many academic and personal strengths, talents, and interests

- **PICTURE BOOK, PICTURE PERFECT—PURPOSE:** To read a number of children's picture books with a school theme in order to examine the picture book genre and how school is portrayed through children's fiction

- **BECOMING A RESPONSIBLE READER—PURPOSE:** To examine student attitudes about reading

- **CALCULATING READING SPEEDS—PURPOSE:** To analyze various reading speeds and when each is appropriate for special circumstances

- **GOING ON A TEXTBOOK SCAVENGER HUNT—PURPOSE:** To discover the various parts of a typical textbook for the middle grades

- **PICTURING THE TEXTBOOK—PURPOSE:** To represent a textbook section or chapter with drawings, diagrams, and illustrations

- **WHO, ULTIMATELY, IS RESPONSIBLE FOR YOUR TEST PERFORMANCE? —PURPOSE:** To determine the causes, consequences, and corrections for test anxiety

- **WRITING AND ANSWERING HIGHER-LEVEL QUESTIONS—PURPOSE:** To introduce a wide variety of question frames for both writing and answering higher-level questions based on Bloom's Taxonomy of Cognitive Development

- **THE FIVE-STEP PARAGRAPH—PURPOSE:** To show students how to construct a comprehensive five-step paragraph on any topic

- **FIVE WAYS TO LOOK AT A CONCEPT OR BIG IDEA—PURPOSE:** To use a variety of graphic organizers to record information about an important concept or big idea learned in any given subject area

- **WELCOMING RESPONSIBLE PARENTS AS SCHOOL PARTNERS— PURPOSE:** To explore ways that parents can become more active and responsible in the school setting

- **HOW ARE YOU AT STUDENT-LED CONFERENCES?—PURPOSE:** To demonstrate how student-led conferences can be an effective and responsible tool for today's middle schooler

- **HOW GOOD IS YOUR ADVISORY PROGRAM?—PURPOSE:** To evaluate the student advisory program

©2004 Incentive Publications, Inc.
Nashville, TN

WRITING PROMPTS/DISCUSSION STARTERS

School Days, School Days
Dear Old Golden Rule Days
Reading, writing, and arithmetic
Taught to the tune of a hickory stick
School Days, School Days
Dear Old Golden Rule Days

Write about the differences there are in your school days and the school days of long ago, portrayed in the words to this song.

_____

_____

_____

_____

_____

_____

_____

_____

"It is the supreme art of the teacher to awaken joy in creative expression and knowledge."
—Albert Einstein, physicist

Write about a teacher you have had that personified this famous scientist's definition of the art of teaching. Tell what this teacher did to "awaken joy in creative expression and knowledge" for you.

_____

_____

_____

_____

_____

_____

_____

SEPTEMBER CALENDAR

***

THEME: SCHOOL   VALUE: RESPONSIBILITY

WEEK ONE

DAY ONE	**"How Are You Smart?"** Completing a self-rating scale to determine individual intelligences
DAY TWO	**"Responsible Goal Setting"** Completing a graphic organizer and assessing its value as a study aid
DAY THREE	**"Who Is Responsible for Your Behavior?"** Planning and participating in a debate related to behavior
DAY FOUR	**"Silence Breeds Violence"** Participating in a case study and role-play
DAY FIVE	**"Building Responsible Relationships"** Creating a journal entry

WEEK TWO

DAY ONE	**"What an Orchestra Can Teach Us About Responsibility"** Preparing and presenting an interactive lecture
DAY TWO	**"How Organized Are You Anyway?"** Self-assessing individual organizational skills
DAY THREE	**"The 'Me I'm Learning to Be' Folder"** Listing and speaking about what personal possessions tell about a person
DAY FOUR	**"Picture Book, Picture Perfect"** Reading and Reviewing picture books with a school theme
DAY FIVE	**"Becoming a Responsible Reader"** Completing written starter statements about reading

SEPTEMBER CALENDAR

---*---

THEME: SCHOOL   VALUE: RESPONSIBILITY

WEEK THREE

DAY ONE	**"Calculating Reading Speeds"** Partnering for a hands-on experiment to determine individual reading speed
DAY TWO	**"Going on a Textbook Scavenger Hunt"** Completing a recording sheet of findings related to investigating a textbook's content
DAY THREE	**"Picturing the Textbook"** Completing a set of study notes
DAY FOUR	**"Who, Ultimately, Is Responsible for Your Test Performance?"** Completing a self-check quiz on computer for test taking
DAY FIVE	**"Writing and Answering Higher-Level Questions"** Completing a set of higher order questions as chapter/test review

WEEK FOUR

DAY ONE	**"The Five-Step Paragraph"** Writing a position paper on a topic of high interest
DAY TWO	**"Five Ways to Look at a Concept or Big Idea"** Producing a variety of graphic organizers to use as study guides
DAY THREE	**"Welcoming Responsible Parents as School Partners"** Producing a questionnaire and graph to evaluate the level of parent involvement in the school
DAY FOUR	**"How Are You at Student-Led Conferences?"** Generating and defending a mock portfolio through a student-led conference
DAY FIVE	**"How Good Is Your Advisory Program?"** Completing a student questionnaire to evaluate effectiveness of the advisory program

THEME: SCHOOL   VALUE: RESPONSIBILITY

HOW ARE YOU SMART?

PURPOSE: To review the eight multiple intelligences and correlate them with appropriate student products and performances to allow "individual selection of the best product or performance based on intelligences as determined by the rating scale"

TARGETED INTELLIGENCE: All Intelligences

CONTENT/STANDARD FOCUS: Social Studies—Individual Development and Identity; Culture

PRODUCT/PERFORMANCE/STUDENT OUTCOME: Multiple Intelligence Self-Rating Scale

"HOW ARE YOU SMART?" (page 30)

Introduce students to the Multiple Intelligences by using the pages in the Appendix for this purpose (pages 353-354). You may want to reproduce them so each student has their own copy, or you may want to make an overhead transparency or power point presentation for the entire class. Then, direct students to complete the self-rating scale on page 30 and tally the results so they become aware of their strong intelligence areas as well as those less dominant. Ask them to then select the most appropriate product or performance task for their unique set of intelligences. If time permits, encourage the students to generate other product or performance ideas that would be useful on future assignments or projects.

RESPONSIBLE GOAL SETTING

PURPOSE: To establish a set of short-term goals for the current school year

TARGETED INTELLIGENCE: Logical/Mathematical

CONTENT/STANDARD FOCUS: Mathematics—Mathematical Connections

PRODUCT/PERFORMANCE/STUDENT OUTCOME: Graphic Organizer

"RESPONSIBLE GOAL SETTING" (page 31)

Poll the students to determine how many of them know how and like to play checkers or chess. Ask what other board games are popular pastimes for them. Encourage students to talk about gamesmanship, sportsmanship, and all the other concepts, skills, and attitudes that can be learned or applied from popular games. Define and describe what a graphic organizer means and how it can be used in the classroom as learning/recording/thinking tool. After students have completed their goal-driven organizer, stage a sharing session for the total group.

WHO IS RESPONSIBLE FOR YOUR BEHAVIOR?

PURPOSE: To determine who is responsible for one's own behavior

TARGETED INTELLIGENCE: Interpersonal

CONTENT/STANDARD FOCUS: Social Studies—Individuals, Groups, & Institutions

PRODUCT/PERFORMANCE/STUDENT OUTCOME: Debate

"WHO IS RESPONSIBLE FOR YOUR BEHAVIOR?" (page 32)

Ask students to think about both good and poor behavior patterns that they observe in school, at home, or while attending activities and events throughout the community. Discuss reasons why it is so difficult to break a bad habit or behavior pattern once it has been established. Encourage students to tell about recent newspaper articles or television news reports that have involved teenagers doing "wrong" deeds or "getting into trouble." Next, review both the resolutions and the debate process described in this activity. As time permits, break students into small groups and have them debate one of the resolutions according to directions given.

SILENCE BREEDS VIOLENCE

PURPOSE: To examine the issue of student violence both in schools and elsewhere

TARGETED INTELLIGENCE: Bodily/Kinesthetic

CONTENT/STANDARD FOCUS: Health, Safety, Wellness & Social Studies—Individuals, Groups, and Institutions

PRODUCT/PERFORMANCE/STUDENT OUTCOME: Case Study/Role-play

"SILENCE BREEDS VIOLENCE" (page 33)

Review some of the tragic events that have occurred in recent years involving student violence in schools locally and nationally—events such as shootings, thefts, vandalism, and suicides. Encourage students to talk about why kids don't readily "rat on one another" or "interfere" in disputes between gangs, groups, and cliques. Finally, have students react to the idea that "silence breeds violence" and, as time permits, informally act out one of the suggested five scenarios.

BUILDING RESPONSIBLE RELATIONSHIPS

PURPOSE: To explore how personal relationships at home and school are formed and how they can be nurtured over time

TARGETED INTELLIGENCE: Interpersonal and Intrapersonal

CONTENT/STANDARD FOCUS: Social Studies—Individual Development and Identity

PRODUCT/PERFORMANCE/STUDENT OUTCOME: Journal Entry

"BUILDING RESPONSIBLE RELATIONSHIPS" (page 34)

Review the cooperative learning structure of "Think/Pair/Share" with students. Tell students that this strategy calls for students to individually respond to an idea, list some thoughts related to the idea, and then share those responses with a partner. Follow this procedure according to the student directions given for this section.

WHAT AN ORCHESTRA CAN TEACH US ABOUT RESPONSIBILITY

PURPOSE: To use the orchestra as a metaphor for teaching harmony with and responsibility to others

TARGETED INTELLIGENCE: Rhythmic/Musical

CONTENT/STANDARD FOCUS: Social Studies—Individuals, Groups, and Institutions

PRODUCT/PERFORMANCE/STUDENT OUTCOME: Interactive Lecturette

"WHAT AN ORCHESTRA CAN TEACH US ABOUT RESPONSIBILITY" (page 35)

Play a recording of a famous orchestra for the students. Help students to understand both the "magic" of classical music and how the conductor orchestrates the different players and instruments to produce a symphony. Emphasize the fact that each player and instrument is only "part of a whole" and is, therefore, responsible for working with others to produce a lovely sound. Encourage students to react to the three quotations and to spend some time outside of class researching more information about famous orchestras, instruments, and composers, sharing their findings in an informal lecturette or presentation.

HOW ORGANIZED ARE YOU ANYWAY?

PURPOSE: Self-assessment of individual organizational skills

TARGETED INTELLIGENCE: Bodily/Kinesthetic

CONTENT/STANDARD FOCUS: Social Studies—Individual Development and Identity

PRODUCT/PERFORMANCE/STUDENT OUTCOME: Cooperative Learning Task

"HOW ORGANIZED ARE YOU ANYWAY?" (page 36)

Introduce students to the "human graph" concept for this activity and follow the directions as given. Emphasize that any human graph requires the students to line up according to their different positions on an identified issue. One end of the continuum attracts students who strongly agree or agree with the stated issue, while the other end of the continuum attracts students who strongly disagree or disagree, leaving the middle for those who are uncertain where they stand on the issue. It is important that the teacher inform the students ahead of time that they must be able to validate or defend their positions. The result of this activity is a visual representation of where the class stands, in relation to organizational skills, both as a group and as individuals.

THE "ME I AM LEARNING TO BE" FOLDER

PURPOSE: To create a list of possessions that best describe a student's many academic and personal strengths, talents and interests

TARGETED INTELLIGENCE: Intrapersonal

CONTENT/STANDARD FOCUS: Social Studies—Individual Development and Identity

PRODUCT/PERFORMANCE/STUDENT OUTCOME: "Me" Folder and Mini-Speech

"THE 'ME I'M LEARNING TO BE' FOLDER" (page 37)

You may want to introduce this activity by first sharing the contents of a "Me" folder that you have compiled ahead of time, and with items representing your special strengths, talents, hobbies, and interests as the teacher.

PICTURE BOOK, PICTURE PERFECT

PURPOSE: To read a number of children's picture books with a school theme in order to examine the picture book genre and how school is portrayed through children's fiction

TARGETED INTELLIGENCE: Verbal/Linguistic

CONTENT/STANDARD FOCUS: Language Arts—Standards 1, 2, 4, 6, and 9

PRODUCT/PERFORMANCE STUDENT OUTCOME: Book Review and Children's Picture Book

"PICTURE BOOK, PICTURE PERFECT" (page 38)

Provide a collection of children's picture books that have the common theme of "school" or ask students to bring one of their own from home. Review the genre of picture books, focusing on the story at both the literal and figurative levels, as well as on the importance of illustrations when conveying the mood and action of the story line. Encourage students to create their own picture books about middle school kids if time permits.

BECOMING A RESPONSIBLE READER

PURPOSE: To examine student attitudes about reading

TARGETED INTELLIGENCE: Intrapersonal

CONTENT/STANDARD FOCUS: Language Arts—Standards 1, 2, and 11

PRODUCT/PERFORMANCE/STUDENT OUTCOME: Written Starter Statement Responses

"BECOMING A RESPONSIBLE READER" (page 39)

Try to set aside some "personal reading time" during the advisory session to complete this activity. Introduce the task by commenting on your own reading habits.

CALCULATING READING SPEEDS

PURPOSE: To analyze various reading speeds and when each is appropriate for special circumstances

TARGETED INTELLIGENCE: Logical/Mathematical

CONTENT/STANDARD FOCUS: Mathematics—Problem Solving & Science—Inquiry

PRODUCT/PERFORMANCE/STUDENT OUTCOME: Partner Hands-On Experiment to determine individual reading speed

"CALCULATING READING SPEEDS" (page 40)

Divide students into pairs or small collaborative groups. Make certain that each subset of students has either a stopwatch or access to a watch/clock with a minute hand so they can use it to time their individual reading speeds.

GOING ON A TEXTBOOK SCAVENGER HUNT

PURPOSE: To discover the various parts of a typical textbook for middle grades

TARGETED INTELLIGENCE: Verbal/Linguistic

CONTENT/STANDARD FOCUS: Language Arts—Standards 1 and 3

PRODUCT/PERFORMANCE/STUDENT OUTCOME: Recording Sheet

"GOING ON A TEXTBOOK SCAVENGER HUNT" (page 41)

Review the concept of a "scavenger hunt" with students as a kind of "treasure hunt" where small groups of individuals are given a list of things to look for in a predetermined space or area. Explain to students that they will be hunting for "treasures"—unique parts of their textbooks.

PICTURING THE TEXTBOOK

PURPOSE: To represent a textbook section or chapter with drawings, diagrams, and illustrations

TARGETED INTELLIGENCE: Visual/Spatial

CONTENT/STANDARD FOCUS: Language Arts—Standards 3 and 12

PRODUCT/PERFORMANCE/STUDENT OUTCOME: Set of Illustrated Study Notes

"PICTURING THE TEXTBOOK" (page 42)

Point out to students that note taking can have many different forms including the recording of ideas through graphics, pictures, drawings, sketches, or illustrations. This method can accomplish the same end results as one gets from taking notes in outline or note card fashion.

WHO, ULTIMATELY, IS RESPONSIBLE FOR YOUR TEST PERFORMANCE?

PURPOSE: To determine the causes, consequences, and corrections for test anxiety

TARGETED INTELLIGENCE: Verbal/Linguistic

CONTENT/STANDARD FOCUS: Language Arts—Standards 5 and 12

PRODUCT/PERFORMANCE STUDENT OUTCOME: Self-Check Quiz

"WHO, ULTIMATELY, IS RESPONSIBLE FOR YOUR TEST PERFORMANCE?" (page 43)

Introduce this activity just before or after a test so that students can relate it to the real testing situation in class. Be certain to spend time discussing the individual results of this Self-Check Quiz, debriefing common student responses and offering positive suggestions for handling test anxiety problems. Conduct a follow-up dialogue with students to analyze the pros and cons of various types of tests, ranging from objective tests to essay tests. Experiment with different testing strategies, including a Bloom Test that has one question at each level of Bloom's Taxonomy, each worth a different point value but whose total count equals 100, or a Cooperative Learning Test that requires students to answer some questions as individual students and others with a partner.

WRITING AND ANSWERING HIGHER-LEVEL QUESTIONS

PURPOSE: To introduce a wide variety of question frames for both writing and answering higher-order questions, based on Bloom's Taxonomy of Cognitive Development

TARGETED INTELLIGENCE: Verbal/Linguistic and Logical/Mathematical

CONTENT/STANDARD FOCUS: Language Arts—Standard 11 & Mathematics—Problem Solving; Communication; Reasoning; Connections & Science—Physical Science; Life Science; Earth and Space Science; Science and Technology & Social Studies—Global Connections; Time, Continuity, and Change; People, Places and Environments; Power, Authority, and Governance; Production, Distribution, and Consumption

PRODUCT/PERFORMANCE/STUDENT OUTCOME: Set of Higher-Level Questions as Chapter/Test Review

"WRITING AND ANSWERING HIGHER-LEVEL QUESTIONS" (page 44)

After students have completed a unit of study or a textbook chapter, have them review the content as individuals or in small groups by using Bloom's Taxonomy of Cognitive Development to create a series of questions on the material covered in class for each level of Bloom. Use the class-generated questions as the basis for a test.

THE FIVE-STEP PARAGRAPH

PURPOSE: To show students how to construct a comprehensive five-step paragraph on any topic

TARGETED INTELLIGENCE: Logical/Mathematical and Verbal/Linguistic

CONTENT/STANDARD FOCUS: Mathematics—Communication & Science—History and Nature of Science; Science in Personal and Social Perspectives & Social Studies—Time Continuity and Change; People, Places, and Environment & Language Arts—Standards 7 and 11

PRODUCT/PERFORMANCE/STUDENT OUTCOME: Position Paper on a topic of high interest

"THE FIVE-STEP PARAGRAPH" (page 45)

Introduce this strategy as a model for writing a short, but concise, position paper on a given topic. Review ways to structure an opening paragraph or lead and a thesis statement. Point out to students that all three paragraphs in the body of the paper are identical in form—one good topic sentence and three supporting details. Finally, help students to understand that it is important to tie the ideas in the paper together by restating the thesis sentence in another way as a summary or conclusion to the ideas presented.

FIVE WAYS TO LOOK AT A CONCEPT OR BIG IDEA

PURPOSE: To use a variety of graphic organizers to record information about an important concept or big idea learned in any given subject area

TARGETED INTELLIGENCE: Logical/Mathematical and Visual/Spatial

CONTENT/STANDARD FOCUS: Science—Unifying Concepts and Processes; Mathematics—Mathematical Connections

PRODUCT/PERFORMANCE/STUDENT OUTCOME: A Variety of Graphic Organizers

"FIVE WAYS TO LOOK AT A CONCEPT OR BIG IDEA" (page 46)

Introduce students to the five different types of graphic organizers that are most commonly used in note taking and in the structuring of major concepts or ideas. Others you might want to cover at the same time would be Venn Diagrams or Webs. If time permits, consider having the students outline a report on a topic of their choice recording information in the format of graphic organizers.

WELCOMING RESPONSIBLE PARENTS AS SCHOOL PARTNERS

PURPOSE: To explore ways that parents can become more active and responsible in the school setting

TARGETED INTELLIGENCE: Interpersonal and Logical/Mathematical

CONTENT/STANDARD FOCUS: Mathematics—Problem Solving; Mathematical Connections

PRODUCT/PERFORMANCE/STUDENT OUTCOME: Questionnaire and Graph

"WELCOMING RESPONSIBLE PARENTS AS SCHOOL PARTNERS" (page 47)

Conduct a discussion with students on the important role of parent participation in the school especially at the middle grade level. Ask students to comment on reasons why parent participation is high in elementary school but much less in both middle and high schools. Discuss the five levels of parent participation in your school setting, as well as ways to increase participation.

28

©2004 INCENTIVE PUBLICATIONS, Inc.
Nashville, TN

HOW ARE YOU AT STUDENT-LED CONFERENCES?

PURPOSE: To demonstrate how student-led conferences can be an effective and responsible tool for today's middle schooler

TARGETED INTELLIGENCE: Interpersonal, Intrapersonal, and Verbal/Linguistic

CONTENT/STANDARD FOCUS: Language Arts—Standards 4, 5, 11, and 12

PRODUCT/PERFORMANCE/STUDENT OUTCOME: Mock Portfolio

"HOW ARE YOU AT STUDENT-LED CONFERENCES?" (page 48)

Talk to students about the trend of encouraging student-led conferences in the middle grades. Ask students to identify what they see as the advantages and disadvantages of this concept from several different perspectives—teacher, parent, and student. Instruct students to use their current work folders or notebooks as sources of artifacts that could be put into a portfolio and that could become a springboard for a parent conference. Dialogue with them about the importance of reflecting on their assigned work and how various pieces can be used to document what students know and can do. Assign students to work with a classmate and simulate the student-led conference scenario, exchanging roles as needed.

HOW GOOD IS YOUR ADVISORY PROGRAM?

PURPOSE: To evaluate the student advisory program

TARGETED INTELLIGENCE: Intrapersonal

CONTENT/STANDARD FOCUS: Social Studies—Individual Development and Identity

PRODUCT/PERFORMANCE/STUDENT OUTCOME: Student Questionnaire

"HOW GOOD IS YOUR ADVISORY PROGRAM?" (page 49)

Discuss the Student Advisory Questionnaire in a total group setting. Encourage students to be candid about feelings and opinions and to engage in a lively exchange of ideas. Complete the questionnaires and use the results to revise, develop, and expand further programs.

THEME: SCHOOL   VALUE: RESPONSIBILITY

HOW ARE YOU SMART?

Multiple Intelligences Self-Rating Scale

Directions: Analyze your own multiple intelligences by rating how well each intelligence describes you on a 1 to 10 scale, with 10 being the highest ranking. Then, try to select two different product or performance research/reporting formats that would be most appropriate for each intelligence, based on its characteristics.

VERBAL/LINGUISTIC   1 2 3 4 5 6 7 8 9 10
Enjoy reading, writing, speaking, word games,
oral presentations, and speeches

LOGICAL/MATHEMATICAL   1 2 3 4 5 6 7 8 9 10
Enjoy problem solving, math, scientific experiments,
brain teasers, logic games, tangrams, and dominoes

VISUAL/SPATIAL   1 2 3 4 5 6 7 8 9 10
Enjoy graphic organizers, maps, drawings, diagrams,
puzzles, mazes, doodling, videos, and photography

BODILY/KINESTHETIC   1 2 3 4 5 6 7 8 9 10
Enjoy sports, role-plays, physical/hands on activities,
building models, body language/gestures, and sewing

MUSICAL/RHYTHMIC   1 2 3 4 5 6 7 8 9 10
Enjoy playing musical instruments, raps, jingles, singing,
listening to CDs, poetry, and all types of sound patterns

INTERPERSONAL   1 2 3 4 5 6 7 8 9 10
Enjoy group work/games/sports, solving conflicts,
social activities, panels, debates, skits, and case studies

INTRAPERSONAL   1 2 3 4 5 6 7 8 9 10
Enjoy journals, diaries, individual hobbies, giving
personal opinions, and reflective activities

NATURALISTIC   1 2 3 4 5 6 7 8 9 10
Enjoy collecting rocks/leaves/shells, exploring outdoors,
bird watching, photographing nature, and the environment

PRODUCTS AND PERFORMANCES TO CHOOSE FROM
Choral reading, bulletin board, cartoon or caricature, collection collage, critique, demonstration, labeled diagram, family tree, flow chart, glossary, interview, lab report with illustrations, museum exhibit, readers theater, and soliloquy

Name: _____

RESPONSIBLE GOAL SETTING

Directions: Think about all the ways that life is like a game of chess or checkers. In both games, there are players, goals, moves, strategic plans, and the potential for a positive outcome if one wins and the potential to learn from mistakes if one loses. In short, there are no "shortcuts" to being a successful player of either board games for fun or life games for real.

Take a few minutes to think about one important goal that you have in mind for being successful at school this semester or year. Use the graphic organizer below to write out your goal and the steps you must take to achieve it. Number each of the boxes in the order you plan to attain your goal.

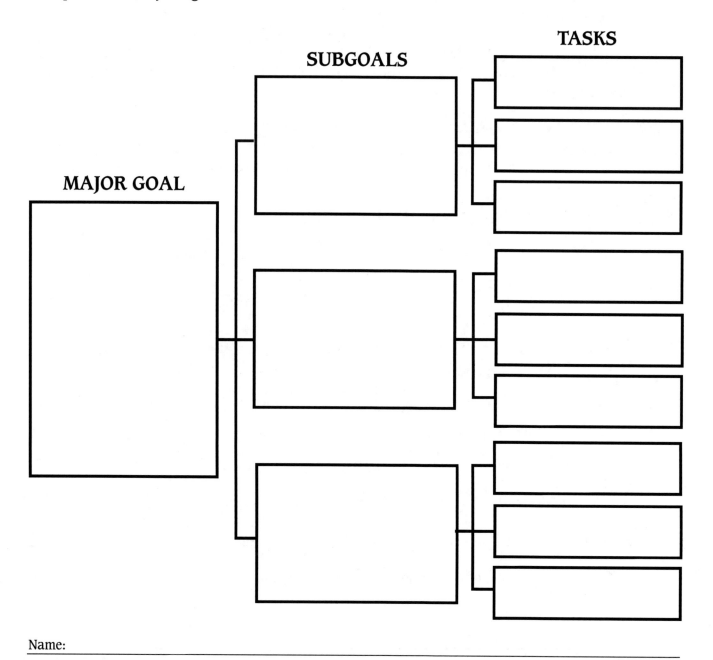

Name:

Advisory Plus!

WHO IS RESPONSIBLE FOR YOUR BEHAVIOR?

Directions: Who is ultimately responsible for your behavior at home, in school, or out in the community? Should parents be held responsible? Should teachers be held accountable? Should law enforcement officers be held answerable? Stage a debate to argue the pros and cons of each of these potential problem areas. Use the debate format outlined here in the preparation and delivery of the debate itself. Be sure to research the issues for each situation. Then generate arguments both for and against the resolution.

RESOLUTION ONE: If a student is expelled from school, the parents or guardians should attend school in the student's place, making certain to take all class notes and take home all class assignments to be completed before student is allowed to return to class.

RESOLUTION TWO: If a student is involved in an unlawful activity such as vandalism, shoplifting, theft, assault, or some other juvenile crime, the parents or guardians should be held accountable for all monetary damages.

RESOLUTION THREE: If a student is responsible for any illegal activity involving damage of any kind to the community in which he/she lives, the parents or guardians should have to spend time doing community service as a form of compensation for the trouble caused.

SUGGESTED RULES FOR A 25-MINUTE DEBATE

1. *3 Minutes:* First Speaker for the affirmative makes opening statement.

2. *3 Minutes:* First Speaker for the negative makes opening statement. (No questions or interruptions allowed during these times.)

3. *3 Minutes:* Second and Third Speakers for the affirmative stand and are questioned by the Second and Third Speakers for the negative.

4. *3 Minutes:* Second and Third Speakers reverse roles. The affirmative side questions, and the negative side answers.

5. *3 Minutes:* Recess for both sides to discuss closing ideas with final speakers.

6. *2 Minutes:* Fourth Speaker for the affirmative side summarizes.

7. *2 Minutes:* Fourth Speaker for the negative side summarizes.

8. *4 Minutes:* Judges withdraw to determine the winner of the debate.

Name:

SILENCE BREEDS VIOLENCE

Directions: Middle and high school students know a simple school fight can turn deadly. They know kids sneak weapons to schools and hurt other kids. They know a teenager who talks about committing suicide might just go ahead and take his own life, and those of others. They know; but they seldom tell. Interviews with kids about violence have shown that many students do not think adults will take them seriously, no matter what they know or are saying. Kids are reluctant to get involved when they hear rumors of violence or suspect something is wrong. Three reasons they often cite are: (1) They fear retaliation and do not want to draw attention to themselves; (2) They don't trust adults to do the right thing in response; and (3) They do not believe their peers are serious when they threaten violence to themselves or others.

Work with a small group of students to create a case study that depicts a potential conflict situation that could become violent if not handled properly at school. You might want to consider one of these scenarios to get you started. Be prepared to act out your skit for others in class and solicit their feedback on how to handle both "silence" and "violence" issues in schools across the country today.

SCENARIO ONE: A boy brings an unloaded handgun to school and uses it to threaten a teacher or another student. What happens?

SCENARIO TWO: Your best friend has been harassed by a group of peers over an extended period of time and has staged a fight with one of the troublemakers after school behind the local supermarket to "settle the score." What happens?

SCENARIO THREE: Someone you know in class has become very depressed due to personal problems at home that are now affecting his/her schoolwork. Because there is no apparent way out, he/she has contemplated suicide. What happens?

SCENARIO FOUR: You have been invited to join a popular gang at school and there is status in becoming a member. As part of the initiation, you are to vandalize school property. What happens?

SCENARIO FIVE: You and a group of friends have witnessed a violent fight after an evening football game where someone has been seriously hurt. School officials and the police are investigating the incident and looking for witnesses who will talk about the tragedy. What happens?

Name:

BUILDING RESPONSIBLE RELATIONSHIPS

Directions: Look up the word "relationship" in the dictionary and write down its multiple definitions. Circle the one that best describes your understanding of the concept. Then, do some reflective thinking about your relationships at home, at school, and out in the community by pondering the questions below. Find a partner to work with, and verbally share your ideas with him/her. Finally, compose a thoughtful paragraph for your journal that summarizes the strengths of a relationship that you currently have with a friend or teacher at school, with a parent/guardian or sibling at home, and with an adult or mentor in the community.

DEFINITIONS OF RELATIONSHIP

_____

_____

_____

_____

POINTS TO PONDER AND DISCUSS

1. How would you describe your relationship with your parents? With your siblings?

2. Describe a time when your parents were very proud of something you did and a time when one or both of your parents let you down.

3. When do you get along best with your brothers and sisters? What are some things you do that irritate them?

4. What are two things about yourself that teachers have said to or about you that made you feel good about yourself?

5. What habits do you have that teachers might criticize or wish were different?

6. Describe the relationship between you and your best friend at school. What makes him/her so special?

7. Describe the relationship between you and someone you don't get along with at school. What seems to be the problem?

8. Think about your experiences outside of home and school. What adult relationships do you most value and why?

9. Strengths of a current relationship I have.

10. Weaknesses of a current relationship I have.

Name: _____

©2004 Incentive Publications, Inc.
Nashville, TN

WHAT AN ORCHESTRA CAN TEACH US ABOUT RESPONSIBILITY

Directions: A full philharmonic or symphony orchestra has 85 to 90 members and performs musical compositions of all types—classical, jazz, theater, rock, etc. Philharmonic means love (phil) of harmony. The conductor leads the orchestra with a baton. The right hand of the conductor is used mainly for beating patterns that indicate the tempo of the music; the left hand is generally used for interpretive instruction (such as the relative loudness of the music) to capture the character of the composition and to effect the composer's direction. A conductor's facial expression and other body movements are essential in communicating his or her performance desires to the orchestra. There are four major types of instruments in the orchestra. The string instruments are violin, viola, cello, double bass, and harp. The woodwinds include piccolo, flute, clarinet, bass clarinet, saxophone, oboe, English horn, and bassoon, while the brasses include the trumpet, trombone, and tuba. The final group of instruments are the percussions, which include such wonders as the drums, cymbals, chimes, triangles, castanets, and tambourines. The secret to a good symphony is total harmony among instruments, with each player assuming full responsibility for his/her part while simultaneously following the lead of the conductor.

Work with a group of peers to uncover more secrets about the magical performance of a quality orchestra. Learn more about seating arrangements; the role of the "concertmaster" and the principal player; important terms such as score, overture, movement, and ensemble; and of the most popular composers such as Beethoven, Mozart, Chopin, and Bach. Prepare a short lecture on the symphony and its contribution to the fine arts, making certain that everyone in your research group plays a "harmonic" part in the delivery of the information. Who will be the conductor of your lecturette? Who will be the principal player? Who will take on the persona of the violin or the bass drum? Finally, use these quotations as springboards for your project, and be sure to follow up by listening to some great orchestra recordings.

QUOTATION ONE:

"Music can name the unnamable and communicate the unknowable."

— Leonard Bernstein

QUOTATION TWO:

*"Music must take rank as the highest of the fine arts—
as the one which more than any other, ministers to human welfare."*

— Herbert Spencer

QUOTATION THREE:

"Music produces a kind of pleasure which human nature cannot do without."

— Confucius

Name:

Advisory Plus!

HOW ORGANIZED ARE YOU ANYWAY?

Directions: It is important for any individual to have basic organizational skills if they are going to be productive in today's world. People who are disorganized waste their valuable time, talent, and treasure—most of which are not renewable resources. Read through each of the items in the checklist below, and determine where you fall on a continuum of 1 to 5. The teacher will ask you and the other students in the class to physically place yourselves on a human graph that pinpoints where you stand in terms of agreement or disagreement for each statement. Do you STRONGLY AGREE, AGREE, STRONGLY DISAGREE, DISAGREE, or are you NOT CERTAIN? Be honest with yourself and then think of ways to improve your organizational skills in areas that could be much better!

STRONGLY AGREE	AGREE	NOT CERTAIN	DISAGREE	STRONGLY DISAGREE
1	2	3	4	5

1 2 3 4 5 | 1. I keep my locker, book bag, and notebook at school neat and orderly.

1 2 3 4 5 | 2. I keep my desktop and study space at home clear of unnecessary papers, magazines, notes, and books.

1 2 3 4 5 | 3. I maintain an assignment book for all classes on a daily basis.

1 2 3 4 5 | 4. I do not procrastinate on long-term assignments.

1 2 3 4 5 | 5. I use a daily calendar to keep track of important school and extracurricular activities.

1 2 3 4 5 | 6. I never fail to turn in assignments on time.

1 2 3 4 5 | 7. I always bring home important information (newsletters, report cards, reminders) from school to my parents/guardians.

1 2 3 4 5 | 8. I usually know where things are (such as glasses, keys, purse, or wallet).

1 2 3 4 5 | 9. My teachers, family members, and friends think of me as an organized person.

Name: _____

THE "ME I AM LEARNING TO BE" FOLDER

Directions: Middle school kids have a number of unique characteristics, strengths, talents, and interests that contribute to their growth intellectually, emotionally, physically, psychologically, spiritually, and ethically. Spend some time thinking about who you are and what things you have or would like to have, to represent things you seek and value. Use this list as a springboard for talking about your current or future strengths, talents, hobbies, interests, career goals, pet peeves, etc. Try to include a wide variety of items and talk about them as you perform a mini "Me I Am Learning To Be" speech. List the items you have selected in the first column below, and then briefly comment on what value each has for you.

COLUMN ONE	COLUMN TWO
Item Selected for Folder	Personal Comments

1. _____   _____

2. _____   _____

3. _____   _____

4. _____   _____

5. _____   _____

6. _____   _____

7. _____   _____

8. _____   _____

9. _____   _____

Name:

PICTURE BOOK, PICTURE PERFECT

Directions: Visit the children's section in the media center of a local elementary school or in the public library of your community. Look for picture books that have something to do with school. Some possible titles to consider are: *Miss Nelson Is Missing* by Harry G. Allard, *Teacher from the Black Lagoon* by Mike Thaler, or any of the *Magic School Bus* series published by Scholastic. Read through one of these books, and then write down the following information on a 4 x 6 file card:

1. Title of Book

2. Author(s) of Book

3. Illustrator of Book

4. Synopsis of Story Line

5. Author's Purpose in Writing Book

6. Your Reaction to Book—both its literary qualities, story, and illustrations

As you read and write about each book, try to determine what message about school the book gives to its reader.

As a follow-up, if time permits, brainstorm a list of possible ideas for authoring an illustrated picture book of your own that focuses on some aspect of middle school. What would you want a young reader or his/her parents to know about middle school? Do you want to write about a particular course of study, a special principal or teacher, an exploratory program, a sporting event, a team celebration, a group assignment, a field trip experience, a homework nightmare, or a classroom project?

You may want to work with a partner so that one of you writes the actual story line, while the other does the illustrations.

Name: _____

BECOMING A RESPONSIBLE READER

Directions: Think about the act of reading at home, at school, or at play. Describe how you feel about each of the situations listed below. Think about your responses before you write them down. Then, reflect back on your thoughts, and draw some conclusions about your attitude towards the reading process. Finally, list three things you could do to become a more effective and responsible reader.

SITUATION ONE: When I read for fun at home, I _____

_____

SITUATION TWO: When I read to complete an assignment in school, I _____

_____

SITUATION THREE: When I receive a book as a present, I _____

_____

SITUATION FOUR: When I go to a bookstore, I _____

_____

SITUATION FIVE: When the teacher asks me questions about what I read, I _____

_____

SITUATION SIX: When I am asked to read aloud in class, I _____

_____

SITUATION SEVEN: When I am given free reading time in class, I _____

_____

SITUATION EIGHT: When it's time to read for information from a textbook, I _____

_____

CONCLUSIONS: _____

_____

_____

TO BECOME A MORE EFFECTIVE AND RESPONSIBLE READER, I COULD:

  1. _____

  2. _____

  3. _____

Name: _____

CALCULATING READING SPEEDS

Directions: There are many reading speeds that people acquire and apply over time, but how fast you read depends largely on the purpose for reading. For example, one would read faster if locating a specific word or reference in the dictionary than if reading technical or scientific material. Review each of the "reading speed" facts below, and think of a situation when each would be appropriate. Then, work with a partner and use a stopwatch to practice reading at each of the designated speeds. Be sure to locate the best type of reading material for each circumstance. How fast can you read for each category?

What level is best for you? What level is best for your friend? What kinds of materials did you choose to use in this experiment?

SPEED READING or Skimming
1000—2000 words per minute

MODIFIED SPEED READING or Very Rapid Reading
500—1000 words per minute

REDUCED SPEED READING or Rapid Reading
350—500 words per minute

MINIMAL SPEED READING or Moderate Reading
250—350 words per minute

SLOWEST SPEED READING or Slow Reading
100—250 words per minute

Name:

©2004 INCENTIVE Publications, Inc.
Nashville, TN

GOING ON A TEXTBOOK SCAVENGER HUNT

Directions: A textbook has many hidden treasures if one wants to take the time to uncover them. Use a textbook from either science, math, or social studies for this activity. Locate each item below, and record an example from the text for each one.

1. State the names of the authors and tell what they teach.

    _____

    _____

2. How many chapters are in your text? Write the title of one that sounds most interesting to you.

    _____

    _____

3. How does each chapter end? What are the common elements?

    _____

    _____

4. How many appendixes does this book contain? Name the topics of each.

    _____

    _____

5. Locate a chart, a graph, and a diagram in the text. Record the figure number and a description of it.

    _____

    _____

6. Find the glossary in the text, and write down the page numbers where it can be found.

    _____

    _____

7. Are there any illustrations in the book? What purpose do they seem to serve for the reader?

    _____

    _____

8. Name and describe one student task, experiment, or assignment that catches your eye.

    _____

    _____

9. List the different sections that you find in each chapter.

    _____

    _____

10. What do you consider to be the strengths of this textbook series? The weaknesses?

    _____

    _____

Name: _____

Advisory Plus!

PICTURING THE TEXTBOOK

Directions: It is important to take notes when reading a section of any textbook to organize information and to see relationships between the concepts presented. Did you know that one can record information from a textbook selection by drawing pictures, illustrations, diagrams, graphs, charts, or even flow charts? This method works as well as taking notes in outline form for some students. Choose a textbook section or chapter, and take a series of visual rather than written notes to see how this strategy works for you. After completing your pictorial ideas, write down a key word or phrase for each graphic item on the lines below. Ask a friend to match each of your visual portrayals with the printed list below.

KEY CONCEPTS/TERMS/IDEAS FROM TEXTBOOK SELECTION

1. _____

2. _____

3. _____

4. _____

5. _____

6. _____

7. _____

8. _____

9. _____

10. _____

11. _____

12. _____

Name: _____

©2004 Incentive Publications, Inc.
Nashville, TN

WHO, ULTIMATELY, IS RESPONSIBLE FOR YOUR TEST PERFORMANCE?

Directions: Test anxiety is not uncommon among students in middle school. Knowing how to take a test is just as important as knowing the information that will be included on the test. It is important to understand the causes of test anxiety, as well as ways to reduce these feelings of stress. Use this self-check quiz to pinpoint your test-taking preferences and skills, as well as things you could do to improve your test-taking abilities. Rate yourself on each of the items below by placing an "A" in front of each statement that describes you most of the time, an "S" in front of each statement that describes you some of the time, and an "N" in front of each item that rarely describes how you feel.

A=ALWAYS

S=SOMETIMES

N=NEVER

1. _____ I get very nervous when taking a test. My hands sweat or shake, my head hurts, and my heart races. I feel very stressed.

2. _____ I take good notes before a test and study them to get ready for a test, so that I am always well prepared.

3. _____ I have mental blocks when I am taking a test, even when I have used study time well.

4. _____ I follow these guidelines for taking a test: I read through the whole test first; I listen carefully if directions are given orally or read the directions to myself carefully; I don't panic when I come across a question I don't know; I answer all questions I know first and then go back over those I am not sure of; I keep track of the time and don't spend too much time on any one item; I take into account the weight or number of points each item or section of the test is worth; I review all questions and answers before turning in the test to my teacher.

5. _____ I do best on objective tests that include multiple choice, true/false, matching, and short answer questions.

6. _____ I do best on essay tests and questions that are open-ended.

7. _____ I recognize the problems I have had taking tests, and am working on how to deal with those problems.

8. _____ I often make careless mistakes on tests.

9. _____ I understand that I am the person most responsible for my test results.

Name: _____

Advisory Plus!

WRITING AND ANSWERING HIGHER-LEVEL QUESTIONS

Directions: Although lower-order thinking is important because it provides students with both a data or factual base of information and a means for understanding and applying the information, it is also important for students to know how to think creatively and critically. A good way to practice higher-level thinking skills is through the art and science of asking good questions of yourself and others as you review a textbook chapter, an Internet site, a videotape, or a reference book. Use this question frame or set of question starters, to help you learn better ways of asking or answering key questions in any subject area.

RECALL OR KNOWLEDGE QUESTIONS
    What or who is _____
    Define or identify _____
    Label or list_____
    Tabulate or reproduce _____

COMPREHEND OR SHOW UNDERSTANDING QUESTIONS
    Describe or explain _____
    Demonstrate or conclude _____
    Rearrange or reorder_____
    Interpret or summarize _____

APPLICATION OR USE QUESTIONS
    Construct or convert _____
    Examine or estimate _____
    Prepare or produce_____
    Solve or show_____

ANALYSIS OR INFERENCE QUESTIONS
    Compare and contrast_____
    Debate or diagram _____
    Form generalizations or make inferences about _____
    Survey or outline_____

SYNTHESIS OR CREATE QUESTIONS
    Compose or construct _____
    Design or develop _____
    Propose or predict _____
    Imagine or create_____

EVALUATION OR ASSESSMENT QUESTIONS
    Argue or criticize _____
    Judge or justify _____
    Rate or recommend _____
    Validate or verify _____

Name: _____

THE FIVE-STEP PARAGRAPH

Directions: A good strategy for writing a short position paper on a given topic is through the format of a "Five-Step Paragraph." This strategy enables you to condense information and/or ideas into a manageable form that has all the elements of a successful paper, including a lead or introductory paragraph and thesis statement, three body paragraphs complete with a topic sentence followed by three detailed statements, and a concluding paragraph that restates the thesis idea and draws a formal conclusion. Use the outline below to write a five-paragraph position paper of your own. Do this on a separate piece of paper. Try it! You will like your result!

PARAGRAPH OF INTRODUCTION

Lead or Opening Statement (Try writing a key definition, startling statement, unusual quotation, important statistic, or some other gimmick to get the reader's attention.)
1. Thesis Statement

BODY PARAGRAPH NUMBER ONE

2. Topic Sentence (Focus on a single main idea for this statement.)
..........3. Detail Sentence
..........3. Detail Sentence
..........3. Detail Sentence

BODY PARAGRAPH NUMBER TWO

2. Topic Sentence (Focus on another main idea for this statement.)
..........3. Detail Sentence
..........3. Detail Sentence
..........3. Detail Sentence

BODY PARAGRAPH NUMBER THREE

2. Topic Sentence (Focus on a third main idea for this statement.)
..........3. Detail Sentence
..........3. Detail Sentence
..........3. Detail Sentence

PARAGRAPH OF CONCLUSION

1. Restatement of Thesis (Think of another way to rewrite the main idea from the Introduction.)
Concluding Statement (Again, try to close this paper with a dramatic ending.)

Name:

Advisory Plus!

FIVE WAYS TO LOOK AT A CONCEPT OR BIG IDEA

Directions: Select an important chapter or chapter section from your math or science textbook that has been assigned to you by the teacher. Try taking notes on the key concepts or big ideas using a series of graphic organizers such as those suggested here. You will need to enlarge and reconstruct each organizer so that it takes up a single page. Notice that each graphic organizer looks at the information to be learned in a slightly different way using the organizing structures of Cause and Effect Chain, Compare and Contrast Diagram, Web (or Concept Map), Organizing Tree, and Attribute Diagram. Many others, such as a Venn Diagram or Scope and Sequence Chart could be used in this activity as well.

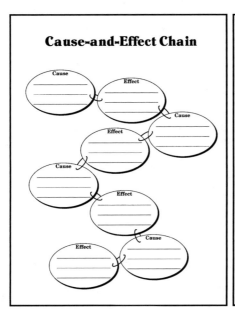

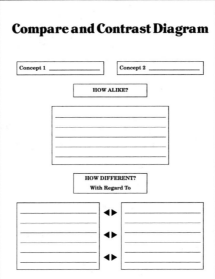

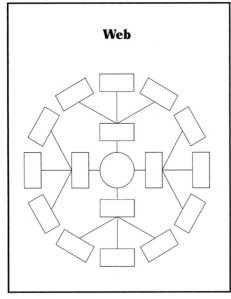

Name: _____

©2004 Incentive Publications, Inc.
Nashville, TN

WELCOMING RESPONSIBLE PARENTS AS SCHOOL PARTNERS

Directions: Work with a group of peers to develop a profile of parent participation in your classroom. Keep in mind that there are five important levels of parent participation in any school, which are (beginning with the lowest level of participation and moving to the highest level of participation):

1. SURVIVAL—Ensuring that child has breakfast, gets a good night's sleep, maintains good health, and attends school regularly and on time;

2. SUPPORT—Making an effort to attend scheduled conferences, return phone calls, and acknowledge notices/reminders sent home by teacher/school;

3. AUDIENCE—Attending child's classroom-participation functions and activities such as open houses, music programs, and sporting events;

4. INVOLVEMENT—Finding time to volunteer at the school or to do things at home for the teacher such as assistance with paperwork, chaperoning field trips, typing newsletters, or duplicating student handouts; and

5. GOVERNANCE—Playing active leadership role through PTA, booster groups, school committees, and parent-initiated programs or projects.

Work in cooperative learning groups to design a simple questionnaire or interview form that one might use with a parent to determine their level of involvement with the school. To get your group started on this project, make a list of the specific things you think are important for a parent to be and do if he/she is to become a responsible partner in the schooling process. Field test the questionnaire or interview form with the members of your group by having each person take turns playing the role first of the parent and then of the student interviewer. Compile a graph of these responses to show the degree of parent involvement representative of your cooperative learning group members. Speculate what the school can do to increase the level of involvement for more families in your school.

Name:

HOW ARE YOU AT STUDENT-LED CONFERENCES?

Directions: A major authentic assessment activity in middle schools today is that of student-led conferences. These are effective communication tools because they provide the student with a leadership role in presenting his/her portfolio of academic artifacts, which in turn reflect one's personal growth over a given period of time.

Student-led conferences involve the student as moderator and facilitator of the conference, with the teacher in a supporting role, and the parent or guardian in a participating role. These conferences are based on the contents of a student's portfolio, which is basically a collection of academic papers, tests, homework assignments, products, performances, worksheets, and reports, selected because they best represent the student's work over a marking period or semester. Each item in the portfolio is chosen because it is representative of what the student knows and is capable of in a given subject area. Likewise, each item in the portfolio contains a reflective statement by the student that explains why each piece was chosen, and what it represents in the academic life of that student. In short, the student-led conference allows the student to direct the conference dialogue and to establish goals for future academic work. Teachers can clarify assignments as needed, and parents can question assignments as needed.

Study the ideas outlined here for conducting a student-led conference with parents sometime in the future. To practice this unique conference format, take a few minutes to look through your current work folder/notebook and choose five or six assignments (homework paper, worksheet, quiz, writing task, journal entry, and some research notes, for example) that you feel are representative of what you can do in a given subject area. Use these to prepare a mock portfolio, making certain to write a simple statement reflecting on why each piece was chosen. Keep in mind that you may organize these items in your portfolio by subject area, theme, topic, genre, or chronological order. Then, sit down with a partner and role-play a student-led conference, letting your peer play the role of your parent.

SOME CONFERENCE PREPARATION QUESTIONS:

1. Explain how your portfolio is organized.

2. What item in your portfolio are you most proud of, and why?

3. What items in your portfolio do you wish didn't have to be there, and why?

4. Of all the assignments included here, which were the easiest? Which were the hardest?

5. What have you been working on this year to improve? How have you progressed?

6. What is the one thing that you would want someone to notice about your portfolio, and why?

7. Do you feel that this collection of work really reflects your abilities and achievements during this past marking period, semester, or year? Why or why not?

8. What would you do differently in putting together a portfolio like this for next time?

Name:

©2004 INCENTIVE Publications, Inc.
Nashville, TN

HOW GOOD IS YOUR ADVISORY PROGRAM?

Student Advisory Questionnaire

Directions: Please read carefully. Circle the number that best represents your response, using this rating scale.

STRONGLY AGREE	AGREE	UNDECIDED	DISAGREE	STRONGLY DISAGREE
1	2	3	4	5

1 2 3 4 5 | 1. My advisory period is important to me.

1 2 3 4 5 | 2. I look forward to my advisory group time.

1 2 3 4 5 | 3. My advisor treats me as an individual of worth in my own right.

1 2 3 4 5 | 4. My advisor believes in and enjoys advisory group time.

1 2 3 4 5 | 5. Advisees are involved in selecting and planning advisory group activities and projects.

1 2 3 4 5 | 6. The lessons are interesting.

1 2 3 4 5 | 7. The activities are meaningful to my age group.

1 2 3 4 5 | 8. My advisor takes time to talk about things that are important to me and my peers.

1 2 3 4 5 | 9. The advisory period helps me be a more well-rounded student.

1 2 3 4 5 | 10. The advisory program is used to take advantage of school and community resources.

1 2 3 4 5 | 11. The advisory program helps me make and keep friends at school.

1 2 3 4 5 | 12. The advisory program helps my parents/guardian know more about and be more involved in the overall school program.

1 2 3 4 5 | 13. My parent/guardian knows and understands the goals of my advisory program.

1 2 3 4 5 | 15. The advisory program encourages school spirit.

1 2 3 4 5 | 16. The advisory program encourages me to be a responsible member of the school community.

1 2 3 4 5 | 17. The advisory program makes school a better place for most students.

Adapted from *Advisory Middle Grades Advisee/Advisor Program* by Imogene Forte and Sandra Schurr. Nashville, TN: Incentive Publications, 1991. Used by permission.

Name:

RUBRIC FOR SEPTEMBER MODULE

SEPTEMBER

RATING SCALE: Best – **1**   Better – **2**   Good – **3**   Fair – **4**   Poor – **5**

____1. I was able to complete the Multiple Intelligences Self-Rating Scale.

____2. I was able to set school goals for the year.

____3. I was able to participate in a debate on the topic of responsible behavior.

____4. I was able to take part in a skit about violence.

____5. I was able to express myself about the important relationships in my life.

____6. I was able to apply the metaphor of an orchestra to the concept of relationships.

____7. I was able to rate my organizational skills using a human graph.

____8. I was able to complete a "Me I Am Learning to Be" speech.

____9. I was able to locate and relate to picture books on the topic of school.

___10. I was able to identify my basic attitudes towards reading.

___11. I was able to calculate reading speeds for different types of reading sources.

___12. I was able to participate in a textbook scavenger hunt.

___13. I was able to take visual notes on a section of my textbook.

___14. I was able to analyze my test-taking strengths and weaknesses.

___15. I was able to apply higher-order questioning skills as needed.

___16. I was able to write a "five-step paragraph" successfully.

___17. I was able to use varied graphic organizers to take notes from a textbook.

___18. I was able to help determine the level of parent participation in my classroom.

___19. I was able to conduct a successful student-led conference with my parents.

___20. I was able to assess the quality of my advisory program using a rating scale.

Name: _____

THEME: SELF-CONCEPT AND RELATIONSHIPS   VALUE: RESPECT

Accepting the premise that the cornerstone on which the foundation of respect for others is built is respect for oneself, what are the building blocks necessary for a firm foundation? Consider courage, compassion, honesty, integrity, wisdom, humor, faith, responsibility, creativity, optimism, commitment, quest for excellence, etc.

- **IDENTIFYING THE "SELF" IN SELF-CONCEPT—PURPOSE:** To explore the many different elements that influence one's self-concept

- **RESPECT AND RELATIONSHIPS—PURPOSE:** To discover the connections between respect and relationships

- **MY BOOK OF LISTS—PURPOSE:** To use lists of ideas as springboards for self-disclosure

- **FROM A-Z, WHAT'S YOUR NAME WORTH?—PURPOSE:** To exchange information about the origin of one's birth name and ways to write it using varied materials

- **WHAT'S THE PLAN?—PURPOSE:** To prepare oneself for making decisions, big and small, that can help to make the school year a success

- **IT'S YOUR LIFE—PURPOSE:** To imagine oneself as the subject of a biography

- **A SPECIAL ONE OF A KIND PERSON—PURPOSE:** To share information about one's personal tastes, special attributes, personality traits, physical characteristics, unusual hobbies/interests, family life, unusual experiences and talents, unique achievements, or future goals and ambitions

- **HOW SNOB-PROOF ARE YOU?—PURPOSE:** To define snobbery in its various forms and determine ways to reduce feelings of snobbery

- **HOW DO YOU MEASURE UP?—PURPOSE:** To explain what is meant by each of these terms when reporting the achievement levels or areas of growth for students: assess, measure, test, and evaluate

- **AN ACTION PLAN FOR IMPROVING THE ENVIRONMENT—PURPOSE:** To promote environmental awareness in school

- **DEVELOPING A HEALTHY RESPECT FOR THE ENVIRONMENT—PURPOSE:** To generate possible solutions for existing ecological problems that are destroying the environment

- **DO YOU PUT YOUR MONEY WHERE YOUR MOUTH IS?—PURPOSE:** To examine our individual habits that show respect or disrespect for the environment

- **THE SEVEN WONDERS OF MY WORLD—PURPOSE:** To identify the seven wonders of the world and then use this concept as a basis for identifying the seven geographic wonders of your state or country

- **IDIOMS SOMETIMES DO TELL IT ALL—PURPOSE:** To understand and create idioms in a group

- **WORDS TO RESPECT—PURPOSE:** To show how humor can be used for vocabulary development through the use of rhyming and lyrical word pairs (usually an adjective and a noun) that present funny word pictures

- **NOW WHAT WOULD YOU DO?—PURPOSE:** To role-play what a student would and would not do in handling several challenging and potential problem situations

- **THE RIGHTS OF THE BILL OF RIGHTS—PURPOSE:** To examine the essentials of the Bill of Rights and its ability to influence one's sense of security, self-respect, and self-concept

- **KEEPING THE "CIVIL" IN CIVIL RIGHTS—PURPOSE:** To review and reflect on the Civil Rights movement in the United States as a means for recognizing and respecting the diversity among cultures

- **SHOWING RESPECT FOR INDEPENDENCE—PURPOSE:** To determine ways the Declaration of Independence brings respect to the citizens of America—yesterday, today, and tomorrow

- **REACHING FOR RESPECT—PURPOSE:** To evaluate accomplished teacher standards regarding respect for students in order to better understand and appreciate the role of the teacher within the framework of the total schooling process

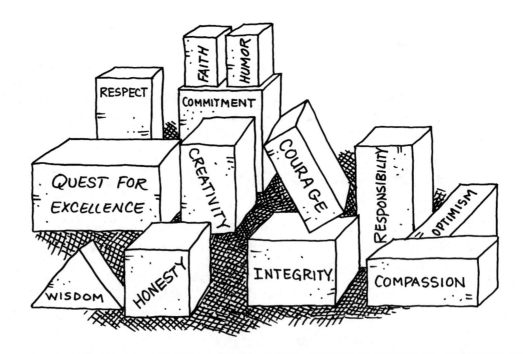

©2004 Incentive Publications, Inc.
Nashville, TN

THEME: SELF-CONCEPT AND RELATIONSHIPS   VALUE: RESPECT

One of the ways teachers show respect for students is by listening to them. Sometimes this is hard to do because they have too many interruptions from other students, or because there is just not enough time to get everything done during the class period. Write about a teacher you have had who listened to you. Tell how it influenced your feelings about school to have a teacher actually make the time to listen.

_____

_____

_____

_____

_____

_____

_____

_____

A person's self-concept is determined largely by personal interpretation of information and feelings derived from his or her environment. This interpretation is influenced by one's opinions at the time about how he or she measures personal talents, abilities, limitations, successes, and failures, as well as one's perception of how he or she is viewed by others. Write an autobiographical sketch reflecting on your own self-concept.

_____

_____

_____

_____

_____

_____

_____

_____

OCTOBER CALENDAR

※

WEEK ONE

DAY ONE	**"Identifying the 'Self' in Self-Concept"** Completing starter statements to define one's self-concept
DAY TWO	**"Respect and Relationships"** Considering the interaction between respect and relationships through answering questions
DAY THREE	**"My Book of Lists"** Creating lists about one's self
DAY FOUR	**"From A-Z, What's Your Name Worth?"** Exploring the origin of one's birth name through writing activities
DAY FIVE	**"What's the Plan?"** Examining the decision-making process

WEEK TWO

DAY ONE	**"It's Your Life"** Answering questions as the subject of a biography
DAY TWO	**"A Special, One-Of-A-Kind Person"** Creating an artifact that documents personal growth.
DAY THREE	**"How Snob-Proof Are You?"** Completing a writing exercise that discusses snobbery as a sign of disrespect
DAY FOUR	**"How Do You Measure Up?"** Completing assessment sheet of academic growth
DAY FIVE	**"An Action Plan for Improving the Environment"** Creating Bulletin Board Sketch of an action plan for improving the school environment

OCTOBER CALENDAR

❋

WEEK THREE

DAY ONE	**"Developing a Healthy Respect for the Environment"** Completing a graphic organizer to propose solutions for ecological problems
DAY TWO	**"Do You Put Your Money Where Your Mouth Is?"** Completing survey of personal behavior as it affects the environment
DAY THREE	**"The Seven Wonders of My World"** Identifying seven geographic wonders of a state or country
DAY FOUR	**"Idioms Sometimes Do Tell It All"** Conducting a writing exercise to relate idioms to personal experiences
DAY FIVE	**"Words to Respect"** Using a creative writing exercise to incorporate humor as a means of self-reflection

WEEK FOUR

DAY ONE	**"Now What Would You Do?"** role-playing several challenging and potential problem situations as a means to practice problem-solving skills
DAY TWO	**"The Rights of the Bill of Rights"** Participating in a cooperative learning activity based on the Bill of Rights
DAY THREE	**"Keeping the 'Civil' in Civil Rights"** Performing a choral reading as a means to reflect on the Civil Rights movement
DAY FOUR	**"Showing Respect for Independence"** Choosing an activity to show a modern interpretation of the Declaration of Independence
DAY FIVE	**"Reaching for Respect"** Rank ordering a checklist related to qualities of a master teacher

IDENTIFYING THE "SELF" IN SELF-CONCEPT

PURPOSE: To explore the many different elements that influence one's self-concept

TARGETED INTELLIGENCE: Interpersonal

CONTENT/STANDARD FOCUS: Social Studies—Individual Development and Identity

PRODUCT/PERFORMANCE/STUDENT OUTCOME: Responses to Starter Statements

"IDENTIFYING THE "SELF" IN SELF-CONCEPT" (page 66)

Introduce students to the theme of "self-concept" by presenting them with this set of six starter statements. Review the intent of each statement, and encourage students to work in pairs to discuss each statement before recording their individual responses. When all six statements have been completed, conduct a group discussion encouraging students to share their ideas within the total group setting.

RESPECT AND RELATIONSHIPS

PURPOSE: To discover the connections between respect and relationships

TARGETED INTELLIGENCE: Interpersonal

CONTENT/STANDARD FOCUS: Health & Social Studies—Individuals, Groups, and Institutions

PRODUCT/PERFORMANCE/STUDENT OUTCOME: Completion of Recording Sheet

"RESPECT AND RELATIONSHIPS" (page 67)

Introduce students to the value of "respect" by asking these two basic questions: Whom do you respect and why? Think about your friends, your teachers, your family or relatives, your heroes, your community leaders, your adult role models, your favorite book characters/author, etc. Why do you respect these individuals, and how have they earned that respect?

Next, have copies of a dictionary available for students and ask them to look up the multiple definitions of both "respect" and "relationships." Write their responses down on the chalkboard, and have them do the same on their recording sheets. Finally, provide them with some quiet time to reflect on these concepts by completing the items on their recording sheet.

Advisory Plus!   56

MY BOOK OF LISTS

PURPOSE: To use lists of ideas as springboards for understanding one's self-concept

TARGETED INTELLIGENCE: Intrapersonal

CONTENT/STANDARD FOCUS: Social Studies—Individual Development and Identity

PRODUCT/PERFORMANCE/STUDENT OUTCOME: Book of Lists

"MY BOOK OF LISTS" (page 68)

Provide students with twelve sheets of lined paper. Have them cut strips eleven inches long and five inches wide to make a ten-page book of lists with a cover. Have them prepare the cover and complete the required ten pages of lists. If time permits, students may want to decorate their covers and pages with simple icons, graphics, or illustrations as well. Staple or paper clip the pages together in booklet form.

FROM A TO Z, WHAT'S YOUR NAME WORTH?

PURPOSE: To explore the origin of students' birth names and self-selected nicknames, and to participate in a fun activity to explore the uniqueness of individual names

TARGETED INTELLIGENCE: Visual/Spatial and Bodily/Kinesthetic

CONTENT/STANDARD FOCUS: Language Arts—Standard 4

PRODUCT/PERFORMANCE/STUDENT OUTCOME: Completion of Creative Worksheet

"FROM A TO Z, WHAT'S YOUR NAME WORTH?" (page 69)

Conduct a short, total group discussion related to the origin of students' birth names. Next, distribute copies of the worksheet and ask students to complete it according to the directions given. Have students determine how much their names are worth in dollars if A = 1 dollar, B = 2 dollars, C = 3 dollars, etc. Students may figure the cost for their first name only, or their entire name, if desired. Determine whose name in the class has the greatest value and the least value.

WHAT'S THE PLAN?

PURPOSE: To prepare oneself for making decisions, large and small, that can help to make the school year a success

TARGETED INTELLIGENCE: Logical/Mathematical and Intrapersonal

CONTENT/STANDARD FOCUS: Language Arts—Standard 11

PRODUCT/PERFORMANCE/STUDENT OUTCOME: Self-Check Question Inventory

"WHAT'S THE PLAN?" (page 70)

Within a group setting, discuss the importance of wise decision making to a successful school year. Emphasize the fact that small decisions are as important as large (major) decisions because of their impact on each other. Distribute the corresponding student page, and ask students to complete it as directed.

IT'S YOUR LIFE

PURPOSE: To imagine oneself as the subject of a biography

TARGETED INTELLIGENCE: Verbal/Linguistic, Visual/Spatial, and Intrapersonal

CONTENT/STANDARD FOCUS: Language Arts—Standards 4, 5, 11, and 12

PRODUCT/PERFORMANCE/STUDENT OUTCOME: Written and Visual Responses in one of the following forms: Book Review, Letter, Descriptive Paragraphs, Map, Mini-Poster, Illustrations

"IT'S YOUR LIFE" (page 71)

Introduce this activity to students by having them talk about a biography they have read in the past. Ask students to speculate on how they would feel if someone wrote a book about their life at some future point in time. Next, review the directions for this activity with students, and point out the optional tasks from which they may choose.

A SPECIAL, ONE-OF-A-KIND PERSON

PURPOSE: To share information about one's personal tastes, special attributes, personality traits, physical characteristics, unusual hobbies/interests, family life, unusual experiences and talents, unique achievements, or future goals and ambitions

TARGETED INTELLIGENCE: Intrapersonal and Verbal/Linguistic

CONTENT/STANDARD FOCUS: Language Arts—Standards 4, 5, and 12 & Social Studies—Individuals, Groups, and Institutions

PRODUCT/PERFORMANCE/STUDENT OUTCOME: Written and Visual Responses in several forms

"A SPECIAL ONE-OF-A-KIND PERSON" (page 72)

Conduct a brief discussion on how and why each individual student is unique and special. Encourage each student to come up with something positive and unusual about themselves that no other person in the class can boast about. Then, review the assignment as written and spend some time discussing what each ABC item would entail if chosen by the student to complete.

HOW SNOB-PROOF ARE YOU?

PURPOSE: To define snobbery in its various forms and determine ways to reduce feelings of snobbery

TARGETED INTELLIGENCE: Verbal/Linguistic and Logical/Mathematical

CONTENT/STANDARD FOCUS: Social Studies—Individual Development and Identity

PRODUCT/PERFORMANCE/STUDENT OUTCOME: Personal Commentary

"HOW SNOB-PROOF ARE YOU?" (page 73)

Write out the definition of snobbery, as well as the meanings of all three types of snobbery on the chalkboard, or on an overhead transparency for students to read. Discuss these three variations of snobbery with the students and give examples of each type as it relates to student life. Instruct students to think about their own attitudes and actions regarding the snobbery concept, and to write a commentary about their reflections.

HOW DO YOU MEASURE UP?

PURPOSE: To explain what is meant by each of the following terms when reporting the achievement levels or areas of growth for students: assess, measure, test, and evaluate

TARGETED INTELLIGENCE: Logical/Mathematical and Bodily/Kinesthetic

CONTENT/STANDARD FOCUS: Mathematics —Communication; Reasoning & Science—Unifying Concepts and Processes

PRODUCT/PERFORMANCE/STUDENT OUTCOME: Self-Assessment Exercise

"HOW DO YOU MEASURE UP?" (page 74)

Display a collection of popular beverage containers with labels in place. Use the questions on the student activity sheet to clarify the special meanings of these concepts: assess, measure, test, and evaluate. Encourage students to apply these four terms to their own performances in math or science.

AN ACTION PLAN FOR IMPROVING THE ENVIRONMENT

PURPOSE: To promote environmental awareness in school

TARGETED INTELLIGENCE: Bodily/Kinesthetic and Visual/Spatial

CONTENT/STANDARD FOCUS: Social Studies—People, Places, and Environments

PRODUCT/PERFORMANCE/STUDENT OUTCOME: Bulletin Board Design

"AN ACTION PLAN FOR IMPROVING THE ENVIRONMENT" (page 75)

Encourage the students to brainstorm some problem areas, within the school setting, that show a lack of respect and concern for appearance and environmental consideration. Divide students into small cooperative learning groups and ask each group to choose a specific area of the school grounds to promote in terms of environmental awareness through a bulletin board design.

DEVELOPING A HEALTHY RESPECT FOR THE ENVIRONMENT

PURPOSE: To generate possible solutions for existing ecological problems that are destroying the environment

TARGETED INTELLIGENCE: Logical/Mathematical and Naturalistic

CONTENT/STANDARD FOCUS: Social Studies—Science, Technology, and Society; Global Connections & Science—Science in Personal and Social Perspectives

PRODUCT/PERFORMANCE/STUDENT OUTCOME: Problem/Solution Graphic Organizer

"DEVELOPING A HEALTHY RESPECT FOR THE ENVIRONMENT" (page 76)

Review the procedure for using the Problem-Solution Graphic Organizer with students, and ask them to use this tool to record possible solutions to the ecological problems identified on the student worksheet.

DO YOU PUT YOUR MONEY WHERE YOUR MOUTH IS?

PURPOSE: To examine individual habits that show respect or disrespect for the environment

TARGETED INTELLIGENCE: Intrapersonal and Naturalistic

CONTENT/STANDARD FOCUS: Social Studies—Science, Technology, and Society & Science—Science in Personal and Social Perspectives

PRODUCT/PERFORMANCE/STUDENT OUTCOME: Individual Survey

"DO YOU PUT YOUR MONEY WHERE YOUR MOUTH IS?" (page 77)

Ask students to complete the personal survey according to directions given. Discuss ways that they, along with their families, could better show respect for the environment.

THE SEVEN WONDERS OF MY WORLD

PURPOSE: To identify the Seven Wonders of the World and then use this concept as a basis for identifying and developing appreciation for seven geographic wonders of your state or country

TARGETED INTELLIGENCE: Visual/Spatial and Naturalistic

CONTENT/STANDARD FOCUS: Social Studies—People, Places, and Environments and Science, Technology, and Society

PRODUCT/PERFORMANCE/STUDENT OUTCOME: Worksheet

"THE SEVEN WONDERS OF MY WORLD" (page 78)

Review the Seven Wonders of the World with students, recounting the various unique features. Next, brainstorm a list of special geographic wonders, natural or man-made, that exist in your own location. Ask each student to complete a descriptive worksheet of the seven wonders of their own world, as determined by natural or man-made phenomena in their own community, state, or country.

IDIOMS SOMETIMES DO TELL IT ALL

PURPOSE: To consider a number of idioms related to relationships, selecting one to apply to a personal experience involving a relationship, which in turn should lead to a better understanding of the varied components of relationships

TARGETED INTELLIGENCE: Verbal/Linguistic and Interpersonal

CONTENT/STANDARD FOCUS: Language Arts—Standards 4, 6, and 12

PRODUCT/PERFORMANCE/STUDENT OUTCOME: Participation in Group Discussion

"IDIOMS SOMETIMES DO TELL IT ALL" (page 79)

Review the definition of an "idiom," and spend a few minutes sharing some popular idioms concerning relationships. Ask students to think of personal experiences they have had that relate to one or more of those idioms listed on the discussion sheet.

WORDS TO RESPECT

PURPOSE: To demonstrate how humor can be used for vocabulary development through the use of rhyming and lyrical word pairs (usually an adjective and a noun) that present funny word pictures, and to use "hink pinks" as springboards to examine feelings related to personal experiences

TARGETED INTELLIGENCE: Verbal/Linguistic and Musical/Rhythmic

CONTENT/STANDARD FOCUS: Language Arts—Standards 4, 6, and 12

PRODUCT/PERFORMANCE /STUDENT OUTCOME: List of Original "Hink Pinks" or Rhyming Pairs

"WORDS TO RESPECT" (page 80)

Define "hink pink" and give students several examples of this rhyming word pattern. Encourage students to think of some of their own to share with the class so as to warm up their creative minds and tickle their sense of humor. Instruct students to follow the directions on the worksheet for relating the predetermined "hink pinks" to some of their personal experiences. If time permits, allow students to share their own original "hink pinks" with the total group.

NOW WHAT WOULD YOU DO?

PURPOSE: To role-play what a student would and would not do in handling one of several challenging and potential problem situations as a means to gathering a heightened self-understanding

TARGETED INTELLIGENCE: Bodily/Kinesthetic and Interpersonal

CONTENT/STANDARD FOCUS: Language Arts—Standard 12

PRODUCT/PERFORMANCE/STUDENT OUTCOME: Role-plays

"NOW WHAT WOULD YOU DO?" (page 81)

Define "role-play" for students as the "acting out" of a realistic or life-like problem scenario, using two or more characters in its portrayal. Ask students to work with a partner to select a scenario, and to dramatize a poor solution to the problem as well as a good one.

THE RIGHTS OF THE BILL OF RIGHTS

PURPOSE: To examine the Bill of Rights and its influence on one's sense of security, self-respect, and self-concept

TARGETED INTELLIGENCE: Verbal/Linguistic and Interpersonal

CONTENT/STANDARD FOCUS: Social Studies—Power, Authority, and Governance; Civic Ideals and Practices

PRODUCT/PERFORMANCE/STUDENT OUTCOME: Cooperative Learning Recording Sheet

"THE RIGHTS OF THE BILL OF RIGHTS" (page 82)

Place students in small cooperative learning groups and direct them to assign appropriate roles and corresponding tasks to complete the recording sheet. Provide each group with a copy of the Bill of Rights, and provide time for completion of the recording sheet.

KEEPING THE "CIVIL" IN CIVIL RIGHTS

PURPOSE: To review and reflect on the Civil Rights movement in the United States as a means for recognizing and respecting the diversity among cultures

TARGETED INTELLIGENCE: Musical/Rhythmic and Naturalistic

CONTENT/STANDARD FOCUS: Social Studies—Power, Authority, and Governance; Civic Ideals and Practices

PRODUCT/PERFORMANCE/STUDENT OUTCOME: Choral Reading Activity

"KEEPING THE 'CIVIL' IN CIVIL RIGHTS" (page 83)

Provide a variety of resources (dictionary, textbooks, encyclopedias, etc.) or print copies or listen to an audio tape of the speech, "I Have A Dream," by Martin Luther King, Jr. Review the characteristics and optional parts of a choral reading presentation. Involve students in the development of an adaptation of the speech to be used as a choral reading activity.

SHOWING RESPECT FOR INDEPENDENCE

PURPOSE: To determine ways the Declaration of Independence has brought respect to the citizens of America

TARGETED INTELLIGENCE: Musical/Rhythmic, Visual/Spatial, Bodily/Kinesthetic, and Naturalistic

CONTENT/STANDARD FOCUS: Social Studies—Power, Authority, and Governance; Civic Ideals and Practices

PRODUCT/PERFORMANCE/STUDENT OUTCOME: Original Drawing, Musical Collage, or Reenactment Drama

"SHOWING RESPECT FOR INDEPENDENCE" (page 84)

Provide students with several copies of the Declaration of Independence, and together read and review its contents. Then, direct students to select and complete one of the optional activities from the student list.

REACHING FOR RESPECT

PURPOSE: To evaluate accomplished teacher standards regarding respect for students in order to better understand and appreciate the role of the teacher within the framework of the total schooling process

TARGETED INTELLIGENCE: Verbal/Linguistic and Interpersonal

CONTENT/STANDARD FOCUS: Language Arts and Social Studies

PRODUCT/PERFORMANCE/STUDENT OUTCOME: Student Outcome; Rank-Order List

"REACHING FOR RESPECT" (page 85)

Direct students to read and follow the directions on the worksheet to rank the outlined standards for teachers. Provide time for a total group discussion to share opinions, insights, and reasons related to rankings. This activity may well be presented as an individual task, a two-person partnering activity, or as a cooperative learning activity for a group of three or four students.

THEME: SELF-CONCEPT AND RELATIONSHIPS   VALUE: RESPECT

IDENTIFYING THE "SELF" IN SELF-CONCEPT

Directions: Think about the term "self-concept" and its importance to you. Let these starter statements serve as springboards for examining your self-concept and recording your thoughts.

1. Formulate the best definition you can think of for self-concept.

    _____

    _____

2. Name some of the major significant factors that might influence the self-concept of a person.

    _____

    _____

3. List some words you could use to explain self-concept.

    _____

    _____

4. What are some ways a person of your age demonstrates a strong self-concept?

    _____

    _____

5. What are some ways a person of your age demonstrates a poor self-concept?

    _____

    _____

6. How does the choice of friends affect one's self-concept?

    _____

    _____

Name: _____

RESPECT AND RELATIONSHIPS

Directions: Look up the words "respect" and "relationships" in the dictionary. Then, complete the set of activities below. Use an extra sheet of paper if you need additional room to write your answers

1. List words used in the dictionary that are key to defining the concept of "respect."

   _____

2. List words used in the dictionary that are key to defining the concept of "relationships."

   _____

3. List three ways that a person can show respect for himself or herself.

   _____

   _____

   _____

4. List three ways that a person can show respect for members of his/her family.

   _____

   _____

   _____

5. List three ways that a person sometimes shows a lack of respect for his/her peers.

   _____

   _____

   _____

6. List three ways that a student can show respect for his/her teachers.

   _____

   _____

   _____

7. Write a personal statement that shows how "respect" and "relationships" fit together or influence one another.

   _____

   _____

   _____

   _____

Name: _____

©2004 INCENTIVE PUBLICATIONS, Inc.
Nashville, TN

Advisory Plus!

MY BOOK OF LISTS

Directions: List making can be lots of fun and completed lists can tell a lot about a person. Divide your paper into strips approximately 11 inches long and 5 inches wide. Make a cover from one strip of paper and title it: "My Book of Lists." Fasten the pages together and use as many suggestions from the list below as possible to fill the pages in your book.

MY BOOK OF LISTS

PAGE ONE:

Make a list of ten people who are or have been important in your life.

PAGE TWO:

Make a list of ten favorite foods.

PAGE THREE:

Make a list of ten favorite heroes.

PAGE FOUR:

Make a list of ten favorite things to do in your free time.

PAGE FIVE:

Make a list of ten favorite words or expressions you use in speaking and writing.

PAGE SIX:

Make a list of ten places you would like to visit before you graduate from high school.

PAGE SEVEN:

Make a list of ten careers you might consider as an adult.

PAGE EIGHT:

Make a list of ten careers you would never want to consider as an adult.

PAGE NINE:

Make a list of ten things you would do if you inherited a million dollars.

PAGE TEN:

Make a list of ten things you worry about.

Name:

©2004 INCENTIVE PUBLICATIONS, Inc.
Nashville, TN

FROM A TO Z, WHAT'S YOUR NAME WORTH?

Directions: Spend some time discussing with peers and class members the origin of your names. Were you named after a favorite relative, a famous actor/actress, a special friend, or someone in the news? Did your parents find your name in a book? Think about the possibility of changing your name to something else. What would it be and why? Divide a clean sheet of paper into two equal boxes. Print your full name on the first line of the top box, and leave the rest of the box blank. Then, write the full name you would choose for yourself if given the opportunity. Write this name on the top line of the bottom box.

Finally, determine the value of both your birth name and your selected name, according to the formula below. Which name is worth the most?

A = $1	H = $8	O = $15	V = $22
B = $2	I = $9	P = $16	W = $23
C = $3	J = $10	Q = $17	X = $24
D = $4	K = $11	R = $18	Y = $25
E = $5	L = $12	S = $19	Z = $26
F = $6	M = $13	T = $20	
G = $7	N = $14	U = $21	

Name: _____

WHAT'S THE PLAN?

Directions: It is time to examine the various decisions, both big and small, that make the school year a success. How are your decisions to date working out? What new decisions need to be made? What old decisions need to be changed or updated? Answer each of the questions below to determine how well your plans are working. Use a separate piece of paper.

EASIER DECISIONS

EASY QUESTION: How and why did you decide to ride the bus, walk, or have someone drive you to school most days this year?

EASY QUESTION: How and why did you decide to pack or buy your lunch on any given day?

EASY QUESTION: How and why did you decide what type of book bag to buy?

EASY QUESTION: How and why did you decide what school supplies to purchase?

EASY QUESTION: How and why did you shop for school clothes, and how do you decide what to wear each day?

HARDER DECISIONS

HARDER QUESTION: How and why do you decide where to sit on the bus and in each of your classes?

HARDER QUESTION: How do you organize your things (books, homework, lunch, supplies, notes to teacher, etc.) to take to school each morning so you don't forget something?

HARDER QUESTION: How do you program yourself to do your homework in a timely manner?

HARDER QUESTION: How do your prepare for tests and special projects?

HARDER QUESTION: How do you set goals for the school year? How do you know when you have reached them and need to set new ones?

HARDER QUESTION: How do you get feedback, in addition to grades and report cards, from the teachers about your academic progress?

Name: _____

IT'S YOUR LIFE

Directions: Assume that a person who knows you well has just written a biography of your life to date. It is rapidly becoming a bestseller. Think about the kinds of things this author might say about your appearance, personality, family life, friends, special hobbies/interests, school activities, community involvement, and personal goals or accomplishments. Then, respond to this author's commentary by completing one of the tasks below.

OPTION ONE: Pretend the book is going to be made into a movie. Who would you choose to play the main characters in your life, including your self? Give reasons for your choices.

OPTION TWO: Write a description of one of the main characters that is likely to be in the book, other than yourself. Paint a portrait or caricature to accompany the description.

OPTION THREE: Write a letter to the school media specialist telling why she or he should buy this book for the school library collection.

OPTION FOUR: Write a letter recommending the book to a special friend or relative.

OPTION FIVE: Write a book review to be printed in the local newspaper.

OPTION SIX: Make a list of questions to ask someone who has just read the book.

OPTION SEVEN: Draw several illustrations to accompany events you know should be in the book.

OPTION EIGHT: Create a mini-poster that advertises the book.

OPTION NINE: Make a list of ten important facts about yourself that you would expect to find in the book.

OPTION TEN: Construct a map or diagram to show where the story about you takes place.

OPTION ELEVEN: Compose both a dedication statement and a thank-you statement that you would have instructed the author to put in the front of the book.

OPTION TWELVE: Design a book jacket for the book.

Name:

A SPECIAL, ONE-OF-A-KIND PERSON

Directions: Think about all of the things that make you a special and unique person. Consider your physical appearance, your special attributes, your personality traits, your hobbies and interests, your family life, your unusual experiences, your varied achievements, your future goals, or anything else that makes you an individual. Then, select one or more products from the ABC list below and develop a plan to construct a special artifact that represents who you were yesterday, who you are today, or who you want to be tomorrow—or all three.

A = Award	M = Menu
B = Billboard	N = Newspaper Headline
C = Certificate	O = Obituary
D = Diary Entry	P = Post Card
E = Epitaph	Q = Quotation
F = Fashion Show Script	R = Real Estate Notice
G = Greeting Card	S = Sign
H = Horoscope	T = Tall Tale
I = Invitation	U/V = Vita
J = Job Application	W/X/Y/Z = Will
K/L = Letter of Commendation	

Briefly describe the artifact or item that you have chosen to represent yourself:

_____

_____

_____

_____

Name: _____

HOW SNOB-PROOF ARE YOU?

Directions: Look up the words "snob" and "snobbery" in the dictionary, and record your own definition on the back of this page. It has been said by experts such as Joseph Epstein in his book, *Snobbery: The American Version,* that there are three basic kinds of snobs: the downward-looking snob, who takes pleasure in the put-down; the fawning snob, who wants to rise to a better world; and the reverse snob, who refuses to do anything others are doing (in other words, "I don't need to play this sport because everyone else is doing it.") Think about your own "snob" tendencies. Do you have any? Which of the three types is most like you? What are the warning signs others might detect in your personality? How could you or anyone else snob-proof yourself? Name a celebrity snob that you see in the movies, on television, in the sports or entertainment world, or in the news. How do you feel about their snobbery tactics?

Write a short commentary below, discussing the issue of snobbery as it relates to how you show respect for other people. Be as honest as possible in your commentary.

MY PERSONAL COMMENTARY ABOUT SNOBBERY

Name: _____

HOW DO YOU MEASURE UP?

Directions: Study the labels on a container designed to hold your favorite beverage. As you focus on the container, try to answer these questions about the container and its contents:

How would you assess its properties or characteristics?

How would you measure its contents?

How would you test for its quality of taste or nutritional components?

How would you evaluate its worth or value when compared to similar products?

Next, try to think about these special terms and how they are used to determine a student's academic growth by answering the questions below.

1. How would you **assess** your overall abilities in math or science?

    _____

    _____

2. How would you **measure** what you know and can do in math or science?

    _____

    _____

3. How would you **test** the quality of your math/science skills and know-how?

    _____

    _____

4. How would you **evaluate** what you know and can do in math/science as compared to other students in the class?

    _____

    _____

5. How do you think a student's achievement level affects his or her self-concept?

    _____

    _____

Name: _____

AN ACTION PLAN FOR IMPROVING THE ENVIRONMENT

Directions: Work with a small group and brainstorm personal actions that you and your classmates could take to enhance the school environment. Think about ways to improve the ambiance of the classroom or hallways, the cleanliness of the bathrooms and common areas, the appearance of the parking lots and outdoor walkways, the attractiveness of the school grounds and entrance, or the friendliness of the school office and campus. Decide on a focus, and then use the space below to sketch out a design for an all-school bulletin board that would present your ideas, along with those of your classmates.

──── OUR BULLETIN BOARD SKETCH: ────

Name:

DEVELOPING A HEALTHY RESPECT FOR THE ENVIRONMENT

Directions: Use the graphic organizer below to record several possible solutions for one or more of the ecological problems that are identified below.

PROBLEM ONE: Paper products contribute to 39% of our solid waste. 85% of the waste produced in schools is paper.

PROBLEM TWO: The United States churns out more than 432,000 tons of garbage daily.

PROBLEM THREE: A plastic six-pack holder has a life expectancy of 450 years.

PROBLEM FOUR: Approximately half of all aluminum cans, one-third of newspapers, and one-tenth of our glass bottles are currently recycled.

Problem-Solution Boxes

PROBLEM	HOW SOLVED

Name:

DO YOU PUT YOUR MONEY WHERE YOUR MOUTH IS?

Directions: The way people treat the environment is often reflective of personal values and feelings. Complete this survey to analyze decisions you and your family make on a daily basis that are likely to affect the amount of waste produced by your household. Choose the most appropriate rating for each stated action or behavior.

RATING SCALE TO USE:

NEVER	RARELY	SOMETIMES	OFTEN	ALWAYS
5	4	3	2	1

1. _____We put into practice the "reduce, reuse, and recycle" motto whenever possible.

2. _____We try to have items repaired before we replace them with new and updated items.

3. _____We use glassware, cloth napkins, and ceramic/plastic plates rather than disposable paper products.

4. _____We recycle all paper and glass/plastic/aluminum products on a regular basis.

5. _____We do not patronize restaurants that depend upon polystyrene products for their meals.

6. _____We do not purchase items that we do not need.

7. _____We read consumer reports before buying something of value.

8. _____We do not litter beaches, parks, roads, and other public places with personal trash.

9. _____When possible, we avoid buying products at the supermarket or elsewhere that are not stored in recyclable containers.

10. _____We promote reducing, reusing, and recycling with others in an effort to become less wasteful and much more "waste wise."

Name:

THE SEVEN WONDERS OF MY WORLD

Directions: Review what you know about the unique features of the highly acclaimed Seven Wonders of the World: The Egyptian Pyramids, The Hanging Gardens of Babylon, The Mausoleum at Halicarnassus, The Temple of Artemis at Ephesus, The Colossus of Rhodes, The Lighthouse of Alexandria, and The Statue of Zeus at Olympia. Speculate as to what makes them so special from a geographic, scientific, and natural point of view. Sometimes we forget to respect and appreciate the wondrous features of our own environment. Think about your own community or state, and what might be declared the seven wonders of your own location. Be sure to select sites that most people can relate to and will respect and protect. Consider everything from statutes, scenic sights, and gardens to buildings and bridges. Show your choices with either a simple drawing or a brief description of each wondrous site!

WONDER ONE:

WONDER TWO:

WONDER THREE:

WONDER FOUR:

WONDER FIVE:

WONDER SIX:

WONDER SEVEN:

Name:

IDIOMS SOMETIMES DO TELL IT ALL

Directions: Idioms are special literary expressions that compare unlike things to convey a visual image. Many times, they refer to relationships. Think of a time when one or more of the idioms used below described a situation that you encountered in a relationship. Explain the situation in some detail, highlighting its humorous side if possible!

1. My brother/sister gets in my hair!

2. He almost bit my head off.

3. I was in a pretty pickle with my family!

4. I was determined to stand by my friend until the bitter end.

5. That particular subject is down my alley.

6. I could see eye-to-eye with my teacher on that issue.

7. I had a bone to pick with the coach.

8. The principal just had to blow off steam.

9. After the argument, things were touch and go.

10. What I say to him/her goes in one ear and out the other.

11. He's as nutty as a fruitcake.

12. I think she bit off more than she could chew.

13. That advisory topic rings a bell with me.

14. She cried "wolf" one too many times.

Name: _____

WORDS TO RESPECT

Directions: Developing a respect for the English language and its unique characteristics can often best be appreciated through the use of creative humor and "play on words." "Hink Pinks" are funny word pairs that present humorous word pictures. For example, if you were asked to give a definition of a "manuscript thief," you might respond with this hink pink, "a book crook." If you were asked, "What is a hink pink for a fraudulent reptile," you might quickly come back with the hink pink, "a fake snake." Do you get the picture? Use the hink pink examples below as a springboard for recalling a personal experience or image, related to the word pair, which has special relevance or meaning for you. Then, make up some hink pinks of your own to tease your peers. You might also want to try illustrating each of the hink pinks you create with silly drawings or exaggerated sketches.

1. What is a hink pink for a "happy boy?" A "glad lad." Tell about a time when you were a glad lad.

   _____

2. What is the definition of a "noisy group?" A "loud crowd." Tell about a time when you were part of a loud crowd.

   _____

3. What is a hink pink for "fair cost?" A "nice price." Tell about a time when you got a bargain for your money.

   _____

4. What is the definition of a "sad or unhappy friend?" A "glum chum." Tell about a time when you were a glum chum.

   _____

5. What is a hink pink for "an intelligent beginning?" A "smart start." Tell about a time when you were ahead of the game and experienced a smart start.

   _____

HERE IS A HINK PINK OF MY OWN

_____

_____

_____

Name: _____

NOW WHAT WOULD YOU DO?

Directions: Work with a partner to select one of the role-playing scenarios outlined below. Act out what you would or would not do in this problem-solving situation. You might even want to do two role-plays each—one demonstrating a poor solution and one demonstrating a positive solution. Try it. You'll be surprised at how much it helps you understand yourself and gain respect for a different point of view!

SCENARIO ONE: You are receiving several unsolicited and suspicious emails from someone you fear may be a potential adult predator.

SCENARIO TWO: You were accused of cheating on an important test when, in fact, you were trying to keep someone else from copying answers off your paper.

SCENARIO THREE: You were playing a musical solo on stage for an audience of peers and you forgot the notes.

SCENARIO FOUR: You won the million dollar lottery after unexpectedly finding the winning ticket, which had been lost by someone else.

SCENARIO FIVE: You found yourself responsible for putting on a party for all the underprivileged kids in town.

SCENARIO SIX: You were appointed to be principal of your school for one whole day.

SCENARIO SEVEN: Your worst enemy nominated you for the Outstanding Humanitarian Award at the end of the school year.

SCENARIO EIGHT: You learned that your best friend had told you a falsehood about a mutual friend, which had affected your relationship with that friend.

Name:

THE RIGHTS OF THE BILL OF RIGHTS

Directions: In your cooperative learning group, refer to a copy of the Bill of Rights to complete one of these tasks, as selected by the group. Be sure to record the names of all members working in your group and what roles they played in completing the assignment.

RECORDING SHEET

NAMES OF GROUP MEMBERS AND THEIR ASSIGNED ROLES

_____

_____

TASK ONE: Speculate on reasons why the Bill of Rights became essential to protecting the freedoms of individuals when it was first adopted in 1791.

_____

_____

_____

_____

TASK TWO: On a separate piece of paper, draw a series of simple illustrations to depict each of the ten amendments in graphic form, using various icons, symbols, and figures.

TASK THREE: Restructure the order of the amendments, from the most important to the least important in the world today, as determined by the members of your group. Record this information on the back of this sheet. State a good reason for your first and last choices below.

First Choice: _____

_____

Last Choice: _____

_____

TASK FOUR: Make a case for constructing a Bill of Rights for kids. How could the existing amendments be modified or rewritten for a younger group of people? Write your ideas below.

_____

_____

_____

_____

Name: _____

KEEPING THE "CIVIL" IN CIVIL RIGHTS

Directions: Consult the resources provided to define the concept of "civil rights" and to locate information about Martin Luther King, Jr. and his famous "I Have A Dream" speech. Then, organize the words of the speech into a choral reading, with some lines designated as "solo" lines, some lines designated as "group A, B, or C" lines, some lines designated as "boys or girls" lines, and some lines designated as "All" lines. Try to include everyone in the class as participants in this choral reading activity. If you can arrange for music to be played in the background, it will enhance the performance, but if not, the combined voices of all class members will suffice.

MY DEFINITION OF CIVIL RIGHTS:

_____

_____

FIVE FACTS TO REMEMBER ABOUT MARTIN LUTHER KING, JR.:

_____

_____

_____

_____

_____

MY LINES OF THE SPEECH TO RECITE:

_____

_____

_____

_____

_____

_____

_____

Name: _____

Advisory Plus!

SHOWING RESPECT FOR INDEPENDENCE

Directions: Obtain a copy of the Declaration of Independence and read through it. Think about how it would translate into contemporary, common language. Choose one of the activities to complete.

ACTIVITY ONE: Imagine you are an artist in 1776, and you are asked to draw a series of pictures that depict the important principle, "All men are created equal," for those who are unable to read. Make a rough sketch of what your painting would look like.

ACTIVITY TWO: Create a reenactment, pantomime, or tableau of the signing of the Declaration of Independence.

ACTIVITY THREE: Sketch a mural of an outdoor setting that would illustrate this fact, presented in the Declaration of Independence, that cites one of the many injuries and usurpations of the King of Great Britain towards the Colonists: "He has excited domestic insurrection among us, and has endeavored to bring on the inhabitants of our frontiers the merciless Indian savages whose known rule of warfare is an undistinguished destruction of all ages, sexes, and conditions." Divide the plan for the mural into panels, so that several members of a group can each work on a section the same time.

ACTIVITY FOUR: Create an outline, including captions, for the illustrations of a simple picture book that would help explain several individual rights to young children.

Name:

REACHING FOR RESPECT

Directions: The list below outlines the eleven facets of accomplished teaching for teachers serving middle-level students, as identified by The National Board for Professional Teaching Standards. From a student's point of view, rank this list of practices from the most essential (1) to the least essential (11) for teachers to show respect for each student as a unique individual of worth and dignity.

_____ KNOWLEDGE OF STUDENTS: Accomplished teachers use their knowledge of child development to understand their students' abilities, interests, aspirations, and values.

_____ KNOWLEDGE OF CONTENT AND CURRICULUM: Accomplished teachers use their knowledge of subject matter and curriculum to make decisions about what is important for students to know and be able to do.

_____ LEARNING ENVIRONMENT: Accomplished teachers establish a caring, inclusive, stimulating, and safe school community so that students can take intellectual risks, practice democracy, and work collaboratively with others.

_____ RESPECT FOR DIVERSITY: Accomplished teachers help students learn to respect and appreciate individual and group differences.

_____ INSTRUCTIONAL RESOURCES: Accomplished teachers create, assess, select, and adapt a rich and varied collection of materials and community resources to support student learning.

_____ MEANINGFUL APPLICATIONS OF KNOWLEDGE: Accomplished teachers engage students in learning within and across the disciplines in such a way as to help students understand how the subjects relate to real-world experiences.

_____ MULTIPLE PATHS TO KNOWLEDGE: Accomplished teachers provide students with multiple paths needed to learn the central concepts, themes, and topics in each school subject and across school subjects.

_____ ASSESSMENT: Accomplished teachers understand the strengths and weaknesses of different assessment methods, and base their instruction on both ongoing assessment and student self-assessment measures.

_____ FAMILY INVOLVEMENT: Accomplished teachers initiate positive interactions and relationships with families of their students.

_____ REFLECTION: Accomplished teachers regularly analyze, evaluate, reflect on, and strengthen the effectiveness and quality of their practice.

_____ CONTRIBUTIONS TO THE PROFESSIONS: Accomplished teachers work with colleagues to improve schools and to advance knowledge and practice in their field.

Name:

THEME: SELF-CONCEPT AND RELATIONSHIPS   VALUE: RESPECT

OCTOBER

RATING SCALE: I think so – **3**   I hope so – **2**   I don't know for sure! – **1**

1. _____ I learned more about the meaning of self-concept.

2. _____ I learned more about the importance of respect and relationships.

3. _____ I learned how to use list making as a means of telling more about myself.

4. _____ I learned more about my birth name and its hypothetical monetary value.

5. _____ I learned how effective decision making can help to make school a success.

6. _____ I learned how a biography can be an interesting way to tell a life story.

7. _____ I learned how many different artifacts can tell something about a person.

8. _____ I learned something about the negative effects of snobbery.

9. _____ I learned how to use the scientific method to analyze people, places, or things.

10. _____ I learned ways students can show more respect for their school environment.

11. _____ I learned how to use a graphic organizer to record ideas for problem solving related to the environment.

12. _____ I learned how to use a rating scale to assess my family's ability to reduce waste.

13. _____ I learned how to use the Internet or encyclopedia to research the Seven Wonders of the World and how to discover the wonders of my own world.

14. _____ I learned about idioms.

15. _____ I learned a unique feature of the English language referred to as "hink pinks."

16. _____ I learned how to stage and participate in a role-playing scenario.

17. _____ I learned some important practices that teachers can use to show respect for their students.

18. _____ I learned more about the Bill of Rights.

19. _____ I learned more about civil rights and Martin Luther King.

20. _____ I learned more about the Declaration of Independence.

Name: _____

THEME: COMMUNICATION   VALUE: HONESTY

In prepared remarks on taking the oath of office as President of the United States on August 9, 1974, President Gerald R. Ford said, "I believe that truth is the glue that holds governments together, not only our government, but civilization itself. That bond, though strained, is unbroken at home and abroad." With the advent of technology that allows people the world over access to actual events even as they are happening, what are some possible reactions to and results of a lack of truth that holds relationships together. Consider both intents and practices of politicians and policy makers domestically and globally, and the cultural and philosophical summits, writings, and events of our day.

- **WHY DISHONESTY RARELY WORKS!—PURPOSE:** To discuss a variety of situations where honest versus dishonest responses or behaviors are analyzed

- **THE ART AND SCIENCE OF QUESTIONING—PURPOSE:** To reflect upon good and bad practices when it comes to questioning during small and large group discussions

- **NOSE FOR THE NEWS—PURPOSE:** To give an informal, sit-down newspaper mini-speech about current events based on a news item of interest to students

- **A PICTURE IS WORTH A THOUSAND WORDS—PURPOSE:** To analyze and create a series of editorial cartoons from the newspaper

- **COMMUNICATION BARRIERS AND BLUNDERS—PURPOSE:** To examine the communication barriers and blunders of profanity, slang, slander, and gossip

- **HOMEWORK HOTLINE—PURPOSE:** To use the popular "Mad Lib" writing format as a basis for completing a humorous fill-in-the-blank paragraph on the value of honesty as it relates to forgotten homework assignments

- **MESSAGES MATTER—PURPOSE:** To give examples when it is more appropriate to communicate with someone through a letter, email, or telephone call

- **ART AND MUSIC AS COMMUNICATION—PURPOSE:** To investigate ways that both art and music are special forms of communication

- **SPONTANEOUS REACTIONS TO COMMUNICATION CHALLENGES— PURPOSE:** To experiment with various springboards that encourage students to engage in spontaneous and personal forms of writing

- **SOME TOPICS TO DISCUSS OR DEBATE—PURPOSE:** To show students how to organize information on a controversial topic

- **IS HONESTY REALLY THE BEST POLICY?—PURPOSE:** To create a television commercial that promotes honesty as an important value in a society

- **GAMBLING AND YOUTH: IS IT REALLY A PROBLEM? BE HONEST!— PURPOSE:** To show how gambling has become a serious problems for many young people

- **DEALING WITH HONESTY IN DIFFICULT SITUATIONS—PURPOSE:** To use case studies as the foundation for dealing with honesty in difficult situations at home, at work, or at play

- **CAFETERIA FOOD FIGHTS: WHO STARTS THEM?—PURPOSE:** To examine the realities of today's cafeteria food and services in school

- **INVENTIONS THAT IMPACTED COMMUNICATION EFFORTS—PURPOSE:** To rank in order various inventions that have influenced communication efforts over time

- **TALKING INSIDE AND OUTSIDE THE CIRCLE—PURPOSE:** To introduce students to the Inside/Outside Circle strategy as a tool for reviewing course content or discussing controversial issues

- **TECHNOLOGICAL INFLUENCES ON COMMUNICATION—PURPOSE:** To demonstrate the multiple influences of technology on forms of communication today

- **COMMUNICATING THROUGH SYMBOLS AND ICONS—PURPOSE:** To demonstrate ways that symbols and icons are used to communicate ideas, information, and locations

- **ACTIONS SOMETIMES SPEAK LOUDER THAN WORDS—PURPOSE:** To give examples of how body gestures and body language can communicate as well as words on many occasions

- **WE ARE ALL MULTICULTURAL TO SOMEONE—PURPOSE:** To introduce students to cultural characteristics that may affect communication among students or between students and adults of different cultures

©2004 Incentive Publications, Inc.
Nashville, TN

WRITING PROMPTS/DISCUSSION STARTERS

*

We are all familiar with the often-recounted story of George Washington's admission to his father, "Yes, Father, I cannot tell a lie. It was I who cut down your prized cherry tree." According to the story, even with the threat of punishment ahead of him, the young lad felt compelled to be honest and admit a serious mistake. The story of the cherry tree may be a myth, but even so, George Washington was known throughout his life as a man of honesty and integrity in all that he said and did. Think about and write about how the pursuit of honesty and willingness to accept responsibility for his actions influenced the course of life for this great statesman, scholar, and president of the United States.

_____

_____

_____

_____

_____

_____

Few, if any, of us would disagree with the quotation, "If you always tell the truth, you never have to bother to remember what you said, or when you said what." Write an original anecdote, funny story, short play, cartoon, or comic strip illustrating a time when failure to tell the truth or behave in an honest manner had unexpected or unusual consequences.

_____

_____

_____

_____

_____

_____

NOVEMBER CALENDAR

✳

WEEK ONE

DAY ONE	**"Why Dishonesty Rarely Works!"** Participating in large group discussion and completing the student activity sheet
DAY TWO	**"The Art and Science of Questioning"** Completing the Effective Questioning Checklist
DAY THREE	**"Nose for the News"** Presenting an informal, sit-down newspaper mini-speech of current events
DAY FOUR	**"A Picture Is Worth a Thousand Words"** Critiquing and creating editorial cartoons
DAY FIVE	**"Communication Barriers and Blunders"** Examining the communication barriers and blunders of profanity, slang, slander, and gossip

WEEK TWO

DAY ONE	**"Homework Hotline"** Completing the Mad-Lib based student activity sheet
DAY TWO	**"Messages Matter"** Examining three types of communication options students have with their friends and family members
DAY THREE	**"Art and Music as Communication"** Discussing ways that art and music serve as cultural and educational forms of communication
DAY FOUR	**"Spontaneous Reactions to Communication Challenges"** Using springboards to encourage student writing
DAY FIVE	**"Some Topics to Discuss or Debate"** Learning to use the Umbrella organizer as a good tool for recording the pros and cons or the advantages and disadvantages of a controversial situation

NOVEMBER CALENDAR

❋

WEEK THREE

DAY ONE	**"Is Honesty Really the Best Policy?"** In cooperative learning groups, creating a television commercial that promotes honesty
DAY TWO	**"Gambling and Youth: Is it Really a Problem? Be Honest!"** Using mathematics to examine gambling activity and completing the self-checklist
DAY THREE	**"Dealing with Honesty in Difficult Situations"** Using case studies as the foundation for dealing with honesty in difficult situations at home, at work, or at play
DAY FOUR	**"Cafeteria Food Fights: Who Starts Them?"** Discussing cafeteria food and services in school
DAY FIVE	**"Inventions that Impacted Communication Efforts"** Discussing inventions that have influenced communication

WEEK FOUR

DAY ONE	**"Talking Inside and Outside the Circle"** Learning to use the Inside/Outside Circle strategy as a tool for reviewing course content or discussing controversial issues
DAY TWO	**"Technological Influences on Communication"** Examining influences of technology on forms of communication and completing mathematical computations as directed on the student activity page
DAY THREE	**"Communicating Through Symbols and Icons"** Discussing symbols and icons and their impact on communication all over the world
DAY FOUR	**"Actions Sometimes Speak Louder Than Words"** Studying body gestures and body language as a form of communication
DAY FIVE	**"We Are All Multicultural To Someone"** Examining how cultural characteristics may affect communication among students or between students and adults of different cultures

WHY DISHONESTY RARELY WORKS!

PURPOSE: To discuss a variety of situations where honest versus dishonest responses/behaviors are analyzed

TARGETED INTELLIGENCE: Logical/Mathematical and Interpersonal

CONTENT/STANDARD FOCUS: Social Studies—Individuals, Groups, and Institutions; Civic Ideals and Practices

PRODUCT/PERFORMANCE/STUDENT OUTCOME: Participation in a large group discussion

"WHY DISHONESTY RARELY WORKS!" (page 102)

Introduce this module as part of a large group discussion based on alternative honest and dishonest reactions to various situations that occur in the real world. Discuss the meaning and inappropriateness of telling "little white lies," which can backfire and set other lies in motion. In preparation for this discussion, ask students to write down their thoughts on the student activity sheet, according to the directions given.

THE ART AND SCIENCE OF QUESTIONING

PURPOSE: To reflect upon good and bad practices when it comes to questioning during small and large group discussions

TARGETED INTELLIGENCE: Verbal/Linguistic and Logical/Mathematical

CONTENT/STANDARD FOCUS: Language Arts—Standards 4, 11, 12

PRODUCT/PERFORMANCE/STUDENT OUTCOME: Completion of Effective Questioning Checklist

"THE ART AND SCIENCE OF QUESTIONING" (page 103)

Instruct students to complete the Effective Questioning Checklist according to directions given on the student activity page. Then, review their responses using the following arguments and rationales: (1) Bad Practice, as questions need to reflect both lower and higher levels of thinking; (2) Bad Practice, as rapid-fire questioning causes confusion and frustration among students, especially ESOL and learning disabled students, because there is not time for personal reflection or thought on one question before they are bombarded by another; (3) Good Practice, as "think time" or "wait time" leads to higher quality responses by students; (4) Bad Practice, as the teacher should alternate between asking questions first, and then calling on students with calling on students first, and then asking questions, to keep students involved and interested at all times; (5) Bad Practice, as there are better ways to handle inattentive students such as shorter discussion times or seating these inattentive students close to teacher and close to front of room where the action is; (6) Good Practice, as both work well and both should be used interchangeably; (7) Good Practice because the goal of a good discussion is to promote interaction between students rather than between a single student and the teacher so that teacher serves as "guide on the side" rather than "sage on the stage;" (8) Good Practice, as many times two or three heads are better than one; (9) Bad Practice, as teacher needs to inform students that they are off the subject now but that "we will come back to their question" later during the discussion; (10) Good Practice, as it is healthy for a teacher to model honesty by admitting to the lack of knowledge on certain subjects, and the interest in and need for further study.

NOSE FOR THE NEWS

PURPOSE: To give an informal, sit-down newspaper mini-speech about current events based on a news item of interest to students

TARGETED INTELLIGENCE: Verbal/Linguistic and Interpersonal

CONTENT/STANDARD FOCUS: Language Arts—Standards 7 and 12 & Social Studies—All Standards

PRODUCT/PERFORMANCE/STUDENT OUTCOME: Preparing a Newspaper Mini-Speech

"NOSE FOR THE NEWS" (page 104)

Direct students to bring in a feature or news story of interest to them. Provide them with copies of file cards on which to take notes according to directions given on the student page. Arrange students in small groups of six and have each student within the groups take turns giving their newspaper mini-speeches, referring to the note cards as needed. Students should remain seated at all times to keep the speech presentations as informal and as non-threatening as possible.

A PICTURE IS WORTH A THOUSAND WORDS

PURPOSE: To analyze and create a series of editorial cartoons from the newspaper

TARGETED INTELLIGENCE: Verbal/Linguistic, Logical/Mathematical, and Visual/Spatial

CONTENT/STANDARD FOCUS: Language Arts—Standards 1, 3, 4, and 11 & Social Studies—All Standards

PRODUCT/PERFORMANCE/STUDENT OUTCOME: Editorial Cartoon

"A PICTURE IS WORTH A THOUSAND WORDS" (page 105)

Make transparencies of several editorial cartoons from the local newspaper to share with students. Use these sample cartoons to lecture students on the characteristics of editorial cartoons listed on the student page. You may want to put students into small groups and have each group analyze an assigned cartoon, using these characteristics to direct the analysis process. If time permits, encourage students to create their own editorial cartoon that reflects one of the social studies standards.

COMMUNICATION BARRIERS AND BLUNDERS

PURPOSE: To examine the communication barriers and blunders of profanity, slang, slander, and gossip

TARGETED INTELLIGENCE: Verbal/Linguistic and Interpersonal

CONTENT/STANDARD FOCUS: Language Arts—Standards 4, 11, and 12 & Social Studies—Individual Development and Identity

PRODUCT/PERFORMANCE/STUDENT OUTCOME: Small Group Discussion

"COMMUNICATION BARRIERS AND BLUNDERS" (page 106)

Help students to understand that effective communication is a two-way street and that one can encounter a number of communication barriers and blunders through the inappropriate use of profanity, slang, slander, and gossip. Divide students into small cooperative learning groups and ask each group to answer the questions listed on the student activity sheet, according to directions given.

HOMEWORK HOTLINE

PURPOSE: To use the popular "Mad Lib" writing format as a basis for completing a humorous fill-in-the-blank paragraph on the value of honesty as it relates to forgotten homework assignments

TARGETED INTELLIGENCE: Verbal/Linguistic and Interpersonal

CONTENT/ STANDARD FOCUS: Language Arts—Standard 12 & Social Studies—Individual Development and Identity

PRODUCT/PERFORMANCE/STUDENT OUTCOME: Creating honesty-based "Mad-Libs"

"HOMEWORK HOTLINE" (page 107)

Bring in sample "Mad-Lib" books from the local bookstore and share this format with students who may not be familiar with the popular "Mad-Lib" type of humorous writing or, if time is limited, display the homework example from the student activity sheet on an overhead transparency to introduce the concept. Instruct students to complete the "Mad-Lib" on their student activity sheet individually. If time permits, encourage students to create original "Mad-Libs" of their own to share with one another.

MESSAGES MATTER

PURPOSE: To give examples of when it is more appropriate to communicate with someone through a letter, email, or telephone call

TARGETED INTELLIGENCE: Verbal/Linguistic, Visual/Spatial, and Bodily/Kinesthetic

CONTENT/STANDARD FOCUS: Language Arts—Standards 4, 8, 11, and 12

PRODUCT/PERFORMANCE/STUDENT OUTCOME: Creating an Outline Graphic Organizer

"MESSAGES MATTER" (page 108)

Ask students to share when and where they are likely to use each of the three types of communication options with their friends and families. Then, instruct students to complete the student activity sheet according to directions given. If necessary, ask students to enlarge the outline form on a separate sheet of paper.

ART AND MUSIC AS COMMUNICATION

PURPOSE: To investigate ways that both art and music are special forms of communication.

TARGETED INTELLIGENCE: Visual/Spatial and Musical/Rhythmic

CONTENT/STANDARD FOCUS: Art and Music

PRODUCT/PERFORMANCE/STUDENT OUTCOME: Composing a short essay

"ART AND MUSIC AS COMMUNICATION" (page 109)

If possible, provide different types of background music and different pieces or pictures of art/sculpture on display as students enter the classroom. Ask students to raise their hands if they have visited an art museum, art show, a concert, symphony, or musical performance. Discuss ways that art and music serve as cultural and educational forms of communication. Finally, instruct students to complete the student activity sheet as directed. If time permits, encourage students to orally share their original essays.

SPONTANEOUS REACTIONS TO COMMUNICATION CHALLENGES

PURPOSE: To experiment with various springboards that encourage students to engage in spontaneous and personal forms of writing

TARGETED INTELLIGENCE: Verbal/Linguistic, Intrapersonal, and Logical/Mathematical

CONTENT/STANDARD FOCUS: Language Arts—Standards 5, 7, 11, and 12 & Social Studies— All Standards

PRODUCT/PERFORMANCE/STUDENT OUTCOME: Piece of Original Writing

"SPONTANEOUS REACTIONS TO COMMUNICATION CHALLENGES" (page 110)

Review the list of springboards suggested on the student activity page and encourage students to select one or more to complete "off the tops of their heads." Review the concept of "spontaneous" writing as a reflection of previously-held thoughts and knowledge as opposed to writing that reflects research prior to the ideas and thoughts being recorded.

SOME TOPICS TO DISCUSS OR DEBATE

PURPOSE: To show students how to organize information on a controversial topic

TARGETED INTELLIGENCE: Verbal/Linguistic and Visual/Spatial

CONTENT/STANDARD FOCUS: Language Arts—Standards 4, 5, 7, 8, 11, and 12 & Social Studies—Culture; Individuals, Groups, and Institutions; Power, Authority, and Governance; Science, Technology, and Society; Civic Ideals and Practices

PRODUCT/PERFORMANCE/STUDENT OUTCOME: Producing a Graphic Organizer

"SOME TOPICS TO DISCUSS OR DEBATE" (page 111)

Explain to students why the Umbrella organizer is a good tool to use for recording the pros and cons, or the advantages and disadvantages, of a controversial situation. The topic should be placed at the top of the umbrella, leaving the sides of the umbrella to be used for listing the pros or advantages on one side and the cons or disadvantages on the other. After students prepare their arguments, organize groups to allow all students in a given group the opportunity to share their opinion on the same issue. Instruct students to use their graphic organizers as a reference for discussing or debating both sides of the issue.

©2004 Incentive Publications, Inc.
Nashville, TN

IS HONESTY REALLY THE BEST POLICY?

PURPOSE: To create a television commercial that promotes honesty as an important value in a society

TARGETED INTELLIGENCE: Verbal/Linguistic, Visual/Spatial, and Bodily/Kinesthetic

CONTENT/STANDARD FOCUS: Language Arts—Standards 4, 5, 6, 8, 11, and 12 & Social Studies—Individual Development and Identity; Science, Technology, and Society

PRODUCT/PERFORMANCE/STUDENT OUTCOME: A Television Commercial

"IS HONESTY REALLY THE BEST POLICY?" (page 112)

Introduce this activity to students by having them share their favorite television commercials within a large group setting. During the discussion, identify various advertising techniques used to market each product or service. Next, divide the students into small cooperative learning groups of six, and ask each group to create their own commercials, promoting the virtue of "honesty" in today's diverse and complex society.

GAMBLING AND YOUTH: IS IT REALLY A PROBLEM? BE HONEST!

PURPOSE: To show how gambling has become a serious problem for many young people

TARGETED INTELLIGENCE: Logical/Mathematical and Intrapersonal

CONTENT/STANDARD FOCUS: Social Studies—Individuals, Groups, and Institutions & Mathematics—Probability; Mathematics as Reasoning

PRODUCT/PERFORMANCE/STUDENT OUTCOME: Self-Checklist

"GAMBLING AND YOUTH: IS IT REALLY A PROBLEM? BE HONEST!"

(pages 113–114) Review the concept of "probability" and how it influences one's chances of winning big in a lottery or other type of large-scale gambling. Encourage students to understand the "odds" when engaging in any type of gambling activity, large or small. Then, instruct students to complete the self-checklist according to the directions given. Encourage volunteers to share their results and relate to the gambling information given on the student page.

DEALING WITH HONESTY IN DIFFICULT SITUATIONS

PURPOSE: To use case studies as the foundation for dealing with honesty in difficult situations at home, at work, or at play

TARGETED INTELLIGENCE: Verbal/Linguistic, Bodily/Kinesthetic, and Intrapersonal

CONTENT/STANDARD FOCUS: Social Studies—Individual Development and Identity

PRODUCT/PERFORMANCE/STUDENT OUTCOME: A Case Study

"DEALING WITH HONESTY IN DIFFICULT SITUATIONS" (page 115)

Review the characteristics of a case study, pointing out to students that it is a life-like scenario with real characters to think about, real problems to address, multiple alternatives to contemplate, and vivid details to consider. Pair students with a partner and have them select one or more of the case studies to discuss between themselves. If time permits, encourage each team to create an original case study to share with the class, or to act out (role-play) one of those described in the activity.

CAFETERIA FOOD FIGHTS: WHO STARTS THEM?

PURPOSE: To examine the realities of today's cafeteria food and services in school

TARGETED INTELLIGENCE: Naturalistic and Logical/Mathematical

CONTENT/STANDARD FOCUS: Science—Life Science; and Science in Personal and Social Perspectives

PRODUCT/PERFORMANCE/STUDENT OUTCOME: Creating an Editorial related to school food services

"CAFETERIA FOOD FIGHTS: WHO STARTS THEM? BE HONEST!" (page 116)

Discuss the problems cafeterias have to deal with in today's schools—problems such as food sourcing, funding/budgets, discipline/behavior disruptions, fast-food options, parent pressures, and nutritional needs. Solicit input from students on likes and dislikes regarding cafeteria food choices, student behavior patterns, parent concerns, and overall quality of dining cafeteria style. Encourage students to work as individuals or in pairs to draft a letter to the principal of the school, or for possible publication in a school newspaper or classroom newsletter.

INVENTIONS THAT IMPACTED COMMUNICATION EFFORTS

PURPOSE: To rank various inventions that have impacted and influenced communication efforts over time

TARGETED INTELLIGENCE: Verbal/Linguistic and Logical/Mathematical

CONTENT/STANDARD FOCUS: Social Studies—Time, Continuity, and Change; Science, Technology, and Society & Science—Unifying Concepts and Processes; Physical Science; Science and Technology; Science in Personal and Social Perspectives

PRODUCT/PERFORMANCE/STUDENT OUTCOME: Think/Pair/Share to Rank Order Inventions Related to Communication

"INVENTIONS THAT IMPACTED COMMUNICATION EFFORTS" (page 117)

Briefly work with students to put the list of inventions on the student page in chronological order. Then, ask students to complete the ranking task according to directions given.

TALKING INSIDE AND OUTSIDE THE CIRCLE

PURPOSE: To introduce students to the Inside/Outside Circle strategy as a tool for reviewing course content or discussing controversial issues

TARGETED INTELLIGENCE: Bodily/Kinesthetic and Interpersonal

CONTENT/STANDARD FOCUS: Science—Science and Technology; Science in Personal and Social Perspectives & Social Studies—Individuals, Groups, and Institutions; Production, Distribution, and Consumption; and Science, Technology, and Society

PRODUCT/PERFORMANCE/STUDENT OUTCOME: Participation in a Large Group Discussion

"TALKING INSIDE AND OUTSIDE THE CIRCLE" (page 118)

Explain the Inside/Outside Circle strategy to students and ask them to apply the strategy to the topic of "technology," using the questions listed on the student page. You may want to put the questions on a transparency for the overhead projector, or on a large piece of chart paper, in order to move quickly from question to question as students change places around the circle. Use music or a whistle to signal when student rotations should begin and end.

TECHNOLOGICAL INFLUENCES ON COMMUNICATION

PURPOSE: To demonstrate the multiple influences of technology on forms of communication today

TARGETED INTELLIGENCE: Logical/Mathematical

CONTENT/STANDARD FOCUS: Mathematics

PRODUCT/PERFORMANCE/STUDENT OUTCOME: Completing Mathematical Computations

"TECHNOLOGICAL INFLUENCES ON COMMUNICATION" (page 119)

Poll the students to determine how many of them have their own cell phones or email addresses. Discuss how personal communication devices have become a way of life for so many adults in the world today. Then, have students complete the mathematical computations as directed on the student page.

COMMUNICATING THROUGH SYMBOLS AND ICONS

PURPOSE: To demonstrate ways that symbols and icons are used to communicate ideas, information, and locations

TARGETED INTELLIGENCE: Verbal/Linguistic and Visual/Spatial

CONTENT/STANDARD FOCUS: Social Studies—Individuals, Groups, and Institutions; Production, Consumption, and Distribution; Global Connections

PRODUCT/PERFORMANCE/STUDENT OUTCOME: Producing a Set of Flash Cards

"COMMUNICATING THROUGH SYMBOLS AND ICONS" (page 120)

Define/explain the concepts of "symbols" and "icons" as forms of communication in today's world. Discuss how these symbols and icons facilitate both communication and interdependence among populations all over the world. Review the directions on the student page and provide note cards, crayons, and/or magic markers for students to use in preparing their flash card sets.

©2004 Incentive Publications, Inc.
Nashville, TN

ACTIONS SOMETIMES SPEAK LOUDER THAN WORDS

PURPOSE: To give examples of how body gestures and body language can communicate as well as words on many occasions

TARGETED INTELLIGENCE: Bodily/Kinesthetic and Intrapersonal

CONTENT/STANDARD FOCUS: Language Arts—Standards 4 and 12

PRODUCT/PERFORMANCE/STUDENT OUTCOME: Reflecting on Body Language

"ACTIONS SOMETIMES SPEAK LOUDER THAN WORDS" (page 121)

To introduce this activity, ask students to discuss ways and times when teachers use body language to get a message across. Review the many different forms of body language such as eye contact, arm/hand gestures, and facial expressions. Instruct students to complete the tasks on the student activity page according to directions given.

WE ARE ALL MULTICULTURAL TO SOMEONE

PURPOSE: To introduce students to cultural characteristics that may affect communication among students or between students and adults of different cultures

TARGETED INTELLIGENCE: Bodily/Kinesthetic and Interpersonal

CONTENT/STANDARD FOCUS: Social Studies—Individuals, Groups, and Institutions; Global Connections

PRODUCT/PERFORMANCE/STUDENT OUTCOME: Role-play

"WE ARE ALL MULTICULTURAL TO SOMEONE" (page 122)

Review the characteristics of various cultures as outlined on the student activity page. Divide students into small cooperative learning groups and have each group develop an original role-play to show the problems a non-English speaking student might have in one of several school-related situations.

THEME: COMMUNICATION   VALUE: HONESTY

WHY DISHONESTY RARELY WORKS!

Directions: Sometimes situations or circumstances arise in our personal lives whereby we think a "little white lie" won't hurt anybody. However, once a lie (even a little one) is set in motion, somebody is likely to be hurt. Take a few minutes to jot down your thoughts and reactions to the questions on the lines below in preparation for a large group discussion on the subject of "Honest vs. Dishonest" decisions about what to say when!

1. What might happen if a kid lies to his/her parents or vice versa?

    _____

    _____

2. What might happen if a student lies to his/her teacher or vice versa?

    _____

    _____

3. What might happen if a client lies to his/her lawyer or vice versa?

    _____

    _____

4. What might happen if a doctor lies to his/her patient or vice versa?

    _____

    _____

5. What might happen if a salesman lies to his/her customer or vice versa?

    _____

    _____

6. What might happen if a politician lies to his/her constituents or vice versa?

    _____

    _____

7. What might happen if a banker lies to his/her depositors or vice versa?

    _____

    _____

8. What might happen if a boyfriend lies to his girlfriend or vice versa?

    _____

    _____

Name: _____

THE ART AND SCIENCE OF QUESTIONING

Directions: When participating in small and large group discussions, whether they are led by the teacher or a student leader, effective questioning techniques are important to the outcome of the discussion itself. Read through each statement on the checklist of questioning practices. From your personal experiences, determine whether you think it indicates a good questioning practice or a bad questioning practice. Write "good" or "bad" in the blank space before each statement. Give a rationale for each choice.

Effective Questioning Checklist:

1. _____Most questions asked during class should be memory questions, not thought questions.

   RATIONALE: _____

2. _____Rapid-fire questioning makes class exciting and interesting.

   RATIONALE: _____

3. _____Students should be given some "think time" before they are expected to answer.

   RATIONALE: _____

4. _____The teacher should call on a student only after stating the question and not before.

   RATIONALE: _____

5. _____The teacher should call on both volunteers and non-volunteers.

   RATIONALE: _____

6. _____Students should be encouraged to question each other during discussions.

   RATIONALE: _____

7. _____Sometimes students should be allowed to work together to answer a question.

   RATIONALE: _____

8. _____Students who ask questions unrelated to the topic of the lesson should be ignored, and their questions left unanswered.

   RATIONALE: _____

9. _____The teacher has an obligation to research and report back to the class when asked a question he/she cannot answer.

   RATIONALE: _____

10. _____The teacher should repeat student answers to be sure everyone heard them.

   RATIONALE: _____

Name: _____

Advisory Plus!

NOSE FOR THE NEWS

Directions: You are to browse through your local newspaper to find a news or feature article of interest to you, which you also think will be of interest to others in the class. Read it carefully, and then prepare a set of five different 3 x 5 file cards to serve as information notes to use when delivering a short mini-speech to a small group of your peers. You are to record the following information from your article on the cards, according to these guidelines:

NOTE CARD ONE: Record the name and date of the newspaper. Record the name of the news service the item is from and the name of the reporter who wrote the article, if available.

NOTE CARD TWO: Briefly explain what the article is about. Tell the Who, What, When, Where, and How of the article.

NOTE CARD THREE: Explain why the article is important, and what you learned from it.

NOTE CARD FOUR: Give your reactions to the article.

NOTE CARD FIVE: Make any additional comments of interest to you using one of the suggestions listed below:

1. Would you like to have been present at this event? Why or why not?

2. What intrigued you most about this event or issue?

3. What could have happened to change the outcome of this event?

4. Suppose a picture of the event or issue were in the newspaper. What might the caption under the photograph have said?

5. Was there a cause and effect relationship to this event? If so, explain.

6. How are today's morals, values, or ethics exhibited in this event or issue?

7. Why is this event or issue newsworthy?

8. Who is most affected by this event or issue?

9. What might a follow-up article to this event or issue be about?

10. How is this event or issue related to something you have studied in school recently?

Name: _____

A PICTURE IS WORTH A THOUSAND WORDS

Directions: Editorial cartoons are found in all newspapers and are important tools for communicating opinions and feelings about important issues or problems that exist in society.

A student, or any newspaper reader, needs to develop certain analysis skills if they are to interpret the message of an editorial cartoon. Bring an editorial cartoon from your local newspaper to class, and use the checklist below to help you become more skilled at making sense out of it. Then, if time permits, try creating an original editorial cartoon of your own on an issue or problem of importance to you. Sketch your cartoon at the bottom of this page.

1. ISSUE: Editorial cartoons have the major purpose of offering an opinion or point of view about some key issue or problem in the news.

2. SYMBOLS: Editorial cartoons make maximum use of symbols to convey their message. A symbol is any object or design that stands for some other thing, person, or idea.

3. EXAGGERATIONS/DISTORTIONS: Editorial cartoons use features that are distorted or exaggerated in some way. They may appear much larger or smaller in size, or they may change in shape or purpose to make the feature look funny or ugly.

4. STEREOTYPES: Editorial cartoons often employ stereotyping to give a more simplistic view of some group in order to make its point quickly.

5. CARICATURES: Editorial cartoons often portray the features of an individual in an exaggerated or distorted way, also to make a point quickly.

6. HUMOR AND IRONY: Editorial cartoons find humor through the use of irony. Irony presents a viewpoint that is expressed in such an odd way as to make that view seem unrealistic, exaggerated, and ridiculous.

7. KNOWLEDGE: Editorial cartoons require the reader to know something about the issue or problem being addressed so that he/she can understand it.

MY SKETCH FOR AN EDITORIAL CARTOON

Name:

COMMUNICATION BARRIERS AND BLUNDERS

Directions: The communication skills of speaking and listening are very important in today's world, for both the student and the adult. If students can't express themselves clearly, accurately, and courteously, many problems can surface. Some barriers to effective communication are the use of profanity, slander, slang, and gossip. Work with members of your cooperative learning group to discuss each of these barriers, using the questions below as the guidelines for the dialogue.

1. How would you define and explain each of these communication terms: profanity, slang, slander, and gossip? How are they alike and how are they different?

2. What do we mean by the concepts of "barriers" and "blunders" when used in the context of being effective communicators?

3. Is there ever a time when the use of profanity in a conversation is acceptable? How do you react to someone who uses profanity on a regular basis? Is profanity a turn-on or a turn-off for you? Explain your thoughts on each of these issues.

4. Have you, or someone you know, ever been a victim of slander? Describe the situation. How does one go about negating slanderous statements that are circulated about him/her? Give examples of what you would do if you found yourself in a similar circumstance.

5. What are your favorite slang expressions and when do you use them? Is slang an appropriate type of language to use in all or most communication settings, or is there a best time and place for slang to be spoken? Give reasons for your answers.

6. It has been said that gossip is inevitable and a way of life for most people. Do you agree or disagree with this philosophy and why? Do you think that most gossip is harmless, or do you think that most gossip is cruel? Is gossip usually based on honest facts? Be specific in your comments.

7. Can your group compose a statement that clearly expresses how profanity, slang, slander, and gossip are real barriers and blunders to effective communication between people?

Name: _____

HOMEWORK HOTLINE

Directions: Have you seen the many books of "Mad Libs" that are popular with kids today and sold in most bookstores? These books contain short essays or stories about many different topics that are composed of sentences with blank spaces in them so that the reader can insert his or her own thoughts. The results are often humorous or silly. Complete the "Mad Lib" outline written below, and then try to create an original "Mad Lib" outline of your own so that others in the class can have fun with it! Write your original piece on the other side of this paper.

"HOMEWORK HASSLES"

If I forgot my homework on any given school day, I would say to my teacher

_____ and he/she would respond by saying _____ .
    (phrase)   *(phrase)*

I would then try discussing the excuse of _____ and he/she would
    (excuse)

tell me to _____ . The dumbest excuse for not doing a homework
    (action)

assignment that I have ever heard in class was _____ and this time
    (excuse)

the teacher agreed to _____ . The cleverest excuse for not doing a
    (action)

homework assignment that I have ever heard in class was _____ , but
    (excuse)

this time the teacher refused to _____ . When my parents heard
    (action)

about the forgotten homework assignment, they told me to _____ and
    (action)

_____ . My advice to any kid who forgets his/her homework in
    (action)

the future is to _____ .
    (action)

Name:

MESSAGES MATTER

Directions: Over time, many people have welcomed the "gift" of a letter as a primary form of communication because letters can be read again and again, can be saved indefinitely, are extremely private and personal, can be composed in segments over time, and can be written on anything from personalized stationery to scrap paper. In fact, some letters have become preserved historical documents found in museums and in private collections. Recently, however, letters are being sent less often in favor of technology and the email option. Today, emails are more widespread for both personal and professional use than are individual letters because of their efficiency and speed. Then, of course, there is the telephone (and cell phone and beeper), which is the communication of choice for people in all age groups and income ranges. Many people enjoy hearing a message rather than reading one, and they thrive on the live, interactive exchange between two or more parties. Using the Three-Level Outline below as a guide, list all of the pros and cons you can think of for each form of communication—letters, emails, and telephone calls. Also, list the circumstances or occasions when each of these tools is really the most appropriate way to communicate with others. Be honest in your assessment.

A Three-Level Outline

I. _____
  A. _____
    1. _____
    2. _____
    3. _____
  B. _____
    1. _____
    2. _____
    3. _____

II. _____
  A. _____
    1. _____
    2. _____
    3. _____
  B. _____
    1. _____
    2. _____
    3. _____

III. _____
  A. _____
    1. _____
    2. _____
    3. _____
  B. _____
    1. _____
    2. _____
    3. _____

Name: _____

©2004 Incentive Publications, Inc.
Nashville, TN

ART AND MUSIC AS COMMUNICATION

Directions: It has been said that both music and art have a language all their own. For example, when you listen to a piece of music or attend a musical performance, does the music conjure up visual images and offer you a basis for conversation with another listener? When you see a piece of sculpture or visit an art museum, does the artistic piece trigger your imagination and offer you a basis for conversation with another viewer? To help you think about these ideas further, ponder each of the questions posed below.

1. What type of music has the greatest appeal to you and why?

2. What type of art has the greatest appeal to you and why?

3. Would you rather attend an art show or a musical production? Give reasons for your answer.

4. How do you explain the rising interest in computer-generated art and music?

5. One problem that technology has caused musicians and artists in our world today is that of copyright violations when individuals download either music selections or art renderings without permission. What do you think can be done about this plagiarism?

6. What special words/terms do you associate with the world of music? List them.

7. What special words/terms do you associate with the world of art? List them.

8. If you could spend a day with a musician or an artist, whom would you choose, and what would you want to know and do?

9. As you think about your favorite record or CD, what song is most special? Why do both the musical score and the lyrics appeal to you? What do they say to you?

10. As you think about your favorite painting or picture, what does the artist say to you? Why do both the subject and the colors appeal to you? What do they say to you?

11. Suppose you were asked to compose a short essay justifying the notion that both music and art are a language of their own. What would you say?

Name:

SPONTANEOUS REACTIONS TO COMMUNICATION CHALLENGES

Directions: Choose one or more of these springboards to use as the foundation for writing a short paragraph based solely on your current knowledge and personal understanding of the topic.

1. Think of some special ways to promote honesty and integrity among students in your school.

2. Tell everything you know about the presidential election process.

3. Explain how music can be used as a communication tool.

4. Expand on this statement: "The only thing we have to fear is fear itself."

5. In what ways can people of one culture show respect for a culture different from their own?

6. State three ecology problems that must be solved by your generation in order to preserve natural resources for the next generation.

7. Tell whether you would rather be rich, famous, or powerful, and why.

8. If you could have taken part in a historical event, which one would it have been and what role would you have wanted to play?

9. Explain why you would or would not make a good candidate for a political office in your community.

10. Talk about a stereotype or prejudice that you have to overcome.

11. Who has more power—a teacher or a politician? Why?

12. Which is likely to be a more honest solution to a disagreement—total agreement of both parties or agreement through compromise?

13. What do you think is most impressive about a democratic society?

14. What is the most important event you can visualize happening in the next 25 years?

15. Imagine a rating machine for honesty. How would it work?

Name:

SOME TOPICS TO DISCUSS OR DEBATE

Directions: Below are several controversial issues about which people have many differing points of view. Learning how to communicate to others one's opinions, feelings, and arguments about something important can best be accomplished through the use of an organizing structure. A good graphic organizer to use in preparing for discussion or debate is an Umbrella Organizer. The problem statement is written under the umbrella, and on either side of the umbrella the pros (or advantages) and the cons (or disadvantages) are written. Enlarge the simple umbrella drawing below to help you plan your arguments.

ISSUE ONE: Many professional sports teams have Indian names and mascots, including the Redskins, Braves, Blackhawks, and Indians. Opponents say that such usage promotes stereotyping, improper labeling, and prejudice. Should such names be permitted? Why or why not?

ISSUE TWO: Men and women should be treated equally in combat. Do you agree or disagree? Explain.

ISSUE FOUR: Does the right to privacy prohibit the government or other institutions from collecting information about you without your permission or knowledge? Discuss.

ISSUE FIVE: In the political arena today, many are challenging the laws that will enable children to divorce their parents. Do you think these laws will protect children or hurt parents trying to raise their own children? Give the pros and cons of such a condition.

ISSUE SIX: Many people think cell phones and pagers are disruptive and should be banned from public places with quiet atmospheres with no or few exceptions. What is good and bad about this situation?

ISSUE SEVEN: Making all schools require uniforms for all students is a good plan because it will improve student attitudes and achievement levels in schools. Is this a good and valid idea? Defend your point of view.

ISSUE EIGHT: Computers, video games, and television are mainly to blame for falling test scores in American schools. Is this true, partly true, or absolutely not true?

The Umbrella

Name:

IS HONESTY REALLY THE BEST POLICY?

Directions: You will be working in cooperative learning groups of six. The assignment for your group is to create a three-minute television commercial that advertises, promotes, or informs the viewer about the importance of honesty in today's society—a virtue that some people feel is declining in the world of advertising. The commercial should include content, a slogan, visuals, and dialogue. To help you get started, take a few minutes to discuss the following questions that involve honesty issues and concerns.

1. Do you think most commercials on television are honest in their promotion of products and services? Why or why not?

2. How would viewers of a television commercial check for honesty in a sales presentation?

3. What are your favorite television commercials? Do you value them because of their honest approach in promoting the product or for some other reason such as humor, cleverness, or creativity?

4. What form of advertising is most appealing to you—magazine advertisements, television commercials, radio sales pitches, billboards, newspaper display ads, or windows of retail outlets? Give reasons for your answer.

5. Which of these advertising techniques do you think is most effective in advertising:
   . . . . . Bandwagon—Everybody is doing it or buying it!
   . . . . . Famous Person—Celebrity promotes the product in a personal way
   . . . . . Impressive Statistics—Five out of every six people use our product
   . . . . . Undermining Competition—Our product outsells every other similar product
            on the market

6. Who are some people today or of the past that you associate with the value of "honesty"?

7. Who are some people today or of the past that you associate with "dishonest" deeds or actions?

8. Does it always pay to be honest in your dealings with people? Is it ever appropriate to tell a little "white lie"? Explain.

9. What types of careers do you associate most with "honesty"? With "dishonesty"? Be specific in your comments.

10. How honest are you in your daily life? Rate yourself on a 1 to 10 scale, with 1 being dishonest most of the time and 10 being honest most of the time.

Name: _____

112

©2004 Incentive Publications, Inc.
Nashville, TN

GAMBLING AND YOUTH: IS IT REALLY A PROBLEM? BE HONEST!

Directions: While gambling is not a new activity, changes in attitudes and access over the past two decades have contributed to its newfound status as a prevalent high-risk activity among youth. Young people today are more exposed to the gambling industry than at any other time in this country's history. Currently, it is difficult to listen to the radio, watch television, or frequent a fast-food restaurant without experiencing the lure of some type of gambling-related activity. Even the household dinner table has become a place where the prospect of "winning big" in the lottery is a common topic of conversation. Youth might engage in a wide range of gambling activities including: bingo, cards, Internet (World Wide Web provides accessibility to online gambling venues), mah jongg, private bets, raffles, scratch and win tickets, sports betting, state-run lotteries, and stock market wagers.

Although adolescent gamblers are by no means a homogeneous population, the characteristics listed below are often symptomatic of young problem gamblers:

- Above-average IQ, but uninterested scholastically
- Resent parental intrusions
- Spend cash liberally
- Very competitive
- Athletic
- Good with numbers
- Hard worker
- Shy
- Easily bored
- Fear criticism and rejection
- Hide feelings
- Easily frustrated
- Low self-esteem
- Believe money will solve problems
- Impulsive
- Obsessive/compulsive behaviors
- Gregarious
- Easily drawn into friendships

(continued . . .)

Name:

GAMBLING AND YOUTH: IS IT REALLY A PROBLEM? BE HONEST! (CONTINUED)

Finally, it should be noted that various forms of gambling are promoted in seemingly harmless ways. Fast-food restaurants promote scratch tabs. Television promotes lotteries. Schools promote raffles. Churches promote bingo. Complete the checklist below to determine if you have ever participated in a gambling activity. Write "Yes" or "No" after each item. Then, use your math textbook to find out more about the concept of "probability" and how it influences one's chances of winning big in a lottery or other type of large-scale gambling.

1. I have played card games for money.. . . . . _____

2. I have flipped coins for money. . . . . _____

3. I have bet on games of personal skill like pool, golf, or bowling. . . . . . . _____

4. I have bet on sports games.. . . . . _____

5. I have played bingo for money. . . . . _____

6. I have played dice games. . . . . _____

7. I have played slot machines. . . . . _____

8. I have played scratch tabs. . . . . _____

9. I have played the lottery by picking numbers. . . . . _____

10. I have played the stock, options, or commodities market for money. . . . _____

11. I have bet on video games. . . . . _____

12. I have bet on horses, dogs, or other animals. . . . . _____

13. I have purchased raffle tickets. . . . . _____

Name:

©2004 Incentive Publications, Inc.
Nashville, TN

DEALING WITH HONESTY IN DIFFICULT SITUATIONS

Directions: Review each of these case studies dealing with the issue of "honesty vs. dishonesty" and decide how you would handle each situation diplomatically, but honestly. Then, if time permits, describe a personal situation dealing with an honesty issue that you or someone you know has experienced. Write out your case study in such a way that it has life-like characters, a problem situation, and alternative methods for approaching and resolving the problem. Give as much detail as possible.

CASE STUDY ONE: Jane and Sally were good friends and did everything together. Jane was very outgoing and very popular in school, and valued Sally for her academic abilities and her willingness to help Jane study for tests. Sally was a quiet, introverted girl who relished being by herself and preferred to spend her free time reading, writing poetry, and exploring on the Internet. Sally enjoyed Jane's company primarily because she found Jane to be an animated conversationalist and a person who could keep a secret. At the end of the school year, Dottie, a mutual friend of Jane and Sally's, was hosting a party, and invited a large group to her home to celebrate moving on to the next grade. Dottie invited Jane but did not invite Sally because of her limitations as a "people person" and a poor "mixer." When Sally questioned Jane about this lack of an invitation, Jane did not know how to respond without hurting Sally's feelings or hurting Dottie. What would you say and do if you were Jane?

CASE STUDY TWO: Mark was not a good student in school, but he was an excellent athlete who needed to maintain his grade point average in order to play on the school's championship basketball team. Sam, on the other hand, was not a good athlete but was a straight A student in all of his subject areas. Both boys knew each other, but were not really good friends. The class was preparing for the upcoming State Assessment Test in math and it was imperative that Mark pass this test if he were to continue on the team, which was playing in the finals of the state championship within the next month. Several kids in the class approached Sam and put pressure on him to let Mark "cheat" on the test by looking at his answers since they sat next to each other in class. Sam wanted to help Mark out, but he had always valued honesty in his dealings with others. What would you say or do if you were Sam?

CASE STUDY THREE: Tanya and her sister, Terri, were three years apart in age and school. Tanya was in 5th grade while her sister was in 8th grade. The girls were pretty good buddies, but they had very different personalities. Tanya was conservative and Terri was a risk-taker. One evening, Tanya discovered that Terri would sneak out of the house after dark without their parents' knowledge in order to meet friends whose reputations made them "off limits" in their parents' opinion. When Tanya confronted her sister about these escapades, Terri tried to bribe Tanya into not telling their parents by giving Tanya half of her allowance each week. Tanya valued her sister's friendship and privacy, but she was very concerned about the situation. What should Tanya say and do?

Name:

CAFETERIA FOOD FIGHTS: WHO STARTS THEM?

Directions: Many school cafeterias today serve chicken nuggets, cheeseburgers, French fries and pizzas along with salads, fruits, and vegetables. The school lunchroom has long been a battleground for food activists and parents concerned about the nutritional quality of students' midday meal. Now, with rising obesity, criticism is escalating from legislators, researchers, and consumer groups who maintain that fast-food vending machines and the troubled economics of school cafeterias are culprits in the alarming growth of children's and youths' waistlines. According to the latest figures from the Centers for Disease Control and Prevention, some 14% of teenagers were overweight in 2000, almost triple the rate of the late 1970s. Among children ages six to eleven, 13% were overweight, almost double the rate of two decades ago. Vending machines are present in 43% of elementary schools, 74% of middle schools, and nearly all high schools. Twenty percent of schools also sell pizza, burgers, and fries.

Are schools doing the right thing, and are they honest about the reasons for their decisions? Take a few minutes to reflect on the questions below, and then compose an editorial for your school newspaper or newsletter on the subject of cafeteria food and services.

1. Behavior of kids in today's school cafeterias leaves much to be desired. Cafeteria food fights are common, and many nutritionists blame such behaviors on "too much sugar and too much processed, full-fat meat and cheese" on the menu. What do you think?

2. Do most kids at your school choose foods from the hot lunch menu and/or salad bar or do they choose items from vending machines and fast food outlets if offered? What do you do?

3. Why do you think that obesity rates in children and teenagers are rising on a yearly basis? How much of this problem is a result of cafeteria food choices? What could be other reasons?

4. In most instances, school cafeterias cannot make a profit on federally subsidized hot lunches, while they can earn a profit margin of 50% or more on a la carte foods, such as chicken fingers or a ham sandwich. Is this fair? What should be done about it?

5. Should schools serve fast food as part of their lunch programs? Why or why not?

6. Some schools are planting elaborate vegetable gardens on school grounds as part of their science and health programs, hoping that kids who pick a tomato or harvest their own carrot or cucumber are more likely to eat such fare if served at school. Do you think this is a good idea?

Name:

INVENTIONS THAT IMPACTED COMMUNICATION EFFORTS

Directions: Work with a partner to review each of the inventions listed below, and rank them from one to fourteen in order of their importance and impact on communication efforts over the years, with 1 being most important and 14 being least important. List the criteria you will use to rank the items, and be prepared to give at least three reasons for your first and last choices.

CRITERIA FOR RANKING _____

Kodak Camera	_____	Television	_____
Talking Movie	_____	Typewriter	_____
Ballpoint Pen	_____	Telephone	_____
Printing Press	_____	Fax Machine	_____
Radio	_____	Microphone	_____
Phonograph	_____	Computer	_____
Telegraph	_____	Pencil	_____

FIRST CHOICE _____

    Reason 1 _____

    Reason 2 _____

    Reason 3 _____

LAST CHOICE _____

    Reason 1 _____

    Reason 2 _____

    Reason 3 _____

Name: _____

Advisory Plus!

TALKING INSIDE AND OUTSIDE THE CIRCLE

Directions: Members of your class are going to be divided into two concentric circles—an inside circle and an outside circle. You are to stand facing each other and move clockwise (inside circle) or counter-clockwise (outside circle) when a signal (such as a whistle or music) is given, making certain to pause in front of another student when that signal is given to stop. Each time the signal is given, you will discuss one of the questions listed below with the person opposite you, taking turns to share thoughts and ideas on the subject. The topic under discussion for this activity is "technology."

QUESTION ONE: Do you have a computer at home? If so, what do you use it for? If not, what would you use it for if you had one?

QUESTION TWO: What are some good and not-so-good ways modern technology has impacted your family and personal life?

QUESTION THREE: What are some good and not-so-good ways modern technology has impacted your academic life at school?

QUESTION FOUR: What do you think about using the Internet for shopping, for travel information, for news/weather, and for entertainment purposes? Can you cite some personal experiences?

QUESTION FIVE: What do you think about using the Internet for research on school assignments? What are its advantages and disadvantages? How do you document your research taken from the Internet?

QUESTION SIX: What are some serious problems that can be caused by dishonest use of the Internet, email, and chat rooms by both kids and adults?

QUESTION SEVEN: How would you control and punish those individuals who misuse technology for wrongdoing, such as through pornography, fraud, false advertising, and misrepresentation of self or product?

QUESTION EIGHT: If you were going to create a home page for your own personal website, what would it look like and what would it say? (If you already have one, describe it.)

QUESTION NINE: What is your favorite website to visit on the Internet? Explain.

QUESTION TEN: What advice would you give to someone who is just learning the magic of the Internet?

Name:

TECHNOLOGICAL INFLUENCES ON COMMUNICATION

Directions: Today, when two adults meet one another for a meeting, conversation, or social event, they are likely to give out contact information for future reference when parting: "Goodbye, here's my office number, home number, cell number, fax number, pager number, work email address, personal email address, and family email address. Please note that I have voice mail, call forwarding, and call waiting." What does this tell you about the influences of technology on the way people communicate with one another at home, at work, and at play? Use the personal information of our imaginary friend, John, to solve a variety of math problems as directed. Have fun playing this numbers game!

Meet John!

   . . . his office phone number is 378-9228;
   . . . his home phone number is 966-5634;
   . . . his cell number is 877-1996;
   . . . his pager number is 344-5544;
   . . . his fax number is 378-9779;
   . . . his email address is john67@meetjohn.com

- Add up all the numbers above. What is their total?

- Subtract his cell number from his home phone number. What is the difference?

- Divide his pager number by the number in his email address.

- Multiply his fax number times his pager number.

- Double his office phone number and add this to his fax number.

- Which is greater? The difference between his home and office phone numbers or the difference between his pager and cell numbers?

Name:

COMMUNICATING THROUGH SYMBOLS AND ICONS

Directions: Many times symbols are used to communicate major ideas or locations of key services. For example, think about patriotic symbols used in the United States, such as the American flag or the Statue of Liberty. Think about the many economic symbols that are used to denote monetary information, such as the dollar sign and the cent sign. Think about science symbols that are used to convey scientific ideas, such as the symbol for male or female. Think about the many icons that are used in technology to facilitate use of the computer, such as the print icon or the cut and paste icon. Think about the travel and safety symbols that you see on the street or highway that indicate the location of a rest stop or a hospital. Finally, think about the symbols used by editors to proofread written materials, such as the symbols for a paragraph or to delete a word. Work with a partner to brainstorm as many different and varied symbols or icons as you can in fifteen minutes. Jot these down on the lines below. Then use 3x5 note cards to prepare a set of flash cards for each symbol/icon on your brainstorming list. On one side of the card draw the symbol or icon, and on the other side define its meaning. See how many of your peers can both identify the symbols and/or icons and classify them according to a given subject area or topic.

_____

_____

_____

_____

_____

_____

_____

_____

_____

_____

Name: _____

ACTIONS SOMETIMES SPEAK LOUDER THAN WORDS

Directions: Body language and gestures can often convey messages and feelings as well as, or even better than, words. For each of the body gestures suggested here, think of a situation when you are likely to elicit such a response from a parent, a teacher, and a friend.

1. The person gives you a great, big smile. What might have caused a smile from a teacher, friend, or parent?

2. The person gives you a huge frown. What might have caused a frown from a teacher, friend, or parent?

3. The person just shrugs their shoulders and gives a sigh. What might have caused a sigh and shrug from a teacher, friend, or parent?

4. The person rolls their eyes backwards. What might have caused this reaction from a teacher, friend, or parent?

5. The person claps their hands to show pleasure. What might have caused hand clapping from a teacher, friend, or parent?

6. The person points their index finger right at you. What might have caused a pointed finger from a teacher, friend, or parent?

Name:

Advisory Plus!

WE ARE ALL MULTICULTURAL TO SOMEONE

Directions: The differences in how people from various cultures communicate (both verbally and nonverbally) are interesting to observe. Eye contact, specific gestures, or unusual behaviors may mean one thing to you, but something completely different to a person from another ethnic background. Some of these differing cultural characteristics are listed below. Work in small cooperative learning groups to role-play some problems a student speaking a language different from the majority of students in your school might have when engaging in conversations or learning experiences with other students or adults. Consider parent/teacher conferences, student/teacher conferences, group learning situations, field experiences, exploratory courses, social or extracurricular activities, or even tutoring sessions.

ANGLO-AMERICAN CULTURE:

- Values informal and face-to-face, eye-to-eye conversations
- Values promptness at meetings and appointments
- Values nuclear family over extended family
- Values competitiveness and individuality in children
- Values control over emotions in public

HISPANIC CULTURE:

- Values physical closeness during conversations more than most cultures
- Values loose interpretation of time
- Values extended family and considers it a priority
- Values showing intense emotions in conversations
- Values demonstrations of affection in activities

AFRICAN-AMERICAN CULTURE:

- Values privacy at first meeting
- Values emotions and personal expressions during conversations
- Values indirect eye contact when listening but direct eye contact when speaking
- Values cultural history
- Values creative semantics and use of language

ASIAN-AMERICAN CULTURE:

- Values silence and control in conversations and interactions
- Values privacy at all costs
- Values formality in addressing one another by name
- Values respect and shows this by bowing head or dropping eyes
- Values differences when greeting males and females

Name:

THEME: COMMUNICATION   VALUE: HONESTY

NOVEMBER

Directions: Draw the rating that best represents your work in this module in the box at the end of each statement.

MY BEST WORK   MY SO-SO WORK   MY NOT SO GOOD WORK?
😊   😐   🙁

1. Quality of my ideas about the issues of honesty and dishonesty . . . . ☐

2. Quality of my responses to questioning checklist . . . . ☐

3. Quality of my mini-newspaper speech . . . . ☐

4. Quality of my editorial cartoon . . . . ☐

5. Quality of my speaking and listening skills . . . . ☐

6. Quality of my original "Mad Lib" . . . . ☐

7. Quality of my outline about forms of communication . . . . ☐

8. Quality of my responses . . . . ☐

9. Quality of my original paragraph . . . . ☐

10. Quality of my facts, opinions, feelings, and arguments on a controversial topic . . . ☐

(continued on next page)

Name:

RUBRIC FOR NOVEMBER MODULE, CONTINUED

11. Quality of my original television commercial about honesty . . . . ☐

12. Quality of my responses to personalized gambling checklist . . . . ☐

13. Quality of my case study responses . . . . ☐

14. Quality of my editorial about the cafeteria in my school . . . . ☐

15. Quality of my rating scale on inventions. . . . . ☐

16. Quality of my participation in an Inside/Outside Circle activity . . . . ☐

17. Quality of my mathematical computations . . . . ☐

18. Quality of my flash cards . . . . ☐

19. Quality of my personal reflections. . . . . ☐

20. Quality of my multicultural role-play . . . . ☐

Name:

MODULE FOUR
DECEMBER

THEME: COMMUNITY   VALUE: GENEROSITY

More than one speaker and/or writer has been credited with originating the saying, "It takes a village to raise a child." Regardless of its origin, it is a statement worthy of reflection. To what extent does the generosity (or lack of generosity) of individuals within a group influence the culture of the community? What impact does this have on the lives of children growing up in the community? How does your opinion relate to the lives of youth in your own community?

- **CONDUCTING A GENEROSITY SEARCH—PURPOSE:** To engage students in a people search activity that focuses on individuals in the class who are generous with their time, talent, and treasure

- **GENEROSITY BEGINS AT HOME—PURPOSE:** To explain the concept of "philanthropy" and assume the role of a philanthropist in the student's home community

- **MAINTAINING A SKETCH JOURNAL OF GOOD & GENEROUS DEEDS—PURPOSE:** To show students how to maintain a sketch journal

- **PEOPLE WHO ARE GENEROUS WITH THEIR TIME, TALENT, OR TREASURE—PURPOSE:** To use the acrostic poetry form as a structure for identifying individuals, past or present, who where generous with their time, talent, or treasure

- **Q IS FOR QUILTS THAT TELL ABOUT OUR COMMUNITY—PURPOSE:** To design a series of paper quilt patches, which highlight people, places, things, and environments representative of the student's local village, town, city, or community

- **PLANNING A DRIVING TOUR OF YOUR COMMUNITY—PURPOSE:** To identify and describe various geographical, institutional, cultural, governmental, and technological sights to see or visit within the local community

- **PROMOTING YOUR COMMUNITY FOR THE CHAMBER OF COMMERCE—PURPOSE:** To discover ways the geographic area of a community can influence the economics and recreational appeal of the area to others

- **CREATING A COMMUNITY WALL CHART—PURPOSE:** To create a colorful and informative wall chart, which celebrates the cultural diversity of a given community

- **A COMMUNITY BOOK TO CHERISH—PURPOSE:** To decide on a novel that should be officially designated as the book for all community members to read

- **HEAR YE! HEAR YE!—PURPOSE:** To give an impromptu speech on a community-related topic

- **HAVING FUN WITH "WHAT-IFS"—PURPOSE:** To promote creative thinking in students by focusing on the skills of fluency, flexibility, originality, and elaboration

- **HOW EFFECTIVE IS YOUR COMMUNITY'S WEBPAGE?—PURPOSE:** To evaluate the effectiveness of the community webpage by making and validating predictions

- **PICTURE POSTCARD PERFECT—PURPOSE:** To design and send a thank-you postcard to a member of the student's community

- **GRAPHS AS STORYTELLERS—PURPOSE:** To construct a graph that gives information and tells a story

- **EVERYTHING YOU WANTED TO KNOW ABOUT SERVICE LEARNING BUT DIDN'T KNOW TO ASK—PURPOSE:** To use the multiple intelligences as a means for introducing students to the concept of service learning

- **SOCIAL SERVICES THAT SATISFY—PURPOSE:** To summarize the major role or function of selected social service agencies and their generous contributions within a given community

- **WHAT WE CAN LEARN ABOUT LIFE FROM THE ANT WORLD—PURPOSE:** To have students compare and contrast the life in ant colonies/communities with those of human communities

- **MUSIC TO OUR EARS—PURPOSE:** To create a musical collage of lyrics and/or types of musical compositions and arrangements

- **TIME CAPSULE—PURPOSE:** To prepare a time capsule of artifacts created by the students to reflect the many dimensions of their advisory and school community

- **THE IDEAL HOMEWORK ASSIGNMENT—PURPOSE:** To give students the opportunity to design the ideal homework assignment for a science, social studies, language arts, or math course that fosters a "sense of community" among students and between student and teacher

©2004 Incentive Publications, Inc.
Nashville, TN

WRITING PROMPTS/DISCUSSION STARTERS

THEME: COMMUNITY   VALUE: GENEROSITY

The famous British statesman, Winston Churchill, is given credit for originating this much-quoted maxim: "We make a living by what we get; we make a life by what we give." Write about your interpretation of this statement and of its application to your life today as well as to your career goals for the future.

_____

_____

_____

_____

_____

_____

_____

_____

The much-revered American humorist and novelist, Mark Twain, wrote, "...to get the full value of a joy you must have somebody to divide it with." Write about an experience you have had either as benefactor or the beneficiary of a shared joy.

_____

_____

_____

_____

_____

_____

_____

_____

©2004 Incentive Publications, Inc.
Nashville, TN

Advisory Plus!

THEME: COMMUNITY   VALUE: GENEROSITY

WEEK ONE

DAY ONE	**"Conducting a Generosity Search"** Conducting a people search activity that focuses on individuals in the class who are generous with their time, talent, and treasure
DAY TWO	**"Generosity Begins at Home"** Explaining the concept of "philanthropy" and exploring the role of a philanthropist
DAY THREE	**"Maintaining a Sketch Journal of Good & Generous Deeds"** Learning to maintain a sketch journal
DAY FOUR	**"People Who Are Generous with Their Time, Talent, or Treasure"** Using the acrostic poetry form as a structure for identifying generous individuals
DAY FIVE	**"Q Is for Quilts that Tell about Our Community"** Designing a series of paper quilt patches which highlight the student's local community

WEEK TWO

DAY ONE	**"Planning a Driving Tour of Your Community"** Identifying and describing various sights to see or visit within the local community
DAY TWO	**"Promoting Your Community for the Chamber of Commerce"** Discovering the relationship between the geographic area of a community and the economic and recreational appeal of that area
DAY THREE	**"Creating a Community Wall Chart"** Creating a colorful and informative wall chart to celebrate cultural diversity
DAY FOUR	**"A Community Book to Cherish"** Choosing a novel that should be officially designated as the book for all community members to read
DAY FIVE	**"Hear Ye! Hear Ye!"** Giving an impromptu speech on a community-related topic

DECEMBER CALENDAR

※

WEEK THREE

DAY ONE	**"Having Fun with 'What-Ifs'"** Promoting creative thinking through skills in fluency, flexibility, originality, and elaboration
DAY TWO	**"How Effective is Your Community's Webpage?"** Evaluating the community webpage
DAY THREE	**"Picture Postcard Perfect"** Designing and send a thank-you postcard to a member of the community
DAY FOUR	**"Graphs as Storytellers"** Constructing a graph that gives information and tells a story
DAY FIVE	**"Everything You Wanted to Know About Service Learning But Didn't Know to Ask"** Using the multiple intelligences as a means for introducing students to the concept of service learning

WEEK FOUR

DAY ONE	**"Social Services that Satisfy"** Summarizing the major role or function of selected social service agencies
DAY TWO	**"What We Can Learn About Life from the Ant World"** Comparing and contrasting the life in ant colonies/communities with those of human communities
DAY THREE	**"Music to our Ears"** Creating a musical collage of lyrics and/or types of musical compositions and arrangements
DAY FOUR	**"Time Capsule"** Preparing a time capsule of artifacts to reflect students' advisory and school community
DAY FIVE	**"The Ideal Homework Assignment"** Designing an ideal homework assignment that fosters a "sense of community"

THEME: COMMUNITY   VALUE: GENEROSITY

CONDUCTING A GENEROSITY SEARCH

PURPOSE: To engage students in a people search activity that focuses on individuals in the class who are generous with their time, talent, and treasures

TARGETED INTELLIGENCE: Interpersonal and Intrapersonal

CONTENT/STANDARD FOCUS: Social Studies—Individual Development and Identity

PRODUCT/PERFORMANCE/STUDENT OUTCOME: Completing a People Search Activity

"CONDUCTING A GENEROSITY PEOPLE SEARCH" (page 140)

Review the rules for a people search activity. Students circulate around the room and look for peers who meet one of the criteria listed on their people search form. Students who qualify for one of the statements sign the sheet on the appropriate line. A student cannot sign for more than one statement on any given student's form. It is important that any student who signs a form on a given line must also be able to give an example of his/her generosity as it relates to the statement.

GENEROSITY BEGINS AT HOME

PURPOSE: To explain the concept of "philanthropy" and assume the role of a mock philanthropist in the student's home community

TARGETED INTELLIGENCE: Verbal/Linguistic and Intrapersonal

CONTENT/STANDARD FOCUS: Mathematics—Computation and Estimation & Language Arts—Standards 7 and 11

PRODUCT/PERFORMANCE/STUDENT OUTCOME: Participating in a Role-Play

"GENEROSITY BEGINS AT HOME" (page 141)

Write the definition of "philanthropy" on the chalkboard or overhead projector. Introduce the activity by discussing the definition of "philanthropy" and "philanthropist." Then, ask students to exchange ideas and supply adjectives that describe this type of person. Instruct students to assume the role of a local philanthropist who is to allocate up to five million dollars for use within the community. Encourage students to make wise decisions as to the amounts they would give to their favorite charities or their favorite social service, educational, cultural, and tourist organizations. Make certain that students keep track of the money spent by maintaining running totals as needed.

©2004 Incentive Publications, Inc.
Nashville, TN

MAINTAINING A SKETCH JOURNAL OF GOOD & GENEROUS DEEDS

PURPOSE: To show students how to maintain a sketch journal

TARGETED INTELLIGENCE: Visual/Spatial, Bodily/Kinesthetic, and Intrapersonal

CONTENT/STANDARD FOCUS: Language Arts—Standards 5 and 12

PRODUCT/PERFORMANCE/STUDENT OUTCOME: Creating a Sketch Journal Entry

"MAINTAINING A SKETCH JOURNAL OF GOOD & GENEROUS DEEDS" (page 142)

Explain the difference between a sketch journal, which uses visual images to record thoughts/observations, and a traditional journal, which uses the written word for this purpose. Ask students to be on the lookout for people in the school who are doing good things for others. Have each student focus on one good deed they observe and then try to convey its nature through visual images rather than words of description. Discuss which type of journal entry is more difficult for students and why.

PEOPLE WHO ARE GENEROUS WITH THEIR TIME, TALENT, OR TREASURE

PURPOSE: To use the acrostic poetry form as a structure for identifying individuals, past or present, who were or are generous with their time, talent, or treasure

TARGETED INTELLIGENCE: Verbal/Linguistic

CONTENT/STANDARD FOCUS: Social Studies—Culture; Time, Continuity and Change & Language Arts—Standards 5 and 11

PRODUCT/PERFORMANCE/STUDENT OUTCOME: Acrostic Poem Format

"PEOPLE WHO ARE GENEROUS WITH THEIR TIME, TALENT, OR TREASURE" (page 143)

Review the concept of an "acrostic poem," in which the letters of a predetermined word or subject of the poem are written in a vertical position and a descriptive statement beginning with each letter in the word is recorded after each letter. Apply this poetry form to the area of social studies, and instruct students to think of generous people, past or present, who have committed generous deeds.

Q IS FOR QUILTS THAT TELL ABOUT OUR COMMUNITY

PURPOSE: To design a series of paper quilt patches which highlights people, places, things, and environments representative of the student's local village, town, city, or community

TARGETED INTELLIGENCE: Visual/Spatial, Bodily/Kinesthetic, and Interpersonal

CONTENT/STANDARD FOCUS: Social Studies—Culture; People, Places, and Environments; Individuals, Groups and Institutions

PRODUCT/PERFORMANCE/STUDENT OUTCOME: A Paper Quilt Patch which represents the community

"Q IS FOR QUILTS THAT TELL ABOUT OUR COMMUNITY" (page 144)

Provide students with a predetermined number of paper quilt squares and art materials with which to create their quilt designs. Work with students to brainstorm a wide variety of subjects for the squares that will reflect the key people, places, things, and environments most representative of their community's history and personality. Combine these individual pieces to make a king-sized quilt design to display in the classroom or a public space.

PLANNING A DRIVING TOUR OF YOUR COMMUNITY

PURPOSE: To identify and describe various geographical, institutional, cultural, governmental, and technological sights to see or visit within the local community

TARGETED INTELLIGENCE: Verbal/Linguistic, Logical/Mathematical, Visual/Spatial, Bodily/Kinesthetic, and Interpersonal

CONTENT/STANDARD FOCUS: Mathematics—Computation and Estimation; Measurement & Social Studies—Culture; Individuals, Groups, and Institutions; People, Places, and Environments; Power, Authority, and Governance; Science, Technology, and Society

PRODUCT/PERFORMANCE/STUDENT OUTCOME: Creating a Travel Brochure

"PLANNING A DRIVING TOUR OF YOUR COMMUNITY" (page 145)

Share several travel brochures with students that depict the various sights and attractions of a community other than their own. Next, tell the students that the class is going to determine what geographical, institutional, cultural, governmental, and technological sights are the most interesting to visit within their own community, for purposes of developing a tourist-oriented driving tour. Divide the students into small cooperative learning groups and have each group design their own tour of at least five stops of interest, complete with estimated mileage from place to place. Ask students to briefly describe their driving tour in a mock travel brochure that they have created to promote their selection of sights. Stress the importance of questioning all information for accuracy, honesty, and a lack of exaggeration.

PROMOTING YOUR COMMUNITY FOR THE CHAMBER OF COMMERCE

PURPOSE: To discover ways the geographic area of a community can influence the economic and recreational appeal of the area to others

TARGETED INTELLIGENCE: Visual/Spatial and Naturalistic

CONTENT/STANDARD FOCUS: Social Studies—People, Places, and Environments

PRODUCT/PERFORMANCE/STUDENT OUTCOME: Creating a Billboard Design

"PROMOTING YOUR COMMUNITY FOR THE CHAMBER OF COMMERCE" (page 146)

Discuss the role of the Chamber of Commerce in any given community as an organization that promotes the area for business people, prospective visitors, potential homeowners, and individuals seeking new lifestyles. Next, work with students to identify the unique geographical features and natural resources of the community that would have appeal to any of these groups. Finally, provide students with a large piece of poster board, oak tag, or drawing paper, on which they are to create a welcoming billboard design that highlights the environmental attractions of the community.

CREATING A COMMUNITY WALL CHART

PURPOSE: To create a colorful and informative wall chart that celebrates the cultural diversity of a given community

TARGETED INTELLIGENCE: Verbal/Linguistic, Logical/Mathematical, and Visual/Spatial

CONTENT/STANDARD FOCUS: Mathematics—Mathematics as Communication; Measurement & Social Studies—Culture

PRODUCT/PERFORMANCE/STUDENT OUTCOME: Wall Chart

"CREATING A COMMUNITY WALL CHART" (page 147)

Assign students to small cooperative learning groups and provide each group with many old magazines, newspapers, textbooks, travel brochures, posters, and any other type of print materials to use as sources for cutting out pictures, photographs, advertisements, diagrams, charts, graphs, headlines, cartoons, excerpts from articles, and captions. Inform students that each group is to construct a wall chart that celebrates the cultural diversity that exists throughout their community. Assist students in the careful measurement and layout of their wall chart items, so that everything fits in its place and reflects their chosen theme. Finally, require the students to use the checklist on the student page as a rubric for informally assessing their work on the wall chart.

A COMMUNITY BOOK TO CHERISH

PURPOSE: To decide on a novel that should be officially designated as the book for all community members to read

TARGETED INTELLIGENCE: Verbal/Linguistic

CONTENT/STANDARD FOCUS: Language Arts—Standards 2, 5 and 11

PRODUCT/PERFORMANCE/STUDENT OUTCOME: Writing a Book Review

"A COMMUNITY BOOK TO CHERISH" (page 148)

Discuss this concept of a community book that is to be read by all young people and adults throughout the area as a means of promoting both literacy and collaboration among diverse groups of people within that community. Instruct students to identify and discuss appropriate book choices with one another and then record their individual choices on the student page. Once the book has been determined, ask each student to write a simple review of their individual book preference to share with others. If time permits, allow students to promote their personal choice with the class, and stage a vote to come up with the winning title!

HEAR YE! HEAR YE!

PURPOSE: To give an impromptu speech on a community-related topic

TARGETED INTELLIGENCE: Verbal/Linguistic and Bodily/Kinesthetic

CONTENT/STANDARD FOCUS: Language Arts—Standards 4 and 12 & Social Studies— Individuals, Groups, and Institutions

PRODUCT/PERFORMANCE/STUDENT OUTCOME: Preparing and Delivering an Impromptu Speech

"HEAR YE! HEAR YE!" (page 149)

Clarify the definition of an impromptu speech as a short, informal, and spontaneous talk that one gives on any topic. Remind students that impromptu speeches do use facts, but that the content is usually focused on the speech giver's own opinions, feelings, attitudes, and experiences. Ask students to select one of the speech titles listed on the student activity page, and then be prepared, after just a few minutes of quiet thinking, to give their impromptu speeches (of no more than one or two minutes) before the class.

©2004 Incentive Publications, Inc. Nashville, TN

HAVING FUN WITH "WHAT-IFS"

PURPOSE: To promote creative thinking in students by focusing on the skills of fluency, flexibility, originality, and elaboration

TARGETED INTELLIGENCE: Verbal/Linguistic and Interpersonal

CONTENT/STANDARD FOCUS: Language Arts—Standards 4, 11, and 12

PRODUCT/PERFORMANCE/STUDENT OUTCOME: Engaging in a Creative Thinking Exercise

"HAVING FUN WITH 'WHAT-IFS'" (page 150)

Divide students into small cooperative learning groups and ask each group to complete the activity according to directions given on the student activity page.

HOW EFFECTIVE IS YOUR COMMUNITY'S WEBPAGE?

PURPOSE: To evaluate the effectiveness of the community webpage by making and validating predictions

TARGETED INTELLIGENCE: Verbal/Linguistic, Visual/Spatial, and Musical/Rhythmic

CONTENT/STANDARD FOCUS: Language Arts—Standards 7 and 8

PRODUCT/PERFORMANCE/STUDENT OUTCOME: Preparing a Prediction Tree Graphic Organizer

"HOW EFFECTIVE IS YOUR COMMUNITY'S WEBPAGE?" (page 151)

Provide students with information regarding the homepage and website location for their local community. Stress the importance of completing the Prediction Tree Graphic Organizer on the student activity page prior to visiting the site. As a concluding task for this activity, engage the students in a discussion on ways the Chamber of Commerce and/or local Tourist Bureau might improve their Internet community marketing program.

PICTURE POSTCARD PERFECT

PURPOSE: To design and send a thank-you postcard to a member of the community

TARGETED INTELLIGENCE: Verbal/Linguistic, Visual/Spatial, and Bodily/Kinesthetic

CONTENT/STANDARD FOCUS: Social Studies—5, 11, and 12

PRODUCT/PERFORMANCE/STUDENT OUTCOME: Creating a Postcard to Express Appreciation

"PICTURE POSTCARD PERFECT" (page 152)

Provide students with sample postcards of the local community so that they can see the variety of visual images projected on these cards. Conduct a brainstorming session with the students to identify various individuals in the community who have made major contributions to its growth and success, giving generously of their time and resources. Then, ask each student to design an original postcard and send it to their person of choice with a thank-you message for his/her contribution.

GRAPHS AS STORYTELLERS

PURPOSE: To construct a graph that gives information and tells a community story

TARGETED INTELLIGENCE: Logical/Mathematical and Visual/Spatial

CONTENT/STANDARD FOCUS: Mathematics—Mathematics as Communication; Mathematics as Reasoning; Statistics; Number and Number Relationships

PRODUCT/PERFORMANCE/STUDENT OUTCOME: Constructing a Graph

"GRAPHS AS STORYTELLERS" (page 153)

Briefly review the characteristics of a line graph, bar graph, and circle graph with students. Have samples to display as needed. Encourage students to discuss historical data, statistics, and numerical information related to their community. Finally, direct students to work in teams to develop an original graph that depicts one set of figures they found of interest during their discussion. If time permits, encourage students to generate a set of questions about their story graph for others to answer.

©2004 Incentive Publications, Inc.
Nashville, TN

EVERYTHING YOU WANTED TO KNOW ABOUT SERVICE LEARNING BUT DIDN'T KNOW TO ASK

PURPOSE: To use the multiple intelligences as a means for introducing students to the concept of service learning

TARGETED INTELLIGENCE: All Intelligences

CONTENT/STANDARD FOCUS: Social Studies—Individuals, Groups, and Institutions; Science, Technology, and Society & Science—Earth and Space Science; Science in Personal and Social Perspectives

PRODUCT/PERFORMANCE/STUDENT OUTCOME: Service Learning Related Task

"EVERYTHING YOU WANTED TO KNOW ABOUT SERVICE LEARNING BUT DIDN'T KNOW TO ASK" (page 154)

Conduct a large group discussion about the purpose of and need for service learning opportunities within the local school and community. Debate the pros and cons of a service learning graduation requirement. Then, encourage students to select one of the service learning tasks suggested on the student activity page to complete. Others may be added to this list as needed.

SOCIAL SERVICES THAT SATISFY

PURPOSE: To summarize the major role or function of selected social service agencies and their generous contributions within a given community

TARGETED INTELLIGENCE: Logical/Mathematical and Interpersonal

CONTENT/STANDARD FOCUS: Social Studies—Individuals, Groups, and Institutions; Power, Authority, and Governance & Mathematics—Mathematics as Communication; Mathematics as Reasoning

PRODUCT/PERFORMANCE/STUDENT OUTCOME: Developing a Questionnaire/Survey

"SOCIAL SERVICES THAT SATISFY" (page 155)

Divide students into small cooperative learning groups and provide a Yellow Pages Directory for each group. Instruct students to locate the information sections on social service agencies and organizations in the community, and to note their purposes, names, and addresses. Next, assign one or more different social agencies or organizations to each group, asking group members to generate a ten-question survey or questionnaire to send for the purpose of learning more about the agencies' activities. Mail the surveys or questionnaires and share results with one another. Set a future date for compiling information from all the respondents. Use the data to draw some conclusions as to what service agencies seem to have the greatest impact on community members.

WHAT WE CAN LEARN ABOUT LIFE FROM THE ANT WORLD

PURPOSE: To have students compare and contrast the life in ant colonies with those of human communities

TARGETED INTELLIGENCE: Verbal/Linguistic and Naturalistic

CONTENT/STANDARD FOCUS: Language Arts—Standards 1 and 3 & Science—Life Science

PRODUCT/PERFORMANCE/STUDENT OUTCOME: Developing a Compare and Contrast Diagram

"WHAT WE CAN LEARN ABOUT LIFE FROM THE ANT WORLD" (page 156)

Provide multiple resources on the subject of ants and ant colonies for students to review. Encourage them to look for similarities between ant communities and human communities. Ask them to record their findings on the Compare and Contrast Diagram provided on the student activity page for this purpose.

MUSIC TO OUR EARS

PURPOSE: To create a musical collage of lyrics and/or types of musical compositions and arrangements

TARGETED INTELLIGENCE: Musical/Rhythmic and Interpersonal

CONTENT/STANDARD FOCUS: Music

PRODUCT/PERFORMANCE/STUDENT OUTCOME: Constructing a Musical Collage

"MUSIC TO OUR EARS" (page 157)

Discuss musical preferences with students and ask them what makes certain kinds of music popular in today's society. Next, talk about the various types of music that are representative of different geographical locations or communities, both in and outside of the United States. Finally, ask students to think of musical groups or song titles that best represent their local community. If possible, have students bring in their favorite recordings to share in a musical collage format.

TIME CAPSULE

PURPOSE: To prepare a time capsule of artifacts created by the students to reflect the many dimensions of their advisory and school community

TARGETED INTELLIGENCE: Visual/Spatial, Bodily/Kinesthetic, Interpersonal, and Naturalistic

CONTENT/STANDARD FOCUS: Social Studies—Culture; Time, Continuity, and Change; Individuals, Groups, and Institutions & Science—Science in Personal and Social Perspectives

PRODUCT/PERFORMANCE/STUDENT OUTCOME: Construction of a Time Capsule

"TIME CAPSULE" (page 158)

Review the purpose of a time capsule with students and discuss the types of artifacts that would best represent the group. Encourage students to contribute appropriate items to be included in the time capsule that would be of interest and help to students entering the school for the first time next year. These artifacts might even play a role in the orientation of new students to the school both now and in the future. Log the artifacts and plans for the time capsule, and make arrangements for a place to store it and a time to share it with newcomers.

THE IDEAL HOMEWORK ASSIGNMENT

PURPOSE: To give students the opportunity to design the ideal homework assignment for a science, social studies, language arts, or math course that fosters a "sense of community" among students and between student and teacher

TARGETED INTELLIGENCE: Intrapersonal and Interpersonal

CONTENT/STANDARD FOCUS: Social Studies—Individual Development and Identity

PRODUCT/PERFORMANCE/STUDENT OUTCOME: Designing an Original Homework Assignment

"THE IDEAL HOMEWORK ASSIGNMENT" (page 159)

Encourage students to talk about their favorite homework assignments in various courses. Ask them to give reasons for their choices. Next, encourage each student to design the "perfect" or "ideal" homework task for a subject area of their choice. Suggest that they consider a homework assignment that has one or more of these characteristics: creative or critical thinking skills, interaction with others, or some application of technology.

THEME: COMMUNITY   VALUE: GENEROSITY

CONDUCTING A GENEROSITY SEARCH

Directions: Use the people search form below to participate in an activity that requires group members to circulate randomly within the group to solicit signatures of peers who fulfill each of the listed "generosity" descriptors. Note that no one can sign his/her name on any form more than once. Note also that the teacher will conduct a group discussion and call on students to give individual responses for any items they acknowledged on the people search forms. For example, if a student named Jane signed her name on the line that says: "Find a person who is generous with their time when someone needs help with a homework assignment," Jane needs to relate a personal example when this has been true.

A PEOPLE SEARCH FOR GENEROUS STUDENTS

1. Find someone in the class who is generous with their academic talent and will help others on an in-class project or task. Describe.

    _____

2. Find someone who has time for helping the teacher with routine tasks related to housekeeping or classroom maintenance. Describe.

    _____

3. Find someone in the class who is generous with their talent in a particular sport and willing to help others improve their skill in that sport. Describe.

    _____

4. Find someone in the class who is generous with their time when someone needs help with a homework assignment. Describe.

    _____

5. Find someone in the class who is generous with their money when someone needs a loan for lunch or a similar school day function. Describe.

    _____

6. Find someone in the class who is generous with their time out of school to serve as a study buddy. Describe.

    _____

7. Find someone in the class who is generous with their talent for making friends. Describe.

    _____

8. Find someone in the class who is generous with their time and talent for overall school improvement in group work. Describe.

    _____

Name: _____

GENEROSITY BEGINS AT HOME

Directions: Write the definition of "philanthropy" in the space provided below. Then, think of some adjectives that would describe a philanthropist such as "kind, unselfish, charitable, generous, and humane," and include these as well. Next, work with others in the class to name one or more people in your community who have performed philanthropic deeds or made philanthropic contributions to your town, village, or city. Finally, assume the role of a philanthropist today, and imagine you had five million dollars to donate to the community for purposes of improving its social services, cultural offerings, educational institutions, or tourist attractions. Decide who or what would receive your dollars, and what amounts you would allocate for their needs or purposes.

DEFINITION OF PHILANTHROPY: _____

_____

_____

PHILANTHROPISTS IN OUR COMMUNITY: _____

_____

_____

PHILANTHROPIC NEEDS: _____

_____

_____

AMOUNT DONATED: _____

Name: _____

MAINTAINING A SKETCH JOURNAL OF GOOD & GENEROUS DEEDS

Directions: A sketch journal requires you to both observe and draw experiences with short entries of personal comments, reflections, notes, and explanations. In short, a sketch journal is an impressionistic and visual representation of a given experience or incident. Sketch journals can include such visuals as diagrams, blueprints, drawings, simplified notes, symbols, icons, rebus statements, stick figures, or even questions. To try your hand at keeping a sketch journal, look for someone you know at school—a teacher, staff member, cafeteria worker, media specialist, custodian, bus driver, school nurse, peer, friend, volunteer, visitor, or parent—who is performing a kind act, good deed, or generous use of time. Carefully watch and note what they are doing. Then, in the space below, sketch out your observations and draw a visual representation of the act/event, filling it in with written comments and reflections as needed.

MY SKETCH JOURNAL ENTRY

Name:

©2004 Incentive Publications, Inc.
Nashville, TN

PEOPLE WHO ARE GENEROUS WITH THEIR TIME, TALENT, OR TREASURE

Directions: A common poetry form is the acrostic poem that spells a word or name down the side of the page vertically rather than across the page horizontally. The poet then writes a list of descriptors or phrases that begin with each letter in the word, making certain that it is related to the subject of the poem.

Use the word "GENEROSITY" as the basis for your original acrostic poem, and write down the name of someone from the past or the present that you admire because they have been generous with their time, talent, or treasure. You may use either the person's first or last name for this activity. Complete each line with a simple description of who they are. Use the example below as a model.

G is for **Ghandi**, the famous religious leader from India who was considered a martyr by some.

E is for **Eloise**, the main character in a wonderful children's book.

N is for **St. Nicholas**, who visits children all over the world during the Christmas holidays.

E is for **Eleanor Roosevelt**, the first lady and wife of President Franklin D. Roosevelt who gave of herself time and time again.

R is for **Rachmaninoff**, the famous Russian composer whose generous talent was ended due to an early death.

O is for **Oprah Winfrey**, a talented African-American talk show host who started book clubs on television.

S is for **Shel Silverstein** who writes wonderful, humorous poetry for children and young people.

I is for **Lee Iacocca**, a successful chief executive officer of Chrysler Corporation who also served on the Statue of Liberty/Ellis Island Foundation.

T is for **Thomas Paine**, who wrote the pamphlet "Common Sense" during the Revolutionary War.

Y is for **Yves St. Laurent**, the brilliant fashion designer from Europe who often donated his profits to local charities.

Name:

Q IS FOR QUILTS THAT TELL ABOUT OUR COMMUNITY

Directions: Work as a group to make a list of the important people, places, things, and events that best tell the story of your home community. Then, with the help of your teacher, decide on the best size for a paper quilt piece and what person, place, thing, or event will be created by each individual student for the quilt project. When all single quilt pieces are completed, paste them on a roll of shelf paper so that the finished quilt design is horizontal and a rectangle rather than a large square. Make certain to autograph your paper quilt square as well. Take turns, with the other participating students of the class, in the retelling of your community's story by using the squares or sections from the quilt project as you go. You may even want to laminate the finished quilt and find a location in the community in which to display it.

SOME IDEAS WE HAVE FOR QUILT SQUARES:

1. _____
2. _____
3. _____
4. _____
5. _____
6. _____
7. _____
8. _____
9. _____
10. _____
11. _____
12. _____
13. _____
14. _____
15. _____

Name: _____

©2004 Incentive Publications, Inc.
Nashville, TN

PLANNING A DRIVING TOUR OF YOUR COMMUNITY

Directions: Many communities promote their area to visitors by compiling a brochure of things to see and do within driving distance of the city limits. Work with members of your cooperative learning group to brainstorm some of the points of interest within your community that would most likely appeal to anyone visiting the area. Think of a theme or focus for your driving tour. Will it be a tour of places that are most appropriate for kids? Will it be a tour of the best shopping spots? Will it be a tour of historic buildings and monuments? Will it be a tour of museums and other places of culture? Will it be a tour of parks, beaches, and other outdoor facilities? Limit your final choices to a "Top Five" list, and arrange the visitation sites according to their geographic locations. Where would you start the tour and where would you end it? Estimate the number of miles from place to place so that you have a practical plan that lends itself to a "driving tour" of the community. Then, prepare a simple brochure that describes each of the five sites chosen. Make certain that the brochure states the theme or focus of the driving tour, has beginning and ending points designated for the tour, and has approximate miles recorded for each site on the tour. The site descriptions should be a short paragraph in length, and may include a simple drawing, sketch, or diagram. Try to make your brochure as interesting as possible, but make sure your information is accurate, honest, and free of exaggerated claims.

BRIEF DESCRIPTION OF SITE ONE:

_____

_____

BRIEF DESCRIPTION OF SITE TWO:

_____

_____

BRIEF DESCRIPTION OF SITE THREE:

_____

_____

BRIEF DESCRIPTION OF SITE FOUR:

_____

_____

BRIEF DESCRIPTION OF SITE FIVE:

_____

_____

Name: _____

PROMOTING YOUR COMMUNITY FOR THE CHAMBER OF COMMERCE

Directions: Are you familiar with the role of the Chamber of Commerce and its job of
promoting the community as a nice place to live, a productive place to work, and a fun
place to play? The type of community that one lives in is often dictated by its geography,
terrain, and natural resources. Think about your own community and its visual and
natural appeal for someone choosing to live, work, and go to school there. Pretend you
have been commissioned by the Chamber of Commerce to design a colorful and creative
billboard to be constructed just outside the city limits. The Chamber of Commerce wishes
to promote the terrain, topography, geography, or natural resources of your community
to welcome visitors to the area. On a large piece of oak tag, poster board, or drawing
paper, draft a design for the billboard that focuses on Mother Nature's influence on your
community. Think of a simple "welcome" message to include as part of the billboard
design. Sketch your ideas below.

──── MY BILLBOARD IDEA ────

Name: _____

CREATING A COMMUNITY WALL CHART

Directions: Many times it is easier to explain things with pictures and labels rather than with words and paragraphs. A wall chart is an elaborate poster that uses labeled pictures, diagrams, or figures to give the viewer information on a given topic. The key to a good wall chart is deciding on a topic and portraying many aspects of the topic through a variety of pictures, labels, mini-texts or passages, captions or headings, and a unique layout displaying the information to the best advantage. Wall charts can be made of poster board, oak tag, or even scrolls of paper. Work with members of your cooperative learning group to design a wall chart around the topic of cultural diversity within your community. Use a variety of magazines and newspapers as the basis for the content of your wall chart. Cut and paste pictures, photographs, advertisements, diagrams, charts or graphs, headlines, cartoons, and excerpts from articles that fit this theme. Embellish several of the visuals with very short written passages that express your thoughts on the topic, as triggered by items on the chart. Give the wall chart a title, and perhaps some appropriate subtitles. You may also want to use letters and borders to add color and interest to the wall chart. Use the checklist below to evaluate the effectiveness of the wall chart.

CHECKLIST FOR EVALUATING OUR GROUP'S WALL CHART

1. Does the wall chart have a title and at least two subtitles?

2. Does the wall chart feature labeled illustrations, diagrams, and/or figures?

3. Does the wall chart contain labels or headings?

4. Does the wall chart use small blocks of written information for interest?

5. Does the wall chart accurately and creatively reflect the topic of cultural diversity?

6. Does the wall chart have an interesting layout?

7. Does the wall chart use connecting arrows and/or lines to move the viewer from item to item so that there is a scope and sequence to the ideas presented?

8. Does the wall chart have eye appeal and color?

Name:

©2004 Incentive Publications, Inc.
Nashville, TN

Advisory Plus!

A COMMUNITY BOOK TO CHERISH

Directions: Many political and educational leaders from places throughout the United States have suggested that every community select a fiction or nonfiction book to be read and discussed by all students and older adults in the area as a means of promoting community literacy and cohesiveness. The motivation behind this effort is to use the book as a tool for bonding together community members of all ages and to encourage a widespread interest in reading. Pretend that you have been selected as the youth representative on a community-wide committee whose responsibility it is to decide on the book choice for your area. Think about the diversity of people who reside in your village, town, or city. Then, think about all of the book titles that you would like the committee to consider. Write your ideas on the lines below. Finally, decide on your book of choice for the committee and write a simple review of it on the back of this paper.

1. Do you think this "community book proposal" is a good idea? Give reasons for your answer.

   _____

   _____

   _____

2. Do you think a fiction or a nonfiction book title would be the best option? Explain.

   _____

   _____

   _____

3. Here are some book titles that I think students would enjoy reading:

   _____

   _____

   _____

4. Here are some book titles that I think adults would enjoy reading:

   _____

   _____

   _____

5. Some advice I would give the committee on book selection from a student's point of view would be: _____

   _____

   _____

Name: _____

HEAR YE! HEAR YE!

Directions: How often have you admired someone in school or in the community who could present information, give speeches, or deliver live demonstrations with ease and confidence? People who speak and present well are not necessarily naturally talented speakers, but rather are those who have had opportunity to learn and develop public speaking skills. Think of those careers that demand public speaking engagements and sophisticated speech-giving techniques. What jobs come to mind? One way to get practice in public speaking is to give short, simple talks on impromptu topics that don't require research, detailed information, speech strategies, or extensive rehearsal. Impromptu speeches often focus more on the expression of personal feelings, opinions, attitudes, and experiences than on factual data. Choose one or more of the community-related topics listed below, and give a one to two minute impromptu speech before a group of peers. Start your impromptu speech with a strong opening statement, and close it by repeating that statement in a different way. Also, try to arrange your thoughts, opinions, and feelings in an organized manner. Consider listing them in numerical order; consider ordering them according to their importance or value to you; consider categorizing them as opinion, feeling, or fact. Or, consider alphabetizing them.

1. The value of community involvement for people my age is . . .

2. Some services my community provides for senior citizens are . . .

3. Some ways my community could serve the homeless are . . .

4. Some community services opportunities I might pursue are . . .

5. Some things I am proud of about my community are . . .

6. Some problems I see in our community related to youth are . . .

7. A summary of why I would or would not want to run for public office in my community is . . .

8. The reasons why (or why not) service learning should be a requirement for middle school students are . . .

9. The five things I like best about where I live are . . .

10. I think my community's services and policies are reflective of generosity and fairness for its citizens of all ages on the part of its law makers and governing body because . . .

Name:

HAVING FUN WITH "WHAT-IFS"

Directions: Sometimes it is fun to look at common things in uncommon ways in order to stimulate our ability to think creatively and "outside the box." Work with members of your cooperative learning group to respond to each of these community-related "WHAT IF" statements, and then think up a few of your own to share with students in your class.

1. <u>WHAT IF</u> all of the streets in your community suddenly became canals like one finds in Venice, Italy? List some possible causes and effects.

   _____

   _____

2. <u>WHAT IF</u> every house that was built in your community had to have a big front porch and a sidewalk? List some possible causes and effects.

   _____

   _____

3. <u>WHAT IF</u> money grew on trees in your community but not in any other community close by? With some of the money, what could people in your community do to improve the lives of people living in neighboring communities?

   _____

   _____

4. <u>WHAT IF</u> all kids in your community had to obey a nine o'clock curfew during the week? List some possible causes and effects.

   _____

   _____

5. <u>WHAT IF</u> all residents of your community had generous hearts and love for each other? How would community life be different?

   _____

   _____

Name: _____

HOW EFFECTIVE IS YOUR COMMUNITY'S WEBPAGE?

Directions: Most communities have websites that people can visit who want to learn more about a given area. These websites are often developed and maintained by either the local Chamber of Commerce or the local Visitor's Bureau for purposes of promoting the assets and appeal of the community for anyone interested in knowing more about it. Before visiting the website of your own village, town, city, or state, try making a series of predictions about what that homepage will look like. What people will it feature? What facts, statistics, or data will it present? What tourist attractions will it highlight? Is there evidence of community generosity toward visitors? What natural resources will it brag about? What pictures will it show? What information will it give to show the community's compassion for its citizens? What incentives will it offer potential businesses? What promises does it make to visitors?

Reconstruct the graphic organizer, Prediction Tree, on a large piece of paper and use it to record your predictions about the contents of the website's homepage. Then, visit the website and test your predictions. How many were correct?

Finally, list some suggestions you would give to the Chamber of Commerce or the Visitor's Bureau to improve the effectiveness of their webpage. Write these down on the other side of this sheet.

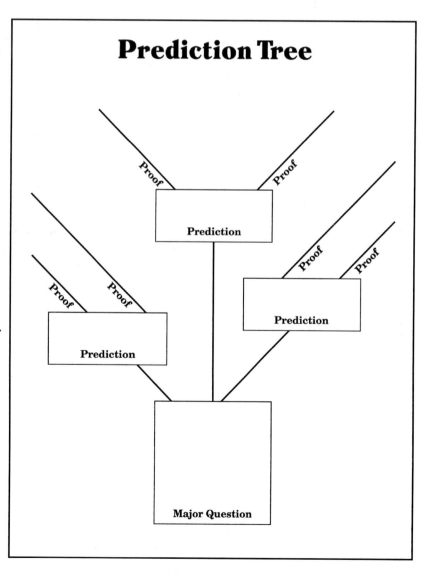

Prediction Tree

Proof   Proof

Prediction

Proof   Proof

Proof   Proof

Prediction

Prediction

Major Question

Name:

PICTURE POSTCARD PERFECT

Directions: Enlarge and reproduce the postcard prototype below on a piece of oak tag or poster board, so that it resembles commercially produced postcards. Think of someone in the area that you respect and would like to thank for his/her contribution of time and resources in making your community a good and safe place to live. Consider an educator, political figure, health care worker, social service staff person, religious leader, recreation leader, school volunteer, local merchant, businessman, computer guru, scout leader, neighbor, community service worker, waiter/waitress, or anyone else important to you. On one side of the postcard, draw a picture, graphic, or colorful symbol that would be appropriate for the recipient of your card. On the other side of the postcard, write a brief thank you message and the recipient's address. Mail your card and surprise a deserving person for his or her positive influence on you in some meaningful way.

Name: _____

©2004 Incentive Publications, Inc.
Nashville, TN

GRAPHS AS STORYTELLERS

Directions: Graphs are great tools for picturing and communicating information with a minimum number of words. Specifically, a graph is a mathematical diagram drawn on a grid that shows how two or more sets of information are related. Three common types of graphs are line graphs, bar graphs, and circle graphs. A line graph has two axes. The vertical axis points upward, and the horizontal axis is drawn from left to right. A bar graph is made up of vertical and horizontal bars. A circle graph has various lines radiating from its center to points along the circumference of the circle. The size of the wedges is in proportion to the size of the number being represented. One important thing about graphs is that they can tell a story. Research interesting numerical data or statistics that interest you about your community. Using this information, construct a graph that tells something about your community. Construct your graph in the space below. Then, develop a set of questions whose answers will tell your story.

MY QUESTIONS TO ANSWER USING THE STORY GRAPH

1. _____
2. _____
3. _____
4. _____
5. _____
6. _____
7. _____
8. _____
9. _____
10. _____

Name:

EVERYTHING YOU WANTED TO KNOW ABOUT SERVICE LEARNING BUT DIDN'T KNOW TO ASK

Directions: Did you know that many high schools in the country are requiring their students to complete up to 50 hours of community service as part of their graduation requirements? Some of these hours can actually be accumulated as part of the middle school experience. Service or community learning projects vary in substance, including everything from volunteerism to heading a petition drive. Complete one or more of the activities listed here to further explore the service learning concept and its potential application for you.

VERBAL/LINGUISTIC TASK: Define the words community, service, and learning. Then combine these meanings and come up with a working definition of "community/service learning."

LOGICAL/MATHEMATICAL TASK: Construct a chart of three columns. Label the first column: Service Learning Tasks I Would Enjoy; the second, Service Learning Tasks I Might Enjoy; and the third, Service Learning Tasks I Would Not Enjoy.

Then, place each of the following service learning activities into one of the three columns and be able to justify each decision: Adopt-A-Highway/Street; Volunteering for a Social Service Agency; Child Care/Tutoring; Visitations to Nursing/Retirement Homes; Create a Petition; Conduct Community Surveys; Fund-Raising; Interviews w/ Public Officials; Letter-Writing Campaigns; Active Role in Youth Organizations; Beautification/Conservation Projects; Social Action Groups; Anti-Crime/Drug Programs; Relief Efforts; Work on Political Campaigns; Outreach Programs for Homeless/Handicapped; and Animal Rights and Protection Efforts.

VISUAL/SPATIAL TASK: Choose one of the service learning tasks listed in the Logical/Mathematical section, and create a simple flow chart to show what would be involved in a typical activity.

BODILY/KINESTHETIC TASK: Role-play a mock interview that you might have with a community official who was looking to recruit student volunteers for an upcoming community service project of great importance to the area.

MUSICAL/RHYTHMIC TASK: Create a cheer, rap, song, or jingle that could be used to promote service learning opportunities for middle level students.

INTERPERSONAL TASK: Work with a partner to write a three-paragraph position paper that discusses a problem or challenge facing your community that might be improved by a service project carried out by students your age.

INTRAPERSONAL TASK: Describe a time when you volunteered to do something for someone else. What did you do and how did it turn out?

NATURALISTIC TASK: Outline a school or surrounding neighborhood beautification project that you would like to see accomplished by a group of students from your school.

Name:

SOCIAL SERVICES THAT SATISFY

Directions: Use the Yellow Pages of your local telephone directory to learn the names and locations of the major social service organizations within your community. Work with a partner to develop a simple questionnaire that can be mailed to these social service organizations in order to find out more about what they do and how they are funded. Set a date in the future for sharing compiled results. Create a balance or ledger sheet of reasons why someone would want to make a generous contribution to each of the agencies that responded to your survey. Try to limit your questions to no more than ten in number, and keep them simple and to the point. Another alternative to mailing the questionnaire would be to conduct a telephone interview using the questions as a guide.

OUR DRAFT LIST OF QUESTIONS FOR SOCIAL SERVICE QUESTIONNAIRE

Question One: _____

Question Two: _____

Question Three: _____

Question Four: _____

Question Five: _____

Question Six: _____

Question Seven: _____

Question Eight: _____

Question Nine: _____

Question Ten: _____

NAME AND ADDRESS OF SOCIAL SERVICE AGENCY TO BE SENT QUESTIONNAIRE

NAME _____

ADDRESS _____

TELEPHONE NUMBER _____

Name:

©2004 Incentive Publications, Inc.
Nashville, TN

Advisory Plus!

WHAT WE CAN LEARN ABOUT LIFE FROM THE ANT WORLD

Directions: Did you know that the ant is one of the most social animals and that ants are distinguished among all insects for their ability to live and work together harmoniously? Use the reference materials provided to locate more information about ants and their lives as part of the ant colonies and communities in which they live. Look for any similarities between human life in communities and ant life in communities. How are they alike and how are they different? What can we learn from our nature pest, the ant, about living together in a common environment? What makes the ant such an unusual species? Enlarge the Compare and Contrast Diagram below and use it to record the results of your findings.

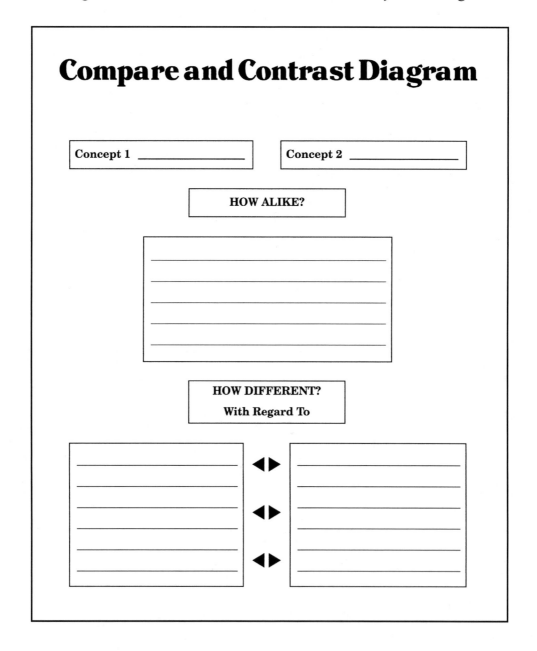

Compare and Contrast Diagram

Concept 1 _____   Concept 2 _____

HOW ALIKE?

HOW DIFFERENT?
With Regard To

MUSIC TO OUR EARS

Directions: It has been said many times over, "music makes the world go 'round." Many communities around the world today have musical identities ranging from opera or classical music (such as one finds in Vienna, Austria) to country music (such as one finds in Nashville, Tennessee). Imagine if music disappeared from our lives. How would this impact members of your local society? Work with a partner to think of some musical types and titles that you think best reflect the personality and makeup of Americans as a national community. List the names of these musical pieces on the lines below, and give reasons for each choice. If time permits, work with others in the class to compose a musical collage of selections that represent all of your classroom suggestions.

MUSIC REPRESENTATIVE OF OUR COUNTRY:

1. TITLE:_____

   Reason: _____

2. TITLE:_____

   Reason: _____

3. TITLE:_____

   Reason: _____

4. TITLE:_____

   Reason: _____

5. TITLE:_____

   Reason: _____

6. TITLE:_____

   Reason: _____

7. TITLE:_____

   Reason: _____

Name:

TIME CAPSULE

Directions: You are to prepare a school-related time capsule for next year's advisory students. This time capsule, like other long-term capsules, will contain a variety of artifacts representing the many dimensions of your school that would be of interest to incoming students or students new to the school community. As an advisory group, try to think of some interesting items that you could place in the time capsule. Consider excerpts from the school newspaper or newsletter; drawings or diagrams of the school facility; original stories, poems, essays, artwork, and personal letters; sample advisory tasks or homework assignments; critiques of the textbooks; or an advice column with words of wisdom to the new arrivals. Try to have eight to ten items for your time capsule, and choose an appropriate container for these items, such as a large brown envelope, accordion folder, shopping bag, loose leaf notebook, or pizza box. Next, it is important to prepare a log that becomes both a checklist and a brief description of all items placed in the time capsule as well as reasons for enclosing each of the items selected. Finally, arrange for the time capsule to be kept in a safe place, so that next year's advisory students will know where to find it. Record your plan below.

PLAN FOR TIME CAPSULE

1. Container to be used_____

2. Items to be included in the time capsule_____

3. Time to assemble capsule _____

4. Place to "plant" capsule_____

5. Instructions for retrieving and using capsule

    1. _____

    2. _____

    3. _____

    4. _____

    5. _____

    6. _____

    7. _____

    8. _____

    9. _____

    10. _____

Name: _____

THE IDEAL HOMEWORK ASSIGNMENT

Directions: Homework is a way of life in school, but students sometimes feel that homework assignments are not as interesting or productive as they could be. Teachers know that the best homework assignments need to be interactive and hands-on in nature. Whenever possible, they require some parent involvement, some application of creative and critical thinking skills, and some use of technology. Discuss the components of effective homework assignments in math, social studies, science, and language arts. Try to give examples to support your choices. Finally, create the ideal homework assignment that you wish a teacher would assign to you. How can you make it a "family affair" or a community effort? How can you make it hands-on or interactive? How can you include the use of technology? How can you infuse problem solving, decision making, or creativity to your task? How would you want the teacher to grade it?
Write your homework assignment below; supply as much detail as possible.

MY THOUGHTS FOR AN IDEAL HOMEWORK ASSIGNMENT

_____

_____

_____

_____

_____

_____

_____

_____

_____

_____

_____

_____

Name:

THEME: COMMUNITY   VALUE: GENEROSITY

DECEMBER

RATING SCALE: Best – **1**   Better – **2**   Good – **3**   Fair – **4**   Poor – **5**

_____1.   I was able to participate in the generosity search.

_____2.   I was able to assume the role of a philanthropist.

_____3.   I was able to maintain a sketch journal of good and generous deeds.

_____4.   I was able to create an acrostic poem using the word generosity.

_____5.   I was able to design an original quilt square telling something about my community.

_____6.   I was able to help plan a driving tour of my community.

_____7.   I was able to think of a special idea for a community-oriented billboard.

_____8.   I was able to work on a group wall chart on the topic of cultural diversity.

_____9.   I was able to think of a good title for a community book.

_____10. I was able to give a community-related impromptu speech.

_____11. I was able to engage in a community "what-if" activity.

_____12. I was able to analyze a community-oriented webpage using a graphic organizer.

_____13. I was able to design an original postcard to send to a special person in my community.

_____14. I was able to construct a graph to share information about my community.

_____15. I was able to learn something about service learning that interested me.

_____16. I was able to help write a community questionnaire to be sent to local social service agencies.

_____17. I was able to learn more about community life through a study of ants.

_____18. I was able to think of some musical compositions that reflect life in our country.

_____19. I was able to help plan and create a school advisory time capsule.

_____20. I was able to describe an ideal homework assignment.

Name: _____

MODULE FIVE

JANUARY

✳

THEME: GLOBAL AWARENESS   VALUE: KNOWLEDGE

How many times do we read or hear these often used quotations related to knowledge and its acquisition, value, and use?

· "Knowledge is Power"
· "Education is something no one can take away from you."
· "Knowing is Growing"
· "Success in life is determined by what you know, not who you know."

Using your own definition of knowledge, how do standardized tests, grades, and parent and teacher expectations contribute (positively or negatively) to your need for knowledge to meet the challenges of daily life?

- **CULTURAL EXPLORATIONS—PURPOSE:** To draw conclusions and encourage dialogue about ways that cultures are alike and different

- **KNOWLEDGE IS POWER WHEREVER YOU LIVE—PURPOSE:** To demonstrate ways that knowledge is of value in today's world, regardless of where you live or what you do

- **WHO SHOULD RULE THE WORLD?—PURPOSE:** To imagine what life would be like if children ruled the world

- **KNOWLEDGE MEANS MANY THINGS TO MANY PEOPLE—PURPOSE:** To associate and validate personal symbols of knowledge from a student's perspective

- **AND THEY LIVED HAPPILY EVER AFTER, HOPEFULLY—PURPOSE:** To depict a conflict/resolution situation through the creation of a comic strip based on children's literature

- **EXAMINING WORLD GOVERNMENT ISSUES FROM A KID'S POINT OF VIEW—PURPOSE:** To examine the pros and cons of various governance issues that exist both in and outside of the United States

- **A GLOBAL GUIDED IMAGERY EXPERIENCE—PURPOSE:** To promote knowledge of the geographical biomes of the world through the use of guided imagery

- **LEARNING MORE ABOUT THIRD WORLD COUNTRIES—PURPOSE:** To identify selected Third World countries and determine what characteristics make them fit this category

- **LEARNING OR LEARNING HOW AND WHERE TO LEARN—PURPOSE:** To question if being able to find information is more valuable than learning, processing, and storing information

- **GENDER REACTIONS TO HEADLINE NEWS—PURPOSE:** To use a series of mock headlines to provoke and explore gender issues

- **THE GENERATION GAP—PURPOSE:** To examine the issues that separate the older generation from the younger generation in today's society

- **STAMP OF APPROVAL—PURPOSE:** To understand and appreciate other cultures

- **ON TRACK TO COMBAT CONFLICT—PURPOSE:** To use the medium of musical recordings to capture feelings and events focused on conflicts among and between individuals or nations

- **MANAGING CONFLICT: ONE SIZE DOESN'T FIT ALL—PURPOSE:** To examine three different conflict management tools that can be effective in the middle-level classroom

- **DEALING WITH CELL YELL AND EMAIL ETIQUETTE AROUND THE WORLD—PURPOSE:** To review the basic cell phone and email guidelines for our emerging wireless world

- **COUNTRY PROUD—PURPOSE:** To demonstrate the use of the acrostic paragraph format to students as a tool for recording information related to one's own country

- **AWARDING THE "QUEST FOR KNOWLEDGE" HONOR—PURPOSE:** To identify and describe a student who exemplifies the individual on a quest for knowledge in all areas of life

- **A GLOBAL TIMELINE—PURPOSE:** To construct a timeline of no more than ten contemporary national or international events

- **NAME THE PERSON, PLACE, OR THING THAT INFLUENCED YOUR CULTURAL HISTORY—PURPOSE:** To use a simple poetry format as the basis for writing about a person, place, or thing of importance in relationship to the student's cultural history

- **QUESTIONING REAL-LIFE ISSUES AS AFFORDED BY SCHOOLWORK—PURPOSE:** To explain how various school subjects can teach skills and concepts for real-life concerns

©2004 Incentive Publications, Inc.
Nashville, TN

THEME: GLOBAL AWARENESS   VALUE: KNOWLEDGE

Gaining knowledge and understanding of cultures and values differing from one's own is one of the best ways for people the world over to learn to live and work together to achieve common and mutually rewarding goals. As dreams, economics, geography, problems, lifestyles, and opportunities are shared and explored, prejudice and malice begin to give way to respect and empathy. Make a list of ten questions you would ask a person of your own age, in a country of your choice, about life in their country. Write a letter to your imaginary pen pal using your questions as a guide for gaining knowledge and understanding of the country and its citizens.

_____

_____

_____

_____

_____

_____

_____

_____

_____

Reread the list of questions and the letter you wrote to your imaginary pen pal. Use the same list of questions to write a letter to the pen pal explaining the life and culture of your own country. What impact do you think letters of this nature could have on knowledge and understanding of cultures, lifestyles, opportunities, challenges, differences, and similarities for you and your pen pal?

_____

_____

_____

_____

_____

_____

_____

_____

JANUARY CALENDAR

✳

WEEK ONE

DAY ONE	**"Cultural Explorations"** Drawing conclusions and encouraging dialogue about ways cultures are alike and different
DAY TWO	**"Knowledge Is Power Wherever You Live"** Demonstrating ways that knowledge is of value in today's world, regardless of where you live or what you do
DAY THREE	**"Who Should Rule the World?"** Imagining what life would be like if children ruled the world
DAY FOUR	**"Knowledge Means Many Things to Many People"** Associating and validating personal symbols of knowledge from a student's perspective
DAY FIVE	**"And They Lived Happily Ever After, Hopefully"** Depicting a conflict/resolution situation through the creation of a comic strip

WEEK TWO

DAY ONE	**"Examining World Government Issues from a Kid's Point of View"** Examining the pros and cons of various governance issues both in and outside of the United States
DAY TWO	**"A Global Guided Imagery Experience"** Stimulating students' imaginations and understanding of the geographical biomes of the world
DAY THREE	**"Learning More About Third World Countries"** Identifying selected Third World countries and determining what characteristics make them fit this category
DAY FOUR	**"Learning or Learning How and Where to Learn"** Examining and discussing learning strategies
DAY FIVE	**"Gender Reactions to Headline News"** Using a series of mock headlines to provoke and explore gender issues

JANUARY CALENDAR
✳

WEEK THREE

DAY ONE	**"The Generation Gap"** Examining the issues that separate the older generation from the younger generation in today's society
DAY TWO	**"Stamp of Approval"** Understanding and appreciating other cultures
DAY THREE	**"On Track to Combat Conflict"** Using the medium of musical recordings to capture feelings and events
DAY FOUR	**"Managing Conflict: One Size Doesn't Fit All"** Examining three different conflict management tools
DAY FIVE	**"Dealing with Cell Yell and Email Etiquette Around the World"** Reviewing basic cell phone and email guidelines for our emerging wireless world

WEEK FOUR

DAY ONE	**"Country Proud"** Demonstrating the use of the acrostic paragraph as a tool for recording information related to one's own country
DAY TWO	**"Awarding the 'Quest for Knowledge' Honor"** Identifying and describing an individual student who exemplifies a quest for knowledge in all areas of life
DAY THREE	**"A Global Timeline"** Constructing a timeline of no more than ten contemporary national or international events
DAY FOUR	**"Name the Person, Place, or Thing that Influenced Your Cultural History"** Using a simple poetry format as the basis for writing about a person, place, or thing of importance in relationship to cultural history
DAY FIVE	**"Questioning Real-life Issues as Afforded by Schoolwork"** Explaining how various school subjects can teach skills and concepts for real-life and real-world uses

THEME: GLOBAL AWARENESS   VALUE: KNOWLEDGE

CULTURAL EXPLORATIONS

PURPOSE: To draw conclusions and encourage dialogue about ways that cultures are alike and different

TARGETED INTELLIGENCE: Verbal/Linguistic and Logical/Mathematical

CONTENT/STANDARD FOCUS: Social Studies—People, Places, and Environments; Global Connections & Language Arts—Standards 4, 9, and 12

PRODUCT/PERFORMANCE/STUDENT OUTCOME: Question and Answer Recording Sheet and Discussion

"CULTURAL EXPLORATIONS" (page 176)

Introduce the topic of "cultural explorations" by asking the students to complete the student activity sheet according to directions given. Then, direct a large group discussion based on students' questions and responses.

KNOWLEDGE IS POWER WHEREVER YOU LIVE

PURPOSE: To demonstrate ways that knowledge is of value in today's world, regardless of where you live or what you do

TARGETED INTELLIGENCE: Verbal/Linguistic, Logical/Mathematical, and Bodily/Kinesthetic

CONTENT/STANDARD FOCUS: Language Arts—Standards 5 and 11

PRODUCT/PERFORMANCE/STUDENT OUTCOME: Role-play

KNOWLEDGE IS POWER WHEREVER YOU LIVE (page 177)

Encourage students to role-play a meeting with a group of tourists to explain the importance of a "knowledge-based" educational system that promotes literacy and encourages learning. Emphasize to students that "knowledge" represents both the content and the skills that are the focus of all areas in the schooling process.

WHO SHOULD RULE THE WORLD?

PURPOSE: To imagine what life would be like if children ruled the world

TARGETED INTELLIGENCE: Verbal/Linguistic and Intrapersonal

CONTENT/STANDARD FOCUS: Language Arts—Standards 4, 5, and 11

PRODUCT/PERFORMANCE/STUDENT OUTCOME: Five-Paragraph Essay

"WHO SHOULD RULE THE WORLD?" (page 178)

Review the moral of the beach ball anecdote with the students. Lead students in a large group discussion on both the character traits and leadership qualities most likely to be representative of mature adults versus young people. Encourage students to stretch their minds and tease their imaginations in this exercise as they develop their thoughts in a five-paragraph essay.

KNOWLEDGE MEANS MANY THINGS TO MANY PEOPLE

PURPOSE: To associate and validate personal symbols of knowledge from a student's perspective

TARGETED INTELLIGENCE: Visual/Spatial, Intrapersonal, and Naturalistic

CONTENT/STANDARD FOCUS: Science—Life Science and Earth/Space Science

PRODUCT/PERFORMANCE/STUDENT OUTCOME: Hanger Mobile

"KNOWLEDGE MEANS MANY THINGS TO MANY PEOPLE" (page 179)

Review universal symbols of knowledge, such as the light bulb and the statue of the *Thinker*, with students and discuss reasons why they were selected. Then, using science as the organizing structure for the symbol, since both science and technology have become the focus of our evolving society, ask students to think of potential symbols of knowledge that might be effective in today's world.

AND THEY LIVED HAPPILY EVER AFTER, HOPEFULLY

PURPOSE: To depict a conflict/resolution situation through the creation of a comic strip based on children's literature.

TARGETED INTELLIGENCE: Verbal/Linguistic and Visual/Spatial

CONTENT/STANDARD FOCUS: Language Arts—Standards 4, 11, and 12

PRODUCT/PERFORMANCE/STUDENT OUTCOME: Comic Strip

"AND THEY LIVED HAPPILY EVER AFTER, HOPEFULLY" (page 180)

Ask students to think about their favorite childhood stories and fairy tales. Discuss the various characters and the differing conflicts, which needed to be resolved as part of the story line. Next, provide students with several examples of comic strips from the local newspaper and discuss how this literary format also involves conflicts among the characters. Finally, have students choose a favorite story or fairy tale and illustrate its major conflict and corresponding resolution through original comic strip creations.

EXAMINING WORLD GOVERNMENT ISSUES FROM A KID'S POINT OF VIEW

PURPOSE: To examine the pros and cons of various governance issues that exists both in and outside of the United States.

TARGETED INTELLIGENCE: Logical/Mathematical and Interpersonal

CONTENT/STANDARD FOCUS: Social Studies—Power, Authority, and Governance; Civic Ideals and Practices

PRODUCT/PERFORMANCE/ STUDENT OUTCOME: Think/Pair/Share Dialogue and Recording Sheet

"EXAMINING WORLD GOVERNMENT ISSUES FROM A KID'S POINT OF VIEW" (page 181)

Help students recognize that there are several universal governance issues facing democratic countries today, including implementation of the death penalty, taxation, immigration, freedom of speech, and gun control decisions. Assign students to work as partners in completing the student activity sheet according to directions given. Enlarge the size of the groups for further discussion, if warranted.

A GLOBAL GUIDED IMAGERY EXPERIENCE

PURPOSE: To stimulate students' mental images and understanding of the geographical biomes of the world through the use of guided imagery

TARGETED INTELLIGENCE: Visual/Spatial, Bodily/Kinesthetic, and Naturalistic

CONTENT/STANDARD FOCUS: Social Studies—People, Places, and Environments & Science—Earth and Space Science

PRODUCT/PERFORMANCE/STUDENT OUTCOME: Guided Imagery Activity

"A GLOBAL GUIDED IMAGERY EXPERIENCE" (page 182)

Explain to students that the earth can be divided into about ten different natural regions or land biomes. Each biome is unique, with a special mixture of physical features—landforms, bodies of water, and climate—and their own forms of plant and animal life. Divide students into pairs and have them challenge one another by following the directions on the student activity page for visualizing different world biomes through a guided imagery experience.

LEARNING MORE ABOUT THIRD WORLD COUNTRIES

PURPOSE: To identify selected Third World countries, and to determine what characteristics make them fit this category

TARGETED INTELLIGENCE: Logical/Mathematical and Visual/Spatial

CONTENT/STANDARD FOCUS: Social Studies—People, Places, and Environments; Global Connections

PRODUCT/PERFORMANCE/STUDENT OUTCOME: Graphic Organizer

"LEARNING MORE ABOUT THIRD WORLD COUNTRIES" (page 183)

Provide a world map and review the location of the seven continents. Ask students to use the map to predict which of the countries shown are most likely to be considered Third World nations, giving reasons for their choices. Next, have them record their predictions on the graphic organizer found on the student activity page.

LEARNING OR LEARNING HOW AND WHERE TO LEARN

PURPOSE: To question if being able to find information is more valuable than learning, processing, and storing information

TARGETED INTELLIGENCE: Verbal/Linguistic

CONTENT/STANDARD FOCUS: Language Arts—Standards 1, 7, and 11

PRODUCT/PERFORMANCE/STUDENT OUTCOME: Student Questionnaire

"LEARNING OR LEARNING HOW AND WHERE TO LEARN" (page 184) Ask students to answer the questions on the student questionnaire. Then, ask them to discuss their beliefs in small groups. After a discussion period, ask a representative from each group to summarize their findings to the entire class.

GENDER REACTIONS TO HEADLINE NEWS

PURPOSE: To use a series of mock headlines to provoke and explore gender issues

TARGETED INTELLIGENCE: Verbal/Linguistic

CONTENT/STANDARD FOCUS: Language Arts—Standards 5, 11, and 12

PRODUCT/PERFORMANCE/STUDENT OUTCOME: Newspaper Article or Editorial

"GENDER REACTIONS TO HEADLINE NEWS" (page 185)

Introduce this topic by asking these questions: Who has life easier today in middle school—boys or girls—and why do you think so? Who has life easier today as adults—males or females—and why do you think so? Who has life easier today in the workplace—men or women—and why do you think so? Then, ask students to select one of the headlines on the student activity page and write a feature article or editorial on the topic, sharing their own thoughts and experiences.

©2004 Incentive Publications, Inc.
Nashville, TN

THE GENERATION GAP

PURPOSE: To examine the issues that separate the older generation from the younger generation in today's society

TARGETED INTELLIGENCE: Verbal/Linguistic

CONTENT/STANDARD FOCUS: Social Studies—Individual Development and Identity; Individuals, Groups, and Institutions

PRODUCT/PERFORMANCE/STUDENT OUTCOME: Recording Sheet and Discussion

"THE GENERATION GAP" (page 186)

Ask students to indicate how many of them still have living grandparents and/or great-grandparents. Discuss how often they see, talk, or email one another. Next, ask students if they think today's society, at least in America, is more youth-oriented or more senior citizen-oriented, and why they feel as they do. Finally, ask students to complete the tasks on the worksheet, using it as the basis for conducting a large group discussion on the topic of conflicts caused by the generation gap.

STAMP OF APPROVAL

PURPOSE: To explore the advantages of travel as a means of learning about, understanding, and appreciating differences in people and their ways of life

TARGETED INTELLIGENCE: Visual/Spatial and Bodily/Kinesthetic

CONTENT/STANDARD FOCUS: Social Studies—People, Places, and Environments; Global Connections

PRODUCT/PERFORMANCE/STUDENT OUTCOME: Original Postage Stamp Design

"STAMP OF APPROVAL" (page 187)

Ask students to talk about their travel experiences within their state or country and about the advantages of travel related to promoting respect and appreciation for differences in people. Next, survey the class to determine if there are any stamp collectors in the group and discuss various postage stamp designs that have "caught their eye" recently. Finally, have students create original stamp designs that promote the idea of traveling to learn more about your world.

ON TRACK TO COMBAT CONFLICT

PURPOSE: To use the medium of musical recordings to capture feelings and events surrounding conflicts among and between individuals, groups, or nations

TARGETED INTELLIGENCE: Musical/Rhythmic and Interpersonal

CONTENT/STANDARD FOCUS: Music

PRODUCT/PERFORMANCE/STUDENT OUTCOME: Mock CD Soundtrack Cover Design

"ON TRACK TO COMBAT CONFLICT" (page 188)

Encourage students to talk about their favorite recording stars and their favorite CDs. Ask students to work in pairs to generate a list of song titles relating to the theme of conflict between people, groups, or nations. Finally, direct them to give their CD a creative name and sketch a colorful and attractive cover for their product.

MANAGING CONFLICT: ONE SIZE DOESN'T FIT ALL

PURPOSE: To examine three different conflict management tools that can be effective in the middle level classroom

TARGETED INTELLIGENCE: Bodily/Kinesthetic and Interpersonal

CONTENT/STANDARD FOCUS: Social Studies—Individuals, Groups, and Institutions

PRODUCT/PERFORMANCE/STUDENT OUTCOME: Small Group Discussion

"MANAGING CONFLICT: ONE SIZE DOESN'T FIT ALL" (page 189)

Encourage students to talk about the various types of conflicts they encounter in the middle school setting. What causes them, and what is the best way to handle them? Next, divide students into small cooperative learning groups to review the three conflict resolution tools discussed on the student activity page and to determine their potential use and effectiveness in their particular classroom setting.

DEALING WITH CELL YELL AND EMAIL ETIQUETTE AROUND THE WORLD

PURPOSE: To review and remember the basic cell phone and email guidelines for our emerging wireless world

TARGETED INTELLIGENCE: Verbal/Linguistic, Bodily/Kinesthetic, and Interpersonal

CONTENT/STANDARD FOCUS: Social Studies—Science, Technology, and Society

STUDENT PRODUCT/PERFORMANCE/STUDENT OUTCOME: Email

"DEALING WITH CELL YELL AND EMAIL ETIQUETTE AROUND THE WORLD"

(page 190) Lead a discussion related to the widespread use and abuse of both cell phone conversations and email messages. Encourage comments on the advantages and disadvantages of both forms of communication. Finally, review the suggested guidelines for cell phones and email behavior on the student activity sheet. Suggest that students practice these guidelines and, if time permits, have students draft an email to send to someone they know.

COUNTRY PROUD

PURPOSE: To demonstrate the use of the acrostic paragraph format to students as a tool for recording information related to one's own country

TARGETED INTELLIGENCE: Verbal/Linguistic

CONTENT/STANDARD FOCUS: Language Arts—Standards 5, 6, 11, and 12

PRODUCT/PERFORMANCE/STUDENT OUTCOME: Acrostic Paragraph

"COUNTRY PROUD" (page 191)

Review the acrostic poetry format for students and show them how this concept can also be used to record information in complete sentences leading to a full and interesting paragraph. Have students compose their own acrostic paragraphs according to directions given on the student activity page.

AWARDING THE "QUEST FOR KNOWLEDGE" HONOR

PURPOSE: To identify and describe a student who exemplifies the individual on a quest for knowledge in all areas of life.

TARGETED INTELLIGENCE: Verbal/Linguistic, Logical/Mathematical, and Interpersonal

CONTENT/STANDARD FOCUS: Social Studies—Global Connections and Science, Technology, and Society

PRODUCT/PERFORMANCE/STUDENT OUTCOME: Nomination Statements and Award Certificates

"AWARDING THE 'QUEST FOR KNOWLEDGE' HONOR" (page 192)

Discuss with students the importance of a constant quest for knowledge as a means to establishing and achieving important life goals, in addition to the acquisition of knowledge in academic and vocational areas. Lead a discussion focusing on skills, attitudes, and work habits required of those special individuals who are effective in identifying and acquiring specific knowledge essential to daily life, as well as more general information related to life enrichment and future planning. Next, challenge the students to think of one individual in the group to whom they would present the "Quest for Knowledge" award, justifying their choice in a written nomination statement. Once the nominations have been made, ask each student to prepare a certificate award for the person they nominated.

A GLOBAL TIMELINE

PURPOSE: To construct a timeline of no more than ten contemporary, national, or international events

TARGETED INTELLIGENCE: Logical/Mathematical and Visual/Spatial

CONTENT/STANDARD FOCUS: Mathematics—Mathematics as Communication & Social Studies—Global Connections

PRODUCT/PERFORMANCE/STUDENT OUTCOME: Timeline

"A GLOBAL TIMELINE" (page 193)

Divide students into small cooperative learning groups and ask each group to generate a list of major national and international events that have occurred in their lifetime. Ask each group to pick the top ten from their list and arrange these events on a timeline, according to when they occurred. Encourage students to add graphics depicting each event for color and interest.

NAME THE PERSON, PLACE, OR THING THAT INFLUENCED YOUR CULTURAL HISTORY

PURPOSE: To use a simple poetry format as the basis for writing about a person, place, or thing of importance in relationship to their cultural history

TARGETED INTELLIGENCE: Verbal/Linguistic

CONTENT/STANDARD FOCUS: Language Arts—Standards 5, 9, 11, and 12

PRODUCT/PERFORMANCE/STUDENT OUTCOME: Original Poem

"NAME THE PERSON, PLACE, OR THING THAT INFLUENCED YOUR CULTURAL HISTORY"

(page 194) Review the simple format for composing a "Name the Person, Place, or Thing" poem. Instruct students to create a poem of their own using some person, place, or thing important to their cultural history.

QUESTIONING REAL-LIFE ISSUES AS AFFORDED BY SCHOOLWORK

PURPOSE: To explain how various school subjects can teach skills and concepts for real-life and real-world uses in the lives of students

TARGETED INTELLIGENCE: Logical/Mathematical

CONTENT/STANDARD FOCUS: All Subject Areas

PRODUCT/PERFORMANCE/STUDENT OUTCOME: Role-Play

"QUESTIONING REAL LIFE ISSUES AS AFFORDED BY SCHOOLWORK" (page 195)

Review the concept of "role-play" as an opportunity to assume the imaginary role of a character in a predetermined scenario. Then, ask students to assume the role of a student meeting with a family from outside their own country that is moving into their community and looking for evidence that the school is teaching students skills and concepts for real-world experiences. Instruct students to follow the directions on the student activity sheet as part of this role-playing scenario. If time permits, ask students to share their work with one another.

CULTURAL EXPLORATIONS

Directions: Answer each of the questions about culture listed on the lines below. Be prepared to use this question and answer sheet as a guide for group discussion.

1. How would you explain the concept of "culture" to a young child so that he/she would understand what it means?

   _____

   _____

2. Are some cultures superior to others, or are all cultures justified in their own special way?

   _____

   _____

3. What would you think of a universal effort to establish a single world culture?

   _____

   _____

4. How do differing cultures develop prejudices and stereotypes of other cultures?

   _____

   _____

5. How is technology impacting cultures to become more alike than they are different? Is this a good thing or not?

   _____

   _____

6. What are some cultural traditions and celebrations from around the world that you would like to know more about, or perhaps adopt into your own culture?

   _____

   _____

7. Why do you think that people with different cultural or ethnic backgrounds sometimes have trouble getting along with each other?

   _____

   _____

Name: _____

KNOWLEDGE IS POWER WHEREVER YOU LIVE

Directions: Pretend that you have been asked to meet with a group of tourists who have come to visit the United States from a different part of the world, and it is your job to convince them that our schools and society place a high value on the "pursuit of knowledge."

Read through the "knowledge-related" statements below, and give at least one real-life example of what is meant by each one, using an experience you or one someone you know has had recently. Prove your point!

1. Knowledge gives you power.

EXAMPLE: _____

_____

_____

2. Knowledge gives you choices.

EXAMPLE: _____

_____

_____

3. Knowledge opens up the world to you.

EXAMPLE: _____

_____

_____

4. Knowledge makes you independent.

EXAMPLE: _____

_____

_____

5. Knowledge makes you interesting.

EXAMPLE: _____

_____

_____

6. Knowledge paves the way for a better life.

EXAMPLE: _____

_____

_____

Name: _____

WHO SHOULD RULE THE WORLD?

Directions: Imagine that two young kids are playing with a big ball at the beach on a windy day, and one of them says, "My beach ball is coming back. That kid on the other side of the world sent it back. Our nations are in harmony!" Her friend firmly says, "No, the wind changed!" She quickly retorts," Two nations using two innocent children and a beach ball have demonstrated to the world that they can live in total harmony." Again, the friend replies, "The wind changed."

Think about the message of this little anecdote. What does it say to you? Who was the optimist? Who was the pessimist? Who was the realist? Who was the idealist? Next, think about how life could or would be different "if children ruled the world." What would they say and do differently than adults? What would they do better? What might they do worse? Write down your thoughts in a five-paragraph essay below. Introduce the idea in the first paragraph. Discuss the pros and cons of the idea in the next three paragraphs. Conclude your ideas on the topic in the last paragraph.

WHAT WOULD HAPPEN IF CHILDREN RULED THE WORLD?

Name: _____

©2004 Incentive Publications, Inc.
Nashville, TN

KNOWLEDGE MEANS MANY THINGS TO MANY PEOPLE

Directions: Over the years, there have been many universal symbols of knowledge ranging from a light bulb to the statue of the *Thinker.* Knowledge means many things to many people, and this activity will give you an opportunity to think of specific objects or things that represent knowledge from your personal perspective. In the squares below, think of a knowledge object or symbol for each category and give a reason for your choice. Then, punch out the hole at the top of each square, cut out the square, and attach a piece of string or colored ribbon or yarn to each one through the hole. Make certain that the pieces of string, ribbon, or yarn are of varied lengths, and tie them to a coat hanger to make a mobile.

TEXTBOOK

Reason . . .

ART MUSEUM

Reason . . .

BUILDING/MONUMENT

Reason . . .

POST OFFICE

Reason . . .

Name:

AND THEY LIVED HAPPILY EVER AFTER, HOPEFULLY

Directions: Examine one of several comic strips on display in the classroom or in your local newspaper. Notice that many of these comic strips focus on some type of conflict situation between two different generations, genders, personality types, outlooks on life, creatures, backgrounds, stereotypes, or attitudes. Recall a simple fairy tale that you know or read as a child, and recreate that story and its main conflict using a comic strip format. Consider such fairy tales as: *Goldilocks and the Three Bears, Little Red Riding Hood, The Three Little Pigs, Jack and the Beanstalk, Cinderella, Snow White and the Seven Dwarfs, The Princess and the Pea, The Ugly Duckling*, or any other favorite from your childhood.

①	②
③	④

Name:

©2004 Incentive Publications, Inc.
Nashville, TN

EXAMINING WORLD GOVERNMENT ISSUES FROM A KID'S POINT OF VIEW

Directions: Write down your thoughts on each of the government-related issues outlined below. Then, share your ideas with a partner and discuss the pros and cons of each situation. If time permits, expand your discussion to include another pair in the classroom.

ISSUE ONE: Should there be a death penalty, and if so, for which types of crimes?

_____

_____

_____

ISSUE TWO: Should the wealthy pay more taxes than the poor, and if so, how should these be determined?

_____

_____

_____

ISSUE THREE: Should our borders be open to anyone wanting to enter our country, or should there be restrictions? Explain.

_____

_____

_____

ISSUE FOUR: Should citizens be able to write and say anything they want to about the government, or should there be restrictions on this freedom of speech?

_____

_____

_____

ISSUE FIVE: How much should the government regulate gun control?

_____

_____

_____

Name: _____

A GLOBAL GUIDED IMAGERY EXPERIENCE

Directions: Guided imagery is a tool that is used to activate your imagination so that you can visualize a given situation, setting, event, or problem scenario. To give you practice in using imagery, work with a partner and one-at-a-time, try to picture the things listed below using your mind's eye. To begin this process, one student reads the description of a scenario briefly outlined below, while the other person closes his/her eyes and describes what he/she is seeing with his/her mind's eye. Try to describe what you see while visiting each of these natural regions or biomes of the world in vivid detail and exciting color. In preparation for this exchange, be sure to take a few moments to elaborate on the image you are trying to form in your mind before sharing it with your partner. Alternate both the guided imagery task and the scenario with one another to avoid unnecessary duplication.

1. Imagine what you think it would be like to visit a tropical rain forest in South America where more species of plants and animals flourish than in all other biomes combined. Here, trees are so thick they fight for the light while their canopies provide homes for reptiles, amphibians, birds, monkeys, parrots, bats, and flying squirrels. The floor of the rain forest is so dark and damp that plants requiring sunlight do not grow quickly.

2. Imagine what you think it would be like to visit the tropical grasslands of Africa where the thick grasses are food to millions of savanna animals, among them antelopes, zebras, giraffes, rhinos, buffaloes, and elephants. These animals in turn feed such predators as cheetahs, leopards, and lions, while still others, including hyenas and jackals, scavenge the remains of dead or dying animals.

3. Imagine what you think it would be like to visit the deserts of Australia, where the land is covered in sand or bare soil and precipitation totals are very small, less than 10 inches each year. Cacti are typical desert plants, and many animals are nocturnal, active only at night when the weather is cooler.

4. Imagine what you think it would be like to visit the polar regions of the Arctic. Powerful icy winds blow across the polar ice caps, causing blizzards of snow and ice to sweep up from the surface. Only migrating animals, such as polar bears and Arctic seals, are found on the Arctic ice mass. What other animals live in the region? What do you think they eat, and how do they survive? Are there seasons?

5. Imagine what you think it would be like to visit the prairies or cool grasslands of the United States where, because of their excellent farming potential, few of these biomes have been left by human beings in their natural state. Instead of serving as natural grazing lands for large herds of wild animals, the grasslands are now covered in wheat, barley, oats, and other grain crops catering to populations of cows, horses, goats, and other domesticated animals that feed on the coarse grasses.

Name:

LEARNING MORE ABOUT THIRD WORLD COUNTRIES

Directions: Use a world map to locate as many countries as you can think of that would classify as Third World countries. Write a country for each letter of the alphabet in the graphic organizer found below. Then, write something that each of these countries has in common to make them qualify as a Third World nation. Try to come up with a Third World country characteristic for most letters of the alphabet as well. Finally, do you think there is such a thing as a First World and Second World country and is there likely to be a Fourth and Fifth World country? How would they differ from one another?

A...	N...
B...	O...
C...	P...
D...	Q...
E...	R...
F...	S...
G...	T...
H...	U...
I...	V...
J...	W...
K...	X...
L...	Y...
M...	Z...

Name:

LEARNING OR LEARNING HOW AND WHERE TO LEARN

In this day of rapid technology and easy access to facts, figures, and history in the making, it is argued by many people, especially technicians, that learning how to find information as needed is more valuable than learning, processing, and storing information. What do you think?

Examine your beliefs related to this issue by recording your reaction to each of the following statements:

1. More can be learned about ancient, as well as modern day, history from Internet sources than can be learned from textbooks and class discussions.

    _____

    _____

2. Every student in middle school should be required to demonstrate computer literacy and competency before moving on to high school.

    _____

    _____

3. Some of the things tested on standardized tests and other assessments in middle schools today are outdated, irrelevant, and unimportant to students' actual life needs.

    _____

    _____

4. When in need of a quotation to use in verbal and/or written communication (conversation, essays, debates, drama presentations, letters, etc.), would you first turn to a book of quotations, to the Internet, or rely on your own memory? _____

    _____

5. Reading and understanding great literature in middle and high school will enrich the individual student's future life. _____

    _____

6. Problem solving skills can best be learned from teacher or parent directed, structured lessons.

    _____

    _____

7. Knowledge acquired is like a savings account at a bank, in that you can deposit and withdraw from your own knowledge bank as needed.

    _____

    _____

8. Regular library visits and check out privileges should be a part of every middle school program.

    _____

    _____

SUMMARY: Which do you think is more important, learning or learning how and where to learn?

_____

_____

_____

_____

Name: _____

GENDER REACTIONS TO HEADLINE NEWS

Directions: Read through this set of mock headline writing prompts dealing with gender issues, and choose one of special interest to you. Compose a short news or feature article agreeing or disagreeing with the selected mock headline. Be certain to include the "who, what, where, when, and why" of the story. Have fun!

RESEARCH SHOWS THAT BOYS ARE SMARTER THAN GIRLS

TEACHERS CATER TO FEMALE LEARNING STYLES IN CLASSROOM

STUDY FINDS THAT GIRLS MAKE BETTER FRIENDS THAN BOYS DO

BOYS PREFER SPORTS THAT DON'T APPEAL TO GIRLS BECAUSE THEY FEAR THE COMPETITION

GIRLS STAGE SIT-IN TO PROTEST MALE FEELINGS OF SUPERIORITY

BOYS ARGUE THAT GIRLS GET BETTER TREATMENT WHEN IN TROUBLE

Name:

THE GENERATION GAP

Directions: Conflicts in values and beliefs between generations are more prevalent in some cultures than in others. Some societies around the world place a high value on the older generations of their culture, while other societies place a high value on the younger generations. Think of some countries or cultures that fall into each category. Where do you think the United States falls in this issue? Read through each of the questions below, and write your responses. Use this worksheet to help you prepare for a group discussion related to the concept of conflicts between the young and the old.

1. Do you think there is a generation gap among members of your family, community, or country? Give reasons for your answer.

    _____

    _____

2. Can you think of a time when you felt discriminated against because you were young? Explain.

    _____

    _____

3. When do you get aggravated with people in your community who are considered senior citizens?

    _____

    _____

4. Is there a difference between maturity and old age? Why do you think as you do?

    _____

    _____

5. What are some common statements that are often made by either a young person talking about an old person or an old person talking about a young person? Add your own expressions to these:

    "They have life so much easier than we ever did."

    _____

    "They are so inflexible and set in their ways."

    _____

6. What are some ways the generations can work together to discourage age-based discrimination and stereotyping?

    _____

    _____

    _____

Name: _____

STAMP OF APPROVAL

Directions: Our global economy, progress through technology, and mutual interdependence with other nations has fostered a universal urge for world travel, while also providing the means for this luxury. One never really understands another culture until experiencing it in some meaningful way, and travel is one of the best options to consider. Pretend the United States Postal Service has created a brand-new stamp to encourage widespread travel among young people throughout the world. Make a sketch of this wonderful stamp creation below, and then write a short paragraph to explain your choice of symbol, color, and design.

Name:

ON TRACK TO COMBAT CONFLICT

Directions: Pretend you are a young recording star who has been hired by a group of teenagers to create a soundtrack CD based on the theme of conflict among people, groups, or nations. Work with a partner to brainstorm possible song titles that capture feelings and events associated with conflict. Write your list of songs on the blank CD outline below. Then, prepare your CD for market by giving it a clever name and creating an attractive cover design to reflect the chosen theme.

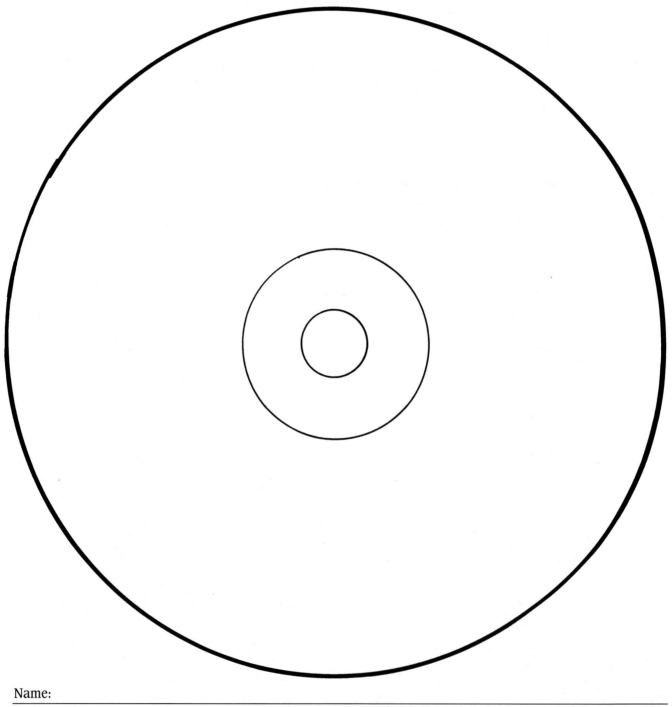

Name:

MANAGING CONFLICT: ONE SIZE DOESN'T FIT ALL

Directions: Review each of the three conflict resolution strategies outlined below, and think about a time when it would have been effective for you or someone you know in solving a problem. Discuss the advantages and disadvantages of each strategy and the most appropriate time to use it with members of your small cooperative learning group.

FIGHT FORM: *To be used for either verbal or physical encounters*

1. With whom did you fight? _____
2. What was the problem? _____
   _____
3. Give one good reason why you started fighting. _____
   _____
4. Think of one good reason why the other person fought with you. _____
   _____
5. Did fighting help or make the problem worse? _____
6. What are two things you might try instead of fighting next time? _____
   _____
7. What can you say to the other person now to make things better? _____
   _____

HASSLE LINE: *To be used with large groups split into factions*

1. Instruct opposing groups to form lines and face one another.
2. Ask students in one line to explain and convince the person facing them of their position.
3. Then, reverse the role and give the other line the same opportunity.
4. Next, instruct the two lines to switch roles completely and argue the other position.
5. Guide students in both lines to come up with a compromise solution they can all support.

THREE-R STRATEGY: *To be used in solving long-standing disagreements or dislikes*

1. RESENTMENT STEP: Ask opposing students to state what they dislike about each other and what has propagated the resentment over time.
2. REQUEST STEP: Ask opposing students to tell the other what must be done to ease the resentment and move towards solving the problem.
3. RECOGNITION STEP: Ask opposing students to negotiate which requests they are willing to honor and why. Then, ask opposing students to think of two or more qualities that they admire in the other.

COMMENTS _____
_____
_____

Name: _____

DEALING WITH CELL YELL AND EMAIL ETIQUETTE AROUND THE WORLD

Directions: Have you noticed lately how many teenagers and adults are busily, and sometimes rudely, engaged in ill-mannered and discourteous behaviors associated with cell phones and email messages? It has been said by many counselors and behavior experts around the world that an insensitive comment or rude gesture can quickly spiral into a confrontation. Incivility, a result of the decline in common courtesy, can be one of the negative results of technology because in a world of cellular phones, email messages, and Internet conversations, common decency and warm personal interaction can fall by the wayside. Unfortunately and ironically, increased connections have actually made people feel disconnected, often leading to uncivil behavior. Finally, it should be noted that recent studies have shown that IM (instant messaging) is as important as a phone call to many young people because those surveyed said that they prefer the Internet for "emotional confrontations" with friends, as they feel more free to express anger online. Review the guidelines for preventing "cell yell" and "email etiquette blunders" below. Then, begin "practicing what you preach" in your next cell phone call or email message!

GUIDELINES FOR COURTEOUS CELL PHONE USE:

1. Keep noise pollution down by making calls only when they are necessary, and require the same of your friends and family members.

2. Keep your calls short and your voice soft so that your conversation won't bother others.

3. Turn your phone off if its ring may disturb someone. Always turn off your cell phone in classrooms, theaters, libraries, houses of worship, hospital rooms, courts of law, and in restaurants.

GUIDELINES FOR EMAIL USE:

1. Respond to every personal message promptly, preferably within 12 to 24 hours.

2. Refrain from sending trivial messages that will impinge on someone else's time to read.

3. Mind both your tongue and fingers so that an email message does not include profanity or abusive language.

4. Proofread all email messages for misspellings and improper grammar.

5. Forward email only with the sender's permission.

6. Understand that your email may be forwarded without your permission, so don't write anything you don't want repeated elsewhere.

7. Realize that email is never an acceptable substitute for a thank-you note or a sensitive face-to-face encounter.

Name:

COUNTRY PROUD

Directions: An acrostic paragraph model is useful for organizing and writing down ideas gleaned from a textbook or other informational source. To compose your acrostic paragraph, select a topic you wish to write about and print its title boldly and vertically down the side of the page (much like you would if you were writing an acrostic poem). Then, record a complete informational sentence about your topic that begins with each bold letter. Your paragraph will have the same number of sentences as you have bold letters for your topic. Choose one of these topics to write about using the acrostic paragraph model. Do your work in the blank space provided below. Topics to consider are: (1) What country, other than your own, do you admire most and why? (Use bold letters of any country of choice.) (2) If you lived in another country, why might you want to immigrate to your country? (Use bold letters in word IMMIGRATE.) (3) What makes you most proud of your own country? (Use bold letters in word PROUD.) (4) What advice would you give a foreign student who had just moved into your neighborhood? (Use bold letters of ADVICE, FOREIGN, or NEIGHBORHOOD.)

———————— MY ACROSTIC PARAGRAPH ————————

Name:

Advisory Plus!

AWARDING THE "QUEST FOR KNOWLEDGE" HONOR

Directions: Think about the different people in your classroom or group who are on a constant quest for knowledge related to a wide array of interests, as demonstrated by their questions, reading, and intellectual curiosity. Nominate someone you know who would qualify as a recipient for the "Quest for Knowledge" honor and describe his/her talents, behaviors, and abilities in the space below. Then, design a special certificate or award to give to this person.

MY NOMINEE FOR THE QUEST FOR KNOWLEDGE HONOR IS …

_____

BECAUSE … _____

_____

_____

_____

_____

_____

_____

_____

_____

Name: _____

©2004 Incentive Publications, Inc.
Nashville, TN

A GLOBAL TIMELINE

Directions: Work with members of your cooperative learning group to brainstorm a number of significant world events that have happened in your lifetime. Retell the story of these happenings by placing them in a ten-event timeline according to when they took place. If time permits, add a simple drawing, diagram, or symbol for each event to add interest and color.

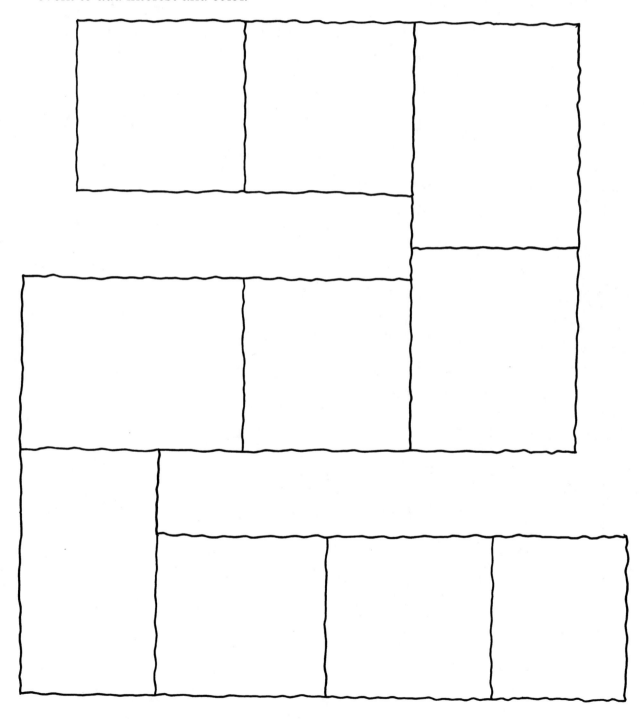

©2004 Incentive Publications, Inc.
Nashville, TN
Advisory Plus!

NAME THE PERSON, PLACE, OR THING THAT INFLUENCED YOUR CULTURAL HISTORY

Directions: There are many different poetry forms to use in writing about important persons, places, or things from your culture or that of another culture. Some popular poetry forms you probably know are couplets, cinquains, haikus, tankas, and free verse poems. This activity introduces you to a "Name the Person, Place, or Thing" poetry form that goes like this:

NAME THE PERSON, PLACE, OR THING

Line 1—descriptive word as clue

Line 2—descriptive word as clue

Line 3—descriptive word as clue

Line 4—descriptive word as clue

Line 5—descriptive sentence as clue

Line 6—answer

One example of this type of poem is written below in the first column. Try creating an original poem of your own that focuses on an important person, place, or thing that is representative of your culture.

NAME THE PERSON, PLACE, OR THING

(Our example)	*(Your example)*
Slave	
Bandanna	
Underground Railroad	
Freedom	
She returned to the South 19 times and used the North Star as a guide to bring some 300 slaves to freedom.	
Harriet Tubman	

Name:

©2004 Incentive Publications, Inc.
Nashville, TN

QUESTIONING REAL-LIFE ISSUES AS AFFORDED BY SCHOOLWORK

Directions: Many students question what is taught in core subject areas such as math, science, English, and social studies because they don't always see the relevance of what they are learning in school. Pretend you have been asked to meet with a family from another part of the world who has just recently been transferred to your community because of the father's superior job skills in technology. You have been asked to meet with this family to talk about what you are learning in school and how useful it is now or will be for real-life experiences. Write your thoughts below concerning each subject area, using the examples as a springboard for your thinking.

1. We are learning fractions and decimals in mathematics . . . . . I use fractions in measuring ingredients for cooking . . . . . . I use decimals for making change in my part-time job at McDonald's.

   _____

   _____

2. We are learning about the Constitution and Bill of Rights in social studies . . . . . . I can use freedom of speech to criticize government actions in letters to the editor of my local newspaper . . . . . I will be able to exercise my right to vote when I am eighteen years old.

   _____

   _____

3. We are learning about simple machines and electrical circuits in science . . . . . . I know how to use a screwdriver, hammer, and wrench safely to make simple repairs and help my parents around the house . . . . . . I understand how circuit breakers and surge protectors work to protect us from fires or damage caused by thunderstorms.

   _____

   _____

4. We are learning about the Internet and the use of email in technology class . . . . . . I know how to type quickly and accurately on the keyboard, and often use the Internet as a source for writing my research reports . . . . . . I can communicate with my grandparents who live out of town by email, saving money on our telephone bill.

   _____

   _____

5. We are learning how to write a business letter in English.. . . . . I can write a business letter to a company when I need to return something by mail and get my money back.

   _____

   _____

Name: _____

THEME: GLOBAL AWARENESS   VALUE: KNOWLEDGE

JANUARY

RATING SCALE:

Best – **1**   Better – **2**   Good – **3**   Fair – **4**   Poor – **5**

1._____I was able to answer the set of questions about culture.

2._____I was able to give real-life examples of the knowledge-related statements.

3._____I was able to speculate on how life would be different if children ruled the world.

4._____I was able to complete the knowledge mobile using my own symbols.

5._____I was able to create a conflict comic strip.

6._____I was able to offer some thoughtful ideas on a set of government issues.

7._____I was able to participate successfully in the guided imagery experience.

8._____I was able to complete the ABC identification chart of Third World countries.

9._____I was able to answer questions about and discuss learning in the age of technology.

10._____I was able to use one of the headlines as the lead for a news/feature story.

11._____I was able to share thoughts on the generation gap in my society.

12._____I was able to create an original design for a travel-related postage stamp.

13._____I was able to design a CD cover on the theme of conflict.

14._____I was able to apply the conflict resolution strategies to my own life.

15._____I was able to apply the guidelines for better cell phone or email use in my family.

16._____I was able to compose an acrostic paragraph according to directions given.

17._____I was able to nominate someone for the "Quest for Knowledge" honor.

18._____I was able to construct a timeline of important global events.

19._____I was able to create an original cultural name poem.

20._____I was able to see the connections between what we need to know in the real world and what we are being taught.

Name: _____

THEME: HEROES AND HEROINES   VALUE: COURAGE

> *"Putting people first has always been America's secret weapon. It's the way we've kept the spirit of our revolution alive—a spirit that drives us to dream and dare, and take great risks for the greater good."*
>
> President Ronald Reagan, 1981

- **A HERO IS MORE THAN A SUB SANDWICH!—PURPOSE:** To define and examine the multiple traits of a hero or heroine

- **WHO IS YOUR HERO?—PURPOSE:** To identify and defend one's personal choice of heroes in many different categories

- **REFLECTIONS ON WHAT MAKES A HERO—PURPOSE:** To recall famous heroes and compare them with the student's own list of personal heroes

- **HEROES WHO REFUSED TO GIVE UP—PURPOSE:** To discuss success stories of heroes that almost weren't

- **UNITED NATIONS: THE PEACEKEEPING HEROES—PURPOSE:** To discover the basic principles, purposes, and projects of the United Nations and its role as a peacekeeper in the world today

- **SEARCHING FOR SOLUTIONS TO WORLD PROBLEMS—PURPOSE:** To describe a personal crusade that a student would like to undertake, if given the time and resources

- **LEARNING FROM HEROES IN THE WORLD OF MUSIC AND ART—PURPOSE:** To explore and interpret the unique minds of artists and musicians through quotations

- **AMERICAN WOMEN WHO BECAME HEROES UNDER DURESS—PURPOSE:** To learn about special American women who became heroes because they championed a cause in which they believed strongly

- **HEROES OF SCIENCE AND TECHNOLOGY—PURPOSE:** To assume the role of a technology or science genius from history as he/she is being recognized for a major contribution to the world

- **MEET SOME EXTRAORDINARY AFRICAN-AMERICAN HEROES—PURPOSE:** To develop a respect for some extraordinary African-American heroes of yesterday

- **TIMELINES HELP US UNDERSTAND EXPLORERS AS HEROES—PURPOSE:** To construct a timeline that represents the discoveries of ten important explorers from around the world

- **CHAMPIONS OF THE ENVIRONMENT—PURPOSE:** To identify professional groups of heroes/heroines and the courageous acts associated with their work roles

- **ATHLETES: HEROES IN THE SPORTS WORLD—PURPOSE:** To examine the world of sports and athletes who are heroes

- **TELL ABOUT A TIME WHEN YOU FELT LIKE A HERO—PURPOSE:** To recall special circumstances or situations when students performed a heroic or courageous deed

- **LITERARY HEROES AND HEROINES—PURPOSE:** To identify literary heroes and heroines from a student's point of view

- **SALUTE TO A PERSONAL HERO—PURPOSE:** To identify and describe an everyday hero or heroine in a student's life

- **WHO ARE THE HEROES IN YOUR FAMILY?—PURPOSE:** To recognize special heroes that exist within one's own family circle

- **FAMOUS LINES FROM FAMOUS PRESIDENTS—PURPOSE:** To analyze some famous quotations of former presidents

- **RATING YOURSELF AS A POTENTIAL LEADER OR HERO—PURPOSE:** To assess one's leadership qualities and potential as a hero in some leadership role

- **YOU MADE THE HEADLINES!—PURPOSE:** To design a mock newspaper story and picture about oneself as a hero

©2004 Incentive Publications, Inc.
Nashville, TN

THEME: HEROES AND HEROINES   VALUE: COURAGE

"Courage is not the absence of fear or despair, but the strength to conquer them." This quotation constitutes the message on the dedication page of the novel *The Kids* by popular author Danielle Steele. Cover notes about the author state that more than 490 million copies of her novels have sold. Can you imagine the impact of this author's writing on readers, many of whom have read dozens of her books? In your own words, tell how you think one of the following people overcame fear or despair to become a legendary hero and how the results of their triumph over fear or despair benefited a wide range of people for years beyond their lifespan: Franklin D. Roosevelt, Albert Schweitzer, or Ludwig van Beethoven.

_____

_____

_____

_____

_____

_____

_____

_____

Agree or disagree with one of the following statements, and support your position with an example from history, fiction, or current events.

1. "Heroes and heroines are made, not born... shaped by the culture of their time and place, the people and events surrounding their daily lives, and the circumstances in which they find themselves."

2. "Certain people are born with traits of greatness, great courage and/or an innate desire to act in a manner resulting in great achievement benefiting the society of their time."

_____

_____

_____

_____

_____

_____

_____

_____

FEBRUARY CALENDAR

WEEK ONE

DAY ONE	**"A Hero Is More Than a Sub Sandwich!"** Defining and examining the multiple traits of a hero or heroine
DAY TWO	**"Who Is Your Hero?"** Students identify and defend their personal choice of heroes in many different categories
DAY THREE	**"Reflections on What Makes a Hero"** Comparing famous heroes with the student's own list of personal heroes
DAY FOUR	**"Heroes Who Refused to Give Up"** Discussing success stories of heroes that almost weren't
DAY FIVE	**"United Nations: The Peacekeeping Heroes"** Discovering the basic principles, purposes, and projects of the United Nations and its role as a peacekeeper in the world today

WEEK TWO

DAY ONE	**"Searching for Solutions to World Problems"** Describing a personal crusade that a student would like to undertake if given the time and the resources
DAY TWO	**"Learning from Heroes in the World of Music and Art"** Explore and interpret the unique minds of artists and musicians through quotations
DAY THREE	**"American Women Who Became Heroes under Duress"** Learning about special American women who became heroes because they championed a cause in which they believed strongly
DAY FOUR	**"Heroes of Science and Technology"** Assuming the role of a technology or science genius from history as he/she is being recognized for a major contribution to the world
DAY FIVE	**"Meet Some Extraordinary African-American Heroes"** Developing a respect for some extraordinary African-American heroes of yesterday

THEME: HEROES AND HEROINES   VALUE: COURAGE

WEEK THREE

DAY ONE	**"Timelines Help Us Understand Explorers as Heroes"** Constructing a timeline that represents the discoveries of ten important explorers from around the world
DAY TWO	**"Champions of the Environment"** Identifying professional groups of heroes/heroines and the courageous acts associated with their work roles
DAY THREE	**"Athletes: Heroes in the Sports World"** Examine the world of sports and athletes who are heroes
DAY FOUR	**"Tell About a Time When You Felt Like a Hero"** Recalling special circumstances or situations when students or their peers performed a heroic or courageous deed
DAY FIVE	**"Literary Heroes and Heroines"** Identifying literary heroes and heroines from their own point of view

WEEK FOUR

DAY ONE	**"Salute to a Personal Hero"** Identifying and describing an everyday hero or heroine in each student's life
DAY TWO	**"Who are the Heroes in Your Family?"** Recognizing special heroes that exist within one's own family circle
DAY THREE	**"Famous Lines from Famous Presidents"** Analyzing famous quotations of former Presidents
DAY FOUR	**"Rating Yourself as a Potential Leader or Hero"** Assessing personal leadership qualities and potential as a hero in some leadership role
DAY FIVE	**"You Made the Headlines!"** Designing a mock newspaper story and picture about the student as a hero

THEME: HEROES AND HEROINES   VALUE: COURAGE

A HERO IS MORE THAN A SUB SANDWICH!

PURPOSE: To define and examine the multiple traits of a hero or heroine

TARGETED INTELLIGENCE: Verbal/Linguistic, Interpersonal, and Intrapersonal

CONTENT/STANDARD FOCUS: Language Arts—Standard 11

PRODUCT/PERFORMANCE/STUDENT OUTCOME: Participating in a Think/Pair/Share Activity

"A HERO IS MORE THAN A SUB SANDWICH!" (page 212)

Assign students to work in pairs and provide dictionaries for each twosome as a reference for helping them define the concept of "hero" and "heroine." Instruct students to generate a comprehensive list of traits they most commonly associate with a hero/heroine and then use this list to identify someone they collaboratively feel best represents their idea of the hero/heroine concept.

WHO IS YOUR HERO?

PURPOSE: To identify and defend one's personal choice of heroes in many different categories

TARGETED INTELLIGENCE: Intrapersonal

CONTENT/STANDARD FOCUS: All Content Areas

PRODUCT/PERFORMANCE/STUDENT OUTCOME: Generating a Personal List of Heroes

"WHO IS YOUR HERO?" (page 213)

Encourage students to use their list of character traits from the activity entitled "A Hero Is More Than a Sub Sandwich" to decide on their personal choice of heroes in many different categories. If this is not available, ask students to decide on their list of heroes and then go back and try to generate a list of character traits that are common to all or most of their personal choices.

REFLECTIONS ON WHAT MAKES A HERO

PURPOSE: To recall famous heroes and compare them with students' own lists of personal heroes

TARGETED INTELLIGENCE: Intrapersonal

CONTENT/STANDARD FOCUS: Social Studies—Individual Development and Identity

PRODUCT/PERFORMANCE/STUDENT OUTCOME: Set of Lists

"REFLECTIONS ON WHAT MAKES A HERO" (page 214)

Introduce the topic of famous heroes and heroines by having students complete the top half of their student activity sheet. Ask students to comment on the difficulty of remembering famous heroes or heroines in each category even though they were once the headliners and the best in their fields. Instruct students to complete the second half of this student activity sheet and to reflect on how much easier this list of personal heroes and heroines is to construct. What makes the difference?

HEROES WHO REFUSED TO GIVE UP

PURPOSE: To discuss the success stories of heroes that almost weren't

TARGETED INTELLIGENCE: Verbal/Linguistic

CONTENT/STANDARD FOCUS: Language Arts—Standards 11 and 12

PRODUCT/PERFORMANCE/STUDENT OUTCOME: Think/Pair/Share Reactions

"HEROES WHO REFUSED TO GIVE UP" (page 215)

Ask students to define the concepts of "courage" and "cowardice" and how they are polar opposites in meaning. Next, introduce the concept of "cliché" through the expression, "If you don't succeed at first, then try, try again." Encourage students to think of personal experiences that illustrate this cliché in their own lives. Finally, instruct students to complete the student activity sheet by giving their reactions to several situations whereby famous heroes overcame failure after failure before they were successful. Emphasize the fact that these individuals were courageous and didn't give in to cowardice in the face of failure.

UNITED NATIONS: THE PEACEKEEPING HEROES

PURPOSE: To discover the basic principles, purposes, and projects of the United Nations and its role as a peacekeeper in the world today

TARGETED INTELLIGENCE: Verbal/Linguistic, Logical/Mathematical, and Interpersonal

CONTENT/STANDARD FOCUS: Language Arts—Standards 1 and 3 & Social Studies— Global Connections; People, Places, and Environments

PRODUCT/PERFORMANCE/STUDENT OUTCOME: Mini-Research/Writing Tasks

"UNITED NATIONS: THE PEACEKEEPING HEROES" (page 216)

Provide students with reference materials, fact sheets, or websites that relate to the United Nations. Instruct students to select one activity from each level of Bloom's Taxonomy to complete. If time permits, provide opportunity for students to share their findings and information within a total class setting.

SEARCHING FOR SOLUTIONS TO WORLD PROBLEMS

PURPOSE: To describe a personal crusade that a student would like to undertake if given the time and the resources

TARGETED INTELLIGENCE: Intrapersonal and Visual/Spatial

CONTENT/STANDARD FOCUS: Language Arts—Standards 5, 7, 8 and 11 & Social Studies— Global Connections

PRODUCT/PERFORMANCE/STUDENT OUTCOME: Graphic Organizer

"SEARCHING FOR SOLUTIONS TO WORLD PROBLEMS" (page 217)

Review methods and sources for conducting research on issues and interests of students, including use of print and non-print sources as well as electronic sources. Next, instruct students to select one of the ten different world issues to research on the student activity sheet, and suggest they record their findings on the Problem-Solution Box Graphic Organizer according to directions given.

LEARNING FROM HEROES IN THE WORLD OF MUSIC AND ART

PURPOSE: To explore and interpret the unique minds of artists and musicians through quotations

TARGETED INTELLIGENCE: Verbal/Linguistic, Visual/Spatial, and Musical/Rhythmic

CONTENT/STANDARD FOCUS: Music and Art & Language Arts—Standards 6 and 11 & Social Studies—Culture

PRODUCT/PERFORMANCE/STUDENT OUTCOME: Interpretations of Quotations

"LEARNING FROM HEROES IN THE WORLD OF MUSIC AND ART" (page 218)
Review the definition and types of figurative language (similes, metaphors, and personification) with students, and relate them to the quotations found on the student activity sheet. Instruct students to interpret each of the quotations as they understand them by writing a brief description of what appears to be in the mind of each author.

AMERICAN WOMEN WHO BECAME HEROES UNDER DURESS

PURPOSE: To learn about special American women who became heroes because they championed a strong cause in which they believed

TARGETED INTELLIGENCE: Verbal/Linguistic and Intrapersonal

CONTENT/STANDARD FOCUS: Social Studies—Individual Development and Identity; Civic Ideals and Practices

PRODUCT/PERFORMANCE/STUDENT OUTCOME: Set of Mini-Tasks

"AMERICAN WOMEN WHO BECAME HEROES UNDER DURESS" (page 219)
Ask students to identify a female hero that they admire in their world today. Encourage students to discuss and defend their modern day choices. Next, review the tasks on the student activity page and instruct students to complete one or more of the tasks according to directions given.

HEROES OF SCIENCE AND TECHNOLOGY

PURPOSE: To assume the role of a technology or science genius from history as he/she is being recognized for a major contribution to the world

TARGETED INTELLIGENCE: Verbal/Linguistic and Logical/Mathematical

CONTENT/STANDARD FOCUS: Social Studies—Science, Technology, and Society & Science—Science and Technology

PRODUCT/PERFORMANCE/STUDENT OUTCOME: Diary Entry

"HEROES OF SCIENCE AND TECHNOLOGY" (page 220)

Review the heroes of science and technology listed on the student activity sheet. Ask students to assume the identity of one of these individuals and compose an original diary entry writing about the personal thoughts of the hero as he or she is being recognized for their genius and contribution to the world.

MEET SOME EXTRAORDINARY AFRICAN-AMERICAN HEROES

PURPOSE: To develop a respect for some extraordinary African-American heroes of yesterday

TARGETED INTELLIGENCE: Logical/Mathematical, Visual/Spatial, and Interpersonal

CONTENT/STANDARD FOCUS: Social Studies—People, Places, and Environment and Sciences, Technology, and Society

PRODUCT/PERFORMANCE/STUDENT OUTCOME: Puzzle

"MEET SOME EXTRAORDINARY AFRICAN-AMERICAN HEROES" (page 221)

Guide students through the accomplishments of the African-American heroes outlined on the student activity sheet. Review the directions for creating word finder, crossword, or logic puzzles and ask them to construct an original puzzle of their own.

©2004 Incentive Publications, Inc.
Nashville, TN

TIMELINES HELP US UNDERSTAND EXPLORERS AS HEROES

PURPOSE: To construct a timeline that represents the discoveries of ten important explorers from around the world

TARGETED INTELLIGENCE: Logical/Mathematical, Visual/Spatial, and Bodily/Kinesthetic

CONTENT/STANDARD FOCUS: Social Studies—People, Places, and Environments; Global Connections & Mathematics— Mathematics as Communication

PRODUCT/PERFORMANCE/STUDENT OUTCOME: Timeline

"TIMELINES HELP US UNDERSTAND EXPLORERS AS HEROES" (page 222)

Provide students with a supply of magic markers and sturdy paper such as: drawing paper, card stock, oak tag, or poster board. Ask students to construct a composite timeline of the explorers' accomplishments as listed on the student activity page. Remind students to include not only the names, dates, and descriptions of the explorers as given, but also to create an original symbol, sketch, or drawing for each explorer that tells something about what they saw or did at the time of their heroic adventure.

CHAMPIONS OF THE ENVIRONMENT

PURPOSE: To identify professional groups of heroes/heroines and the courageous acts associated with their work roles

TARGETED INTELLIGENCE: Interpersonal and Naturalistic

CONTENT/STANDARD FOCUS: Science—Science in Personal and Social Perspectives

PRODUCT/PERFORMANCE/STUDENT/OUTCOME: Small Group Discussion

"CHAMPIONS OF THE ENVIRONMENT" (page 223)

Introduce the concept of guarding our natural resources and protecting our delicate environment by focusing on the workers hired and trained to perform a wide range of dangerous and important jobs related to this topic. Divide the students into small cooperative learning groups, and have each group discuss the clusters of careers on the student activity sheet, making certain to write down the various skills and tasks required of each of these courageous acts.

ATHLETES: HEROES IN THE SPORTS WORLD

PURPOSE: To examine the world of sports and athletes who are heroes

TARGETED INTELLIGENCE: Bodily/Kinesthetic and Intrapersonal

CONTENT/STANDARD FOCUS: Social Studies—Individual Development and Identity

PRODUCT/PERFORMANCE/STUDENT OUTCOME: Set of "This Is How I Feel . ." Statements

"ATHLETES: HEROES IN THE SPORTS WORLD" (page 224)

Lead a discussion about the world of sports in our global society, including the most popular sports today, the most recognized athletes, the high salaries of superstars, and the privileges that go with being a sports celebrity. Then, ask students to complete the student activity sheet according to directions given. Provide class time to discuss both student athlete preferences and the controversial issues often associated with celebrity athletes.

TELL ABOUT A TIME WHEN YOU FELT LIKE A HERO

PURPOSE: To recall special circumstances or situations when students performed a heroic or courageous deed

TARGETED INTELLIGENCE: Verbal/Linguistic and Intrapersonal

CONTENT/STANDARD FOCUS: Language Arts—Standards 4, 5, and 11

PRODUCT/PERFORMANCE/STUDENT OUTCOME: Personal Anecdotes

"TELL ABOUT A TIME WHEN YOU FELT LIKE A HERO" (page 225)

Take a few minutes to review with the students the list of twenty different springboards listed on the student activity sheet. Present the idea that many of us do small but important heroic deeds on a day-to-day basis. Then, instruct students to select one or more of the anecdote starter statements to complete according to directions given.

LITERARY HEROES AND HEROINES

PURPOSE: To identify literary heroes and heroines from a student's point of view.

TARGETED INTELLIGENCE: Verbal/Linguistic and Intrapersonal

CONTENT/STANDARD FOCUS: Language Arts—Standards 2 and 11

PRODUCT/PERFORMANCE/STUDENT OUTCOME: List of Literary Heroes and Heroines

"LITERARY HEROES AND HEROINES" (page 226)

Spend a few minutes talking with students about the books they have read throughout their schooling process, beginning with the primary grades, and continuing through their current grade level. Discuss the role of the protagonist and antagonist in each of these stories as heroes and as non-heroes. Then, instruct the students to work individually or with a partner to write down ten of their favorite books from elementary grades to the present and describe the heroes/heroines of each one, as well as their courageous deeds.

SALUTE TO A PERSONAL HERO

PURPOSE: To identify and describe an everyday hero or heroine in a student's life

TARGETED INTELLIGENCE: Logical/Mathematical and Visual/Spatial

CONTENT/STANDARD FOCUS: Language Arts—Standards 5 and 11

PRODUCT/PERFORMANCE/STUDENT OUTCOME: Graphic Organizer

"SALUTE TO A PERSONAL HERO" (page 227)

Describe an adult hero that you had during your growing up years. Discuss his/her role as a mentor, coach, friend, pastor, health care worker, babysitter, etc. Next, introduce the "Person Pyramid" graphic organizer and ask students to complete it, using an adult hero from their own lives.

WHO ARE THE HEROES IN YOUR FAMILY?

PURPOSE: To recognize special heroes that exist within one's own family circle

TARGETED INTELLIGENCE: Intrapersonal

CONTENT/STANDARD FOCUS: Social Studies—Individual Development and Identity; People, Places, and Institutions; Culture

PRODUCT/PERFORMANCE/STUDENT OUTCOME: Set of Mini-Tasks

"WHO ARE THE HEROES IN YOUR FAMILY?" (page 228)

Share with students a "personal hero" in your family. Ask them to reflect upon the members of their immediate family as well as their relatives from previous generations—grandparents, great-grandparents, aunts, uncles, cousins, etc. Next, instruct students to complete one of the family-oriented activities for each level of Bloom's Taxonomy on the student activity page, according to the directions given.

FAMOUS LINES FROM FAMOUS PRESIDENTS

PURPOSE: To analyze the famous quotations of some former presidents.

TARGETED INTELLIGENCE: Verbal/Linguistic

CONTENT/STANDARD FOCUS: Language Arts—Standard 11 & Social Studies—Power, Authority and Governance

PRODUCT/PERFORMANCE/STUDENT OUTCOME: Agree/Disagree Statements

"FAMOUS LINES FROM FAMOUS PRESIDENTS" (page 229)

Lead a group discussion focusing on the role and importance of the president of the United States and the influence of their actions and words on future generations of Americans. Then, ask students to read through the three well-known quotations on the student page and write a brief paragraph reflecting their interpretation of the statement as it applies to people of their age today.

©2004 Incentive Publications, Inc.
Nashville, TN

RATING YOURSELF AS A POTENTIAL LEADER OR HERO

PURPOSE: To assess one's leadership qualities and potential as a hero in some leadership role

TARGETED INTELLIGENCE: Intrapersonal and Interpersonal

CONTENT/STANDARD FOCUS: Social Studies—Individual Development and Identity

PRODUCT/PERFORMANCE/STUDENT OUTCOME: Rating Scales

"RATING YOURSELF AS A POTENTIAL LEADER OR HERO" (page 230)

Brainstorm the desired qualities and character traits of a leader and a hero. How are they alike and how are they different? Then, instruct students to complete the hero/leadership rating scales outlined on the student activity sheet according to directions given. Encourage students to share their results with one another.

YOU MADE THE HEADLINES!

PURPOSE: To design a mock newspaper story and picture about oneself as a hero

TARGETED INTELLIGENCE: Verbal/Linguistic and Visual/Spatial

CONTENT/STANDARD FOCUS: Language Arts—Standards 5 and 12

PRODUCT/PERFORMANCE STUDENT OUTCOME: Un-Coloring Book Page

"YOU MADE THE HEADLINES!" (page 231)

Lead a group discussion focusing on the concept and qualifications of a hero or heroine as defined by the exploration of heroes and heroines in past sessions. Discuss individual interpretations of these qualifications and personal beliefs related to courage and commitment. Introduce the concept of an "un-coloring book page" as a page that contains a set of simple directions with a large space for the student to draw or color in a graphic responding to that set of directions. Then, have students draw and color in their own reactions as directed on the student activity sheet.

THEME: HEROES AND HEROINES   VALUE: COURAGE

A HERO IS MORE THAN A SUB SANDWICH !

Directions: In your own words, define the concept of "hero" and "heroine." Then, look these terms up in the dictionary and write down their multiple definitions. Finally, try to think of a set of character traits that you commonly associate with a hero and record your top ten ideas on the lines below. Compare your list with that of a friend, and work together to agree on both the top ten traits of a hero and on someone living today who has most of those traits.

MY DEFINITION OF HERO AND HEROINE:

_____

_____

DICTIONARY DEFINITION OF HERO AND HEROINE:

_____

_____

OUR TOP TEN LIST OF TRAITS FOR A HERO OR HEROINE:

1. _____

2. _____

3. _____

4 _____

5. _____

6. _____

7. _____

8. _____

9. _____

10. _____

PERSON CHOSEN AS OUR PRESENT DAY HERO: _____

BECAUSE: _____

_____

Name: _____

WHO IS YOUR HERO?

Directions: Decide on your hero (past or present) in each of the categories listed below, and give reasons for each selection.

POLITICS: My hero in politics is _____ because

_____

_____

SPORTS: My hero in sports is _____ because

_____

_____

MILITARY: My military hero is _____ because

_____

_____

FILM: My hero in film is _____ because

_____

_____

ACADEMIC: My hero in science or math is _____ because

_____

_____

AUTHOR/POET: My hero as a poet or author is _____ because

_____

_____

ARTIST: My hero as an artist is _____ because

_____

_____

ENTERTAINMENT: My hero as an entertainer is _____because

_____

_____

MUSICIAN: My hero as a musician is _____ because

_____

_____

Name: _____

©2004 Incentive Publications, Inc.
Nashville, TN

Advisory Plus!

REFLECTIONS ON WHAT MAKES A HERO

Directions: The word "hero" means different things to different people, and not all heroes are people with the best credentials, the most money, or the greatest number of awards. To test this theory, write the names of as many people described below as you can.

1. Name one of the wealthiest people in the world. _____

2. Name a recent Academy Award winner for best actress or actor. _____

3. Name a recent inductee to the baseball Hall of Fame. _____

4. Name a recent gold record recording star. _____

5. Name a recent Wimbledon tennis winner. _____

6. Name a well-known military leader living today. _____

How did you do? Now try to name a person who, in your opinion, fits each description below. Which is easier, and why?

1. Name a teacher who has greatly influenced your success as a student. _____

2. Name a friend who has helped you get through a difficult time. _____

3. Name an adult who has served as a mentor to you. _____

4. Name a person who has taught you something important outside of school. _____

5. Name a person with whom you enjoy spending time. _____.

6. Name a person who makes you feel good about yourself. _____

7. Name a person who is a good role model for you. _____

Name: _____

HEROES WHO REFUSED TO GIVE UP

Directions: How many times have you heard the expression: "If you don't succeed at first, then try, try again." While this is an old cliché, it certainly seems to be as meaningful today as ever. Lives of great people seem to bear out the belief that persistence appears to be the first requisite for living the heroic life. The examples below are stories about famous people who refused to take "rejection" seriously and, because of their persistence, came out ahead of others in their field. Work by yourself first to read through each anecdote, jotting down your personal reactions to each one. Then, work with a partner to share and discuss your individual responses.

1. Madeleine L'Engle's book, *A Wrinkle in Time*, was rejected by every major publisher before it was finally accepted by Farrar, Strauss, and Giroux publishing house. Today it has been back to print over 40 times and won the Newbery Medal for children's literature.

   YOUR REACTION:

   _____

2. Abraham Lincoln lost twenty-three elections during his lifetime, but he won three, including the presidential election.

   YOUR REACTION:

   _____

3. Walt Disney, who once worked as a reporter on a newspaper, was fired from his job by a senior editor because he was "uncreative" and "spent too much of his time doodling the day away."

   YOUR REACTION:

   _____

4. Dr. Robert Jarvik, the famous heart surgeon, was rejected by fifteen American medical schools before he was accepted at New York University, which ultimately led to his invention of the world's most successful artificial heart.

   YOUR REACTION:

   _____

5. Babe Ruth struck out 1,330 times before he began his trek to hitting an amazing 714 home runs.

   YOUR REACTION:

   _____

Name: _____

UNITED NATIONS: THE PEACEKEEPING HEROES

Directions: Complete one of these activities for each level of Bloom's Taxonomy to learn more about the basic principles, purposes, and projects of the United Nations and its role as a peacekeeper in the world today. You may use the Internet or print reference materials to help you with your work.

KNOWLEDGE LEVEL TASKS:

1. Identify the main goal or purpose established for the United Nations in its Charter.
2. Name at least three different agencies created by the United Nations to promote social progress.

COMPREHENSION LEVEL TASKS:

1. Group ten countries that are members of the United Nations by the continent on which they are located.
2. Infer the reasons that the United Nations has offices all over the world and six official languages.

APPLICATION LEVEL TASKS:

1. Examine the role of the United Nations in making the world a better place for children. Plan how you would utilize United Nations Children's Fund money to solve a particular problem facing the world's children.
2. Construct a simple timeline showing the development of the United Nations from the League of Nations to the present day.

ANALYSIS LEVEL TASKS:

1. Find a representation of the United Nations logo. Deduce the reasons that the logo designer had for including the picture of the world surrounded by olive branches.
2. You have just been selected to be a candidate for the position of United States representative to the United Nations. Develop a resume identifying why you are the best candidate for the job. Identify the qualities and characteristics that you will need to be a good ambassador.

SYNTHESIS LEVEL TASKS:

1. UNICEF, an agency created by the United Nations, helps kids around the world. Plan a UNICEF Halloween fundraiser.
2. Modify the symbol of the United Nations to include your ideas about the role of the organization. Invent a slogan for the United Nations that captures the spirit of its work.

EVALUATION LEVEL TASKS:

1. State what you think is the greatest strength of the United Nations. Defend your opinion.
2. Judge the effectiveness of the United Nations in helping to maintain peacefulness throughout the world.

Name:

SEARCHING FOR SOLUTIONS TO WORLD PROBLEMS

Directions: Choose any four of these world issues that you would want to address if given the time and resources to do so. Then, complete the Problem-Solution Box Graphic Organizer, stating the problems you have selected, and how you would go about addressing them. Problems to consider are: (1) Helping the homeless in your community; (2) Helping people with AIDS or other infectious diseases; (3) Helping the starving children and adults in countries other than your own; (4) Helping people endangered and suffering in war-torn countries find new homes in other countries; (5) Helping abused women and children in shelters; (6) Saving endangered species; (7) Treatment of inmates in prisons and penitentiaries; (8) Helping orphans in orphanages around the world; (9) Teaching literacy to those who cannot read or write.

Problem-Solution Boxes

PROBLEM	HOW SOLVED

Name:

LEARNING FROM HEROES IN THE WORLD OF MUSIC AND ART

Directions: Read each of these quotations by famous artists and musicians, heroes to many art and music lovers, who are trying to express the passion they feel for their work. In your own words, interpret what you think they mean.

QUOTATION 1:

"I dream my painting, and then I paint my dream."

—Vincent van Gogh

_____

_____

_____

QUOTATION 2:

"Music is the shorthand of emotion."

—Leo Tolstoy

_____

_____

_____

QUOTATION 3:

"Painting is just another way of keeping a diary."

—Pablo Picasso

_____

_____

_____

QUOTATION 4:

"The truest expression of a people is in its dances."

—Agnes De Mille

_____

_____

_____

QUOTATION 5:

"All the sounds of the earth are like music."

— Oscar Hammerstein, II

_____

_____

_____

QUOTATION 6:

"A great artist can paint a great picture on a small canvas."

—Charles Dudley Warner

_____

_____

_____

QUOTATION 7:

"Drawing is speaking to the eye; talking is painting to the ear."

—Joseph Joubert

_____

_____

_____

Name: _____

©2004 Incentive Publications, Inc.
Nashville, TN

AMERICAN WOMEN WHO BECAME HEROES UNDER DURESS

Directions: Use this list of American women and their accomplishments as the basis for completing one or more of the tasks outlined below.

1. Harriet Beecher Stowe writes the famous book, *Uncle Tom's Cabin,* in 1852.

2. Lucy Stone, Susan Anthony, and Elizabeth Cady Stanton found national associations for women's suffrage in 1869.

3. Clara Barton founds the American Red Cross in 1881.

4. Annie Oakley shocks the world with her shooting skills in Buffalo Bill's Wild West Show in 1885.

5. Helen Keller, blind and deaf, graduates from college and begins her career in 1904.

6. Dolores Huerta plays a key labor role in founding the United Farm Workers in 1962.

7. Sandra Day O'Connor becomes the first woman justice on the Supreme Court in 1981.

8. Sally Ride is America's first woman astronaut in 1983.

9. Geraldine Ferraro is the first woman to run for vice president on a major party ticket in 1984.

TASK ONE: Name another female hero, not on this list, that you would add to it. Give reasons for your choice.

TASK TWO: Give an example of two different character or personality traits that each of these women would most likely have had in order to accomplish what they did.

TASK THREE: If you were going to interview each of these women, what is one special question you would like to ask them?

TASK FOUR: Imagine yourself as one of these female heroes. Which one would you choose to be, and why?

TASK FIVE: Design a creative award, trophy, or monument for one of these women.

TASK SIX: Rank the accomplishments of each of these American heroes from the most important to the least important. Defend your first and last choices.

TASK SEVEN: Create a one-day diary entry for one of these women that could have been written at the height of their achievement.

Name:

HEROES OF SCIENCE AND TECHNOLOGY

Directions: Assume the role of a famous technology or science genius, and write non-stop for five minutes in your diary about your personal thoughts and feelings as you are being recognized for your genius and contribution to one of the fields of technology or science outlined below. Try to focus on the particular personal traits and/or values that enabled the person to achieve hero status. Also, consider the value of their accomplishment for society.

1. **1728:** John Bartram creates the first botanical gardens in America. What do they look like and where are they located?

2. **1770:** Benjamin Banneker builds the first wooden pendulum clock, which keeps time for more than 50 years. Who is the first to own one, and how is it used?

3. **1798:** Eli Whitney invents a machine that produces weapons with interchangeable parts, a process that begins mass production and the building of factories around the world. Who makes and buys the weapons, and how are they used?

4. **1830:** Peter Cooper builds the nation's first steam engine, but it loses a race to a horse. How fast does the engine go, where does it go, and how does it lose the race with the horse?

5. **1838:** Samuel Morse introduces the first code for sending telegraph messages. Who sends and receives the first telegram, and what does it say?

6. **1851:** Isaac Singer is the first to patent a successful sewing machine. Who purchases the sewing machine, and what things do they mend and sew with it?

7. **1852:** Elisha Otis brags about his new invention, the passenger elevator. Where do they install the elevator, and what happens when it gets stuck for the first time?

8. **1878:** Thomas Edison invents the first phonograph recording, and the first electric light the following year. How do the electric lights change the way people live today?

9. **1903:** Orville and Wilbur Wright complete the first manned flight. Who flies the plane, where do they go, and what problems do they have?

10. **1962:** John Glenn is the first American to orbit the Earth. How does he feel just before and after takeoff?

Name: _____

MEET SOME EXTRAORDINARY AFRICAN-AMERICAN HEROES

Directions: Read through the names and accomplishments of the extraordinary African-American heroes listed below, and then create a crossword puzzle, word finder puzzle, or logic puzzle using the information given. Be prepared to talk about each of these questions in a group discussion.

1. Which of the individuals did you already know something about?

2. Which hero and his/her accomplishments surprised you the most, and why?

3. Which hero would you like to know more about?

4. Which hero exhibited traits that you would like to have? Why? Give reasons for your answer.

5. What part of the country do most of these heroes come from?

---

1. Benjamin Banneker (1731–1806) was a famous astronomer, mathematician, and surveyor from the state of Maryland.

2. Captain Paul Cuffe (1759–1817) was a merchant, mariner, and ship owner from Cuttyhund Island in Massachusetts.

3. Booker T. Washington (1856–1910) was an educator, and the founder of the Tuskegee Institute. He was born in Hale's Ford, Virginia.

4. Matthew A. Henson (1866–1955) was an explorer and co-discovered the North Pole. He was born in Charles County, Maryland.

5. Marian Anderson (1902–1993) was a famous concert and opera singer born in Philadelphia, Pennsylvania.

6. Joe Louis (1914–1981) was a boxer known as the "Brown Bomber" from Lafayette, Alabama.

7. Bessie Coleman (1892–1926) was a Negro aviatrix (or pilot) born in Atlanta, Texas.

8. Garrett A. Morgan (1875–1963) invented the first traffic signal and the gas mask. He was born in Paris, Kentucky.

9. Granville T. Woods (1856–1910) was considered the "Black Edison" because of his inventions of important electrical items and appliances. He was born in Columbus, Ohio.

10. Harriet Tubman (1820–1913) was a slave born in Dorchester County, Maryland who was active in freeing others through the Underground Railroad.

Name: _____

TIMELINES HELP US UNDERSTAND EXPLORERS AS HEROES

Directions: Review the dates and discoveries of these ten explorers who became heroes after scouting out new territories. Construct a simple timeline on sturdy paper that represents these heroes, dates, and discoveries. For each date, write down the name and discovery of each explorer, and add a simple picture or illustration that depicts what you think they saw or found at the time of their heroic adventures.

1. **1492:** Christopher Columbus sails to the Americas from Spain looking for a trade route to the East.

2. **1497:** Vasco da Gama of Portugal sails for India with four ships and 150 sailors.

3. **1488:** Bartolomeu Dias was the first Portuguese sailor to sail around Africa after reaching the Indian Ocean.

4. **1513:** Juan Ponce de Leon discovers Florida and claims it for his country, Spain.

5. **1521:** Spanish conquistador, Hernan Cortes, conquers the Aztec empire in Mexico.

6. **1533:** Francisco Pizarro captures the Inca empire of Peru.

7. **1596:** Willem Barents led the Dutch explorers in an unsuccessful attempt to find the Northeast Passage from Asia to Europe, but was trapped in Arctic ice.

8. **1608:** Samuel de Champlain founded the first permanent settlement in New France, known as Quebec.

9. **1682:** Sieur de La Salle reached the mouth of the Mississippi from Canada and gave Louisiana its name.

10. **1741:** Russia's Vitus Bering and Aleksandr Chirikov were the first two men to reach Alaska.

Name:

CHAMPIONS OF THE ENVIRONMENT

Directions: Guarding our natural resources and protecting our delicate environment demands considerable time, talent, and resources from those commissioned and trained to do the job. Work with members of your cooperative learning group to discuss and record the various responsibilities associated with each of these career clusters, noting also the acts of courage which are most often associated with these occupation-related tasks.

1. Park rangers _____

    _____

    _____

2. Smoke jumpers and forest fire fighters _____

    _____

    _____

3. Hurricane spotters and trackers _____

    _____

    _____

4. Environmentalists who clean up oil spills _____

    _____

    _____

5. Scientists who protect the rain forests and its wildlife _____

    _____

    _____

6. Animal control workers _____

    _____

    _____

Name: _____

ATHLETES: HEROES IN THE SPORTS WORLD

Directions: Think about the world of sports and the superstar athletes who receive the most attention and the most recognition in their fields. List your favorite athletes, or heroes of the sports world, for each category listed below. Then, share your feelings about each of the sports-related situations described.

1. My favorite sports heroes are:

    In football _____

    In basketball _____

    In baseball _____

    In hockey _____

    In soccer _____

    In tennis _____

    In golf _____

2. What do you think about the issue of eligibility for sports being tied directly to an athlete's grade point average and academic performance in school?

    This is what I think: _____

    _____

    _____

3. What do you think about athletes who take steroids or other performance-enhancing drugs?

    This is what I think: _____

    _____

    _____

4. What do you think about athletes who receive multi-million dollar contracts in advance, before they finish out a season, based on what they are expected to do rather than what they actually are able to do?

    This is what I think: _____

    _____

    _____

5. What do you think about athletes who receive as much money for their endorsement of products as they do from their actual performance in the sport?

    This is what I think: _____

    _____

    _____

Name: _____

TELL ABOUT A TIME WHEN YOU FELT LIKE A HERO

Directions: Good people often perform mini-heroic or mini-courageous actions when challenged to do so, without even realizing the bravery these actions require. Read through the discussion topics listed below and select one or more of the incidents that applies to you. On the back of this sheet, write a good paragraph that describes each of the incidents that made you a "hero" in the eyes of someone else.

1. A time I tried to make someone special and it worked

2. A time I gave someone something money couldn't buy

3. A time I did a favor for someone without them asking

4. Something I got that I had to take a risk for

5. A time I hid my true feelings because it would hurt someone else

6. A time I handled a choice I made that didn't work out as I had hoped it would

7. Something I planned with other people that didn't turn out as expected

8. A time I should have been afraid but wasn't

9. A time I got into trouble, and what I did to get out of trouble

10. A time I stood up for a friend

11. A problem I solved on my own

12. A time my friend took a risk by sticking up for me

13. A time I was honest about something that was hard to admit

Name: _____

LITERARY HEROES AND HEROINES

Directions: On the lines below, make a list of five different books including novels, plays, biographies and autobiographies, stories, songs, or poems that you have read that feature a courageous hero or heroine as the main character. Identify the hero or heroine of each piece of writing. After each title, write a brief statement describing a courageous act that he/she performed, and the character traits or value system exemplified by the act.

1. TITLE: _____

    HERO/HEROINE: _____

    COURAGEOUS DEED: _____

    _____

2. TITLE: _____

    HERO/HEROINE: _____

    COURAGEOUS DEED: _____

    _____

3. TITLE: _____

    HERO/HEROINE: _____

    COURAGEOUS DEED: _____

    _____

4. TITLE: _____

    HERO/HEROINE: _____

    COURAGEOUS DEED: _____

    _____

5. TITLE: _____

    HERO/HEROINE: _____

    COURAGEOUS DEED: _____

    _____

Name: _____

©2004 Incentive Publications, Inc.
Nashville, TN

SALUTE TO A PERSONAL HERO

Directions: Think about the important adults in your life who, over time, have contributed to your growth as an individual. It might be a relative or a neighbor, a doctor or teacher. It might be the parent of a friend, or a mentor, a pastor or a coach, or someone else. Select someone who has, indeed, become a personal hero or heroine to you and complete the Person Pyramid graphic organizer below to describe your hero. Be ready to share your "salute" with others in the class.

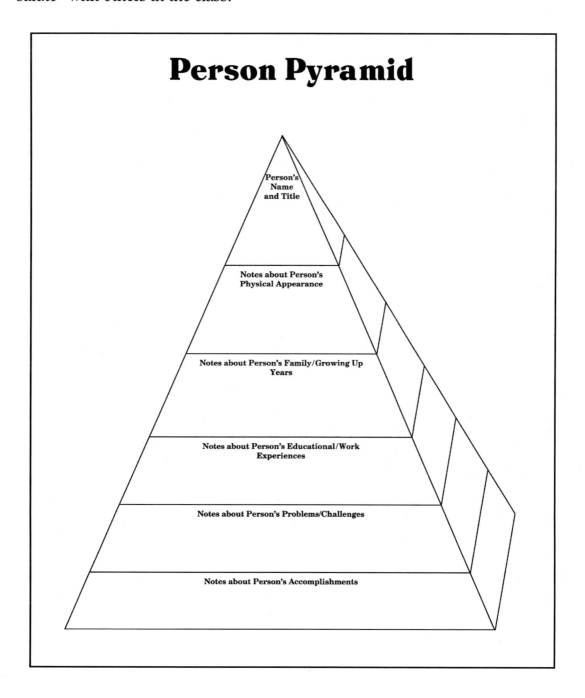

Person Pyramid

Person's Name and Title

Notes about Person's Physical Appearance

Notes about Person's Family/Growing Up Years

Notes about Person's Educational/Work Experiences

Notes about Person's Problems/Challenges

Notes about Person's Accomplishments

Name:

Advisory Plus!

WHO ARE THE HEROES IN YOUR FAMILY?

Directions: Sometimes we can find special heroes among our own immediate family members or distant relatives. Complete one task at each level below, and determine if there is someone in your family who could be considered a hero in his/her own right.

KNOWLEDGE LEVEL TASKS:

1. Identify an important family tradition that you honor each year. Who is responsible for starting or maintaining this tradition?

2. Recall a special event that you have had in your family. Who was involved?

COMPREHENSION LEVEL TASKS:

1. List the members in your immediate family, and describe one special quality about each family member.

2. Describe a favorite relative, and explain why you appreciate this person.

APPLICATION LEVEL TASKS:

1. Construct a timeline of the important events in your life to date. Reflect back upon those events, and determine what individuals made them stand out in your mind.

2. Investigate your surname by questioning family members or using the Internet. What does it mean and what is the country of its origin? Who in the family values this information the most?

ANALYSIS LEVEL TASKS:

1. Select one favorite family member or relative and create a riddle about him/her.

2. If you were in trouble, what family member or relative would you ask to come to your rescue? Why?

SYNTHESIS LEVEL TASKS:

1. Envision a family reunion. Who would you invite and where would you have it? Who could you depend on to help you make the plans?

2. Pretend that you would honor a particular family member or relative at the reunion. Who is it most likely to be? Why would this person be chosen?

EVALUATION LEVEL TASKS:

1. Elaborate on this statement: "Home is where the heart is." What family member or relative makes your home close to your heart?

2. Decide which family member or relative has made the greatest and most positive impact on your life. Give reasons for your answer.

Name:

©2004 Incentive Publications, Inc.
Nashville, TN

FAMOUS LINES FROM FAMOUS PRESIDENTS

Directions: The office of the president of the United States is the nation's highest office. Every four years, voters select the person to fill this position. They examine the candidates' records of past service to the country to find evidence of courage, honesty, integrity, and commitment to the country's best interest. Each holder of this office faces the challenge of leaving a strong legacy behind for future generations to learn from and live up to. Since one of the ways presidents are best remembered is by their words, these words are often quoted for years to come. Read through each quotation below attributed to a former president of the United States, and write a brief paragraph reflecting your interpretation of the statement as it applies to people of your age today.

PRESIDENT: **John F. Kennedy**

QUOTATION:

"Compromise need not mean cowardice."

I AGREE or I DISAGREE (circle one) with this statement because: _____

_____

_____

PRESIDENT: **Harry Truman**

QUOTATION:

"It is amazing what you can get done if you don't care who gets the credit."

I AGREE or I DISAGREE (circle one) with this statement because: _____

_____

_____

PRESIDENT: Ronald Reagan

QUOTATION:

"History teaches that wars begin when governments believe the price of aggression is cheap."

I AGREE or I DISAGREE (circle one) with this statement because: _____

_____

_____

Name: _____

RATING YOURSELF AS A POTENTIAL LEADER OR HERO

Directions: Have you ever thought about your interest in and potential for becoming a leader and/or a hero in some leadership role? Do you think most people seek out these roles because they want to be in control, because they want others to look up to and respect them, or because they want to make a contribution to society in some small way? Test your leadership/hero potential by completing each item on the rating scale below. Think reflectively to select the most appropriate number as it relates to you at this point in life.

1. My courage level: *(10 = I am a risk taker.)*

   1   2   3   4   5   6   7   8   9   10

2. My energy level: *(10 = I am very energetic most of the time.)*

   1   2   3   4   5   6   7   8   9   10

3. My common sense level: *(10 = I can see simple solutions to everyday problems.)*

   1   2   3   4   5   6   7   8   9   10

4. My self-discipline level: *(10 = I am extremely self-disciplined.)*

   1   2   3   4   5   6   7   8   9   10

5. My cool-headedness level: *(10 = I can keep a level head when I need to.)*

   1   2   3   4   5   6   7   8   9   10

6. My loyalty and honesty level: *(10 = I am consistently loyal and honest.)*

   1   2   3   4   5   6   7   8   9   10

7. My creativity level: *(10 = I am a creative thinker and problem solver.)*

   1   2   3   4   5   6   7   8   9   10

8. My communication skill level: *(10 = I am a good speaker and a good listener.)*

   1   2   3   4   5   6   7   8   9   10

Name: _____

YOU MADE THE HEADLINES!

Directions: Pretend you have just performed a heroic deed worthy of being published in your local newspaper. This is the story and the picture recounting the heroic deed you would like to be remembered for. Think about your talents and abilities and opportunities to demonstrate courage and bravery on behalf of another.

Name:

THEME: HEROES AND HEROINES   VALUE: COURAGE

FEBRUARY

RATING SCALE: **1** – I think so   **2** – I hope so   **3** – I don't know for sure!

1. _____ I learned something about what makes a hero/heroine and the character traits most commonly associated with these special people.

2. _____ I learned how to identify some personal heroes of my own.

3. _____ I learned that heroes are different things to different people.

4. _____ I learned how many heroes had to overcome defeat or rejection before they finally met with success.

5. _____ I learned much about the United Nations and its many roles as a peacekeeping hero in today's world.

6. _____ I learned how important it is for individuals to be courageous and persistent when searching for solutions to world problems.

7. _____ I learned more about heroes in the world of music and art.

8. _____ I learned how women have become heroes by championing causes that were important to them.

9. _____ I learned more about heroes in the world of science and technology.

10. _____ I learned more about the extraordinary accomplishments of African-American heroes.

11. _____ I learned how timelines can help us organize historical information about explorers.

12. _____ I learned much about the risks that are taken by those whose job it is to protect our environment.

13. _____ I learned how athletes are considered to be heroes in the sports world.

14. _____ I learned more about myself and how mini-heroic or mini-courageous actions can make me a hero in the eyes of someone else.

15. _____ I learned ways that literary characters can be perceived as heroes and heroines.

16. _____ I learned that I, too, have everyday heroes who have contributed to my growth as a person.

17. _____ I learned that there can be heroes within my own circle of family or friends.

18. _____ I learned how American presidents can be viewed as heroes through their courageous words and deeds.

19. _____ I learned how to use a self-inventory as a tool for helping me to understand my own potential as a hero or leader.

20. _____ I learned how interesting it is to promote oneself as a hypothetical hero through a mock newspaper article.

Name: _____

MODULE SEVEN
MARCH
✳

THEME: ENVIRONMENT   VALUE: STEWARDSHIP

"On Spaceship Earth there are no passengers; everybody is a member of the crew.
We have moved into an age in which everybody's activities affect everybody else."

Marshall McLuhan, Understanding Media, 1964

What responsibilities do you as a crew member on "Spaceship Earth" have to conserve and protect the natural resources of our planet for generations to come? How effectively are you carrying out these responsibilities? Do you think that people of your generation are more or less aware of and committed to being good caretakers of the environment than people of your parents' generation? Summarize your thoughts by developing a checklist of activities related to stewardship of our earth's treasures. Use the checklist to assess your own personal commitment to responsible behavior in regard to reducing, reusing, and recycling natural resources.

- **STEWARDSHIP: WHAT DOES IT MEAN?—PURPOSE:** To examine the multiple definitions of the concepts "steward" and "stewardship"

- **THE INTERCONNECTEDNESS OF MAN AND BEAST—PURPOSE:** To illustrate the relationship and interconnectedness of man and beast

- **TYPES OF ENVIRONMENTAL POLLUTION— PURPOSE:** To discover the multiple causes and effects of air, water, and sound pollution

- **CONSERVATION AND RECYCLING—PURPOSE:** To determine the driving and opposing forces that are related to conservation and recycling efforts

- **TECHNOLOGICAL ADVANCES HINDER STEWARDSHIP EFFORTS— PURPOSE:** To analyze the content of a famous quotation about our lack of stewardship when it comes to protection of the environment

- **CREATING "I URGE YOU" TELEGRAMS—PURPOSE:** To create a series of telegrams that express concerns students have about the environment

- **AMERICA THE BEAUTIFUL—PURPOSE:** To identify the land forms and special places within the environment that are named in the famous and patriotic composition, "America the Beautiful"

- **THE SOLID WASTE DILEMMA—PURPOSE:** To create an original sculpture made out of solid waste products

- **BEAUTY IS ABOVE AND BELOW ME—PURPOSE:** To construct a collage, montage, or poster of beauty that reflects various forms of nature and the environment

- **PARTICIPATING IN AN ENVIRONMENTAL STEWARDSHIP CAMPAIGN— PURPOSE:** To simulate a mock stewardship campaign created to improve sites of the local environment

- **STAMP OUT POLLUTED THINKING—PURPOSE:** To rank those things/activities that can pollute a student's thinking or negatively affect his/her relationship with others

- **A DIFFERENT KIND OF POLLUTION: IS HAIKU WHAT IT USED TO BE?— PURPOSE:** To review the traditional Japanese haiku pattern and its humorous or "tongue in cheek" application to the world of technology

- **WAYS THAT THE WEB CAN POLLUTE STUDENT LEARNING—PURPOSE:** To explore ways that the Web and the Internet have contributed to the problem of cheating in the schools

- **A WORD ABOUT BODY POLLUTANTS—PURPOSE:** To discuss the special medical problems faced by many adolescents today, especially those that involve polluting the body with undesirable substances

- **CAN BOOKS REALLY UPSET THE ECOLOGY OF THE MIND?—PURPOSE:** To study the issues of banning books from the library because they "endanger, pollute, or upset" the ecology of the minds of children and young adults

- **SEEKING THE IDEAL ENVIRONMENT—PURPOSE:** To invent an ideal environmental area of the future

- **ARBOR DAY ANY DAY—PURPOSE:** To plan an Arbor Day celebration for the class or school that could be held on any day of the year

- **ENERGY CONSERVATION BRINGS CHAOS!— PURPOSE:** To create an original comic strip depicting one humorous solution to the energy crisis that threatens many modern societies

- **ROLE-PLAYING AN ECOLOGY COUNCIL FOR YOUR CLASS—PURPOSE:** To role-play the creation and operation of an environmental council for the classroom

- **CHOOSE A CONSERVATION MINI-ACTIVITY TO DO—PURPOSE:** To select and complete a conservation-related mini activity

©2004 Incentive Publications, Inc.
Nashville, TN

WRITING PROMPTS/DISCUSSION STARTERS

✳

Read and react to the statement below by agreeing or disagreeing with its application to life in your community today. Write a brief paragraph telling why you feel that people of your acquaintance respect and protect the natural environment or take for granted and waste the earth's natural resources.

"We have forgotten how to be good guests,
how to walk lightly on the Earth as its other creatures do."

(*Only One Earth*, The United Nations Conference on the
Human Environment in Stockholm, Sweden, 1972)

_____

_____

_____

_____

_____

In a speech delivered at the state fairgrounds in Richmond, Virginia in 1989, George Bush, the 41st president of the United States said,

"The natural beauty that you and I enjoy today is a sacred trust.
So, we must do more than simply limit the damage we've already done.
We must work to preserve and restore the integrity and richness
of this continent's natural splendor."

Compose a brief paragraph for your school newspaper urging students of your school to read and heed these words.

_____

_____

_____

_____

_____

MARCH CALENDAR

✳

WEEK ONE

DAY ONE	**"Stewardship: What Does it Mean?"** Examining the multiple definitions of the concepts "steward" and "stewardship"
DAY TWO	**"America the Beautiful"** Identifying the land forms and special places within the environment that are named in the famous and patriotic composition, "America the Beautiful"
DAY THREE	**"Ways that the Web can Pollute Student Learning"** Exploring in a class discussion ways that the Web and the Internet have contributed to the problem of cheating in the schools
DAY FOUR	**"Beauty Is Above Me and Below Me"** Constructing a collage, montage, or poster of beauty that reflects various forms of nature and the environment
DAY FIVE	**"Can Books Really Upset the Ecology of the Mind?"** Studying the issues of banning books from the library because they "endanger, pollute, or upset" the ecology of the minds of children and young adults

WEEK TWO

DAY ONE	**"Creating 'I Urge You' Telegrams"** Creating a series of telegrams that express concerns students have about the environment
DAY TWO	**"The Interconnectedness of Man and Beast"** Illustrating the relationship and interconnectedness of man and beast
DAY THREE	**"The Solid Waste Dilemma"** Creating an original sculpture made out of solid waste products
DAY FOUR	**"Conservation and Recycling"** Determining in a class discussion the driving and opposing forces that are related to conservation and recycling efforts
DAY FIVE	**"Technological Advances Hinder Stewardship Efforts"** Analyzing the content of a famous quotation about our lack of stewardship when it comes to protection of the environment

MARCH CALENDAR
✳

WEEK THREE

DAY ONE	**"Stamp Out Polluted Thinking"** Ranking those things/activities that can pollute a student's thinking or negatively affect his/her relationship with others
DAY TWO	**"A Different Kind of Pollution: Is Haiku What it Used to Be?"** Reviewing the traditional Japanese haiku pattern and its humorous or "tongue in cheek" application to the world of technology
DAY THREE	**"Types of Environmental Pollution"** Discovering the multiple causes and effects of air, water, and sound pollution
DAY FOUR	**"A Word About Body Pollutants"** Discussing the special medical problems faced by many adolescents today, especially those that involve polluting the body with undesirable substances
DAY FIVE	**"Participating in an Environmental Stewardship Campaign"** Simulating a mock stewardship campaign created to improve the local environment

WEEK FOUR

DAY ONE	**"Seeking the Ideal Environment"** Inventing an ideal environmental area of the future
DAY TWO	**"Arbor Day Any Day"** Planning an Arbor Day celebration for the class or school that could be held on any day of the year
DAY THREE	**"Energy Conservation Brings Chaos"** Creating an original comic strip depicting one humorous solution to the energy crisis that threatens many modern societies
DAY FOUR	**"Role-Playing an Ecology Council for Your Class"** Role-playing the creation and operation of an environmental council for the classroom
DAY FIVE	**"Choose a Conservation Mini-Activity to Do"** Selecting and completing a conservation-related mini-activity

THEME: ENVIRONMENT   VALUE: STEWARDSHIP

STEWARDSHIP: WHAT DOES IT MEAN?

PURPOSE: To examine the multiple definitions of the concepts "steward" and "stewardship"

TARGETED INTELLIGENCE: Verbal/Linguistic

CONTENT/STANDARD FOCUS: Language Arts—Standards 3 and 5

PRODUCT/PERFORMANCE/STUDENT OUTCOME: Short Paragraph

"STEWARDSHIP: WHAT DOES IT MEAN?" (page 248)
Provide dictionaries for students to use in locating definitions for the concepts of "steward" and "stewardship." Encourage students to discuss their multiple uses and/or applications to a variety of careers and/or professions. Ask students to write a comprehensive paragraph on both of these terms as related to the environment. Finally, encourage students to design an original symbol to represent the idea of "environmental stewardship."

THE INTERCONNECTEDNESS OF MAN AND BEAST

PURPOSE: To illustrate the relationship and interconnectedness of man and beast

TARGETED INTELLIGENCE: Visual/Spatial, Bodily/Kinesthetic and Naturalistic

CONTENT/STANDARD FOCUS: Social Studies—People, Places and Environment & Science— Life Science

PRODUCT/PERFORMANCE/STUDENT OUTCOME: Personal Drawings

"THE INTERCONNECTEDNESS OF MAN AND BEAST" (page 249)
Discuss how Native Americans and other peoples of the past had such great respect for the environment in which they lived because of their dependency on natural resources and wildlife for their very survival on a day-to-day basis. Contrast this attitude towards nature with that of many people in the world today who hunt animals as much for sport, entertainment, luxury items, and unnecessary economic rewards as they do for food, clothing, and shelter. Then, instruct students to create personal drawings or other creative expressions to interpret the words of Chief Seattle of the Duwamish tribe. If possible, provide time for sharing and discussion of projects.

TYPES OF ENVIRONMENTAL POLLUTION

PURPOSE: To discover the multiple causes of air, water, and sound pollution

TARGETED INTELLIGENCE: Logical/Mathematical, Visual/Spatial, and Naturalistic

CONTENT/STANDARD FOCUS: Science—Science as Inquiry; Life Science; Earth and Space Science; Science in Personal and Social Perspectives

PRODUCT/PERFORMANCE/STUDENT OUTCOME: Chart and Graphic Organizer

"TYPES OF ENVIRONMENTAL POLLUTION" (page 250)

Review the definition and types of pollution with students. Assign students to work in pairs to complete the chart on air, water, and sound pollution drawing upon their own ideas, opinions, and knowledge base of the topics. Finally, instruct students to construct a Venn Diagram showing the overlaps in causes and effects of the three types of pollution.

CONSERVATION AND RECYCLING

PURPOSE: To determine the driving and opposing forces that are related to conservation and recycling efforts

TARGETED INTELLIGENCE: Logical/Mathematical, Visual/Spatial, Intrapersonal, and Naturalistic

CONTENT/STANDARD FOCUS: Social Studies—Individual Development and Identity; Science, Technology, and Society & Science—Life Science; Earth and Space Science; Science in Personal and Social Perspectives

PRODUCT/PERFORMANCE/STUDENT OUTCOME: Graphic Organizer

"CONSERVATION AND RECYCLING" (page 251)

Introduce the topic of conservation and recycling by asking students to comment on what they do at home and for their community when it comes to conservation and recycling efforts. Next, assign students to complete the Opposing Forces Chart on the student activity sheet that asks them to think about both the driving and opposing forces that impact their recycling and conservation habits.

TECHNOLOGICAL ADVANCES HINDER STEWARDSHIP EFFORTS

PURPOSE: To analyze the content of a famous quotation about our lack of stewardship when it comes to protection of the environment

TARGETED INTELLIGENCE: Verbal/Linguistic, Visual/Spatial, Bodily/Kinesthetic, Naturalistic, and Interpersonal

CONTENT/STANDARD FOCUS: Language Arts—Standard 7 and 8, Social Studies— Individuals, Groups, and Institutions; Science, Technology, and Society & Science—Science and Technology; Science in Personal and Social Perspectives; Global Connections

PRODUCT/PERFORMANCE/STUDENT OUTCOME: Group Mural

"TECHNOLOGICAL ADVANCES HINDER STEWARDSHIP EFFORTS" (page 252)

Introduce this activity by posing the question to students: "How has technology advanced our society and global community, and how has technology hindered our stewardship efforts in protecting the environment of our society and global community?" Guide students through completion of the activities on the student activity sheet. Finally, assign students to cooperative learning groups, and ask each group to illustrate one of the images presented in the Toffler passage using large drawing paper and magic markers.

CREATING "I URGE YOU" TELEGRAMS

PURPOSE: To create a series of telegrams that express concerns students have about the environment

TARGETED INTELLIGENCE: Bodily/Kinesthetic, Visual/Spatial, and Interpersonal

CONTENT/STANDARD FOCUS: Language Arts—Standards 4 and 11, Social Studies—Science, Technology, and Society; Global Connections & Science—Science in Personal and Social Perspectives

PRODUCT/PERFORMANCE/STUDENT/OUTCOME: Set of Telegrams

"CREATING 'I URGE YOU' TELEGRAMS" (page 253)

Review the concept of the "telegram" as it has been used over time and explain how telegrams have, for the most part, been replaced by emails as a major form of communication. Place students in small cooperative learning groups and have each group create and categorize their "I URGE YOU" telegrams according to directions specified on the student activity sheet. Encourage groups to draw conclusions as to those environmental issues that are of most concern to students.

AMERICA THE BEAUTIFUL

PURPOSE: To identify the land forms and special places within the environment that are named in the famous and patriotic composition, "America the Beautiful"

TARGETED INTELLIGENCE: Visual/Spatial, Musical/Rhythmic, and Naturalistic

CONTENT/STANDARD FOCUS: Music & Social Studies—People, Places, and Environments; Civic Ideals and Practices

PRODUCT/PERFORMANCE/STUDENT OUTCOME: Graphic Word Forms

"AMERICA THE BEAUTIFUL" (page 254)

Play a recording of "America the Beautiful," or have students sing the song as a group. Provide copies of the lyrics for students to use as they write down all of the land forms or special places that are named in the song. Encourage students to write each selected word using a visual representation of the word's meaning. If time permits, ask students to try writing additional lines or verses to the song, focusing on other land forms such as deserts, lakes, rivers, islands, forests, or plateaus.

THE SOLID WASTE DILEMMA

PURPOSE: To create an original sculpture made out of solid waste products

TARGETED INTELLIGENCE: Bodily/Kinesthetic and Visual/Spatial

CONTENT/STANDARD FOCUS: Art

PRODUCT/PERFORMANCE/STUDENT OUTCOME: Sculpture of Solid Waste Products

"THE SOLID WASTE DILEMMA" (page 255)

Ask students to bring in several examples of solid waste products from home (or use the contents of wastebaskets and trash containers on school campus with help from the custodian) such as: candy wrappers, newspapers, soda cans, milk cartons, bottle caps, food package containers, straws, aluminum or Styrofoam items, etc. Provide students with tape and glue, and have them create small, simple sculptures showcasing the solid waste products commonly found around the home and school. Display these as reminders of the solid waste dilemma.

BEAUTY IS ABOVE AND BELOW ME

PURPOSE: To construct a collage, montage, or poster of beauty that reflects various forms of nature and the environment

TARGETED INTELLIGENCE: Visual/Spatial, Bodily/Kinesthetic, and Naturalistic

CONTENT/STANDARD FOCUS: Art & Social Studies—People, Places, and Environments

PRODUCT/PERFORMANCE/STUDENT OUTCOME: Collage, Montage, or Display Poster

"BEAUTY IS ABOVE AND BELOW ME" (page 256)

Lead students in a brainstorming session on the places of beauty that exist in their neighborhood, community, state, and country. Consider everything from parks and gardens to countrysides and landscapes. Next, instruct students to locate pictures of varied, beautiful scenarios using the Internet, magazines, old calendars and posters, or travel brochures (you may want to ask students to bring contributions for this collection from home) to create individual, small group, or even a large group collage, montage, poster, or bulletin board for display in the classroom. Be certain to leave room for them to add the words of this popular Navajo Indian Chant: "Beauty is before me and beauty is behind me. Above and below me hovers the beautiful. I am surrounded by it."

PARTICIPATING IN AN ENVIRONMENTAL STEWARDSHIP CAMPAIGN

PURPOSE: To simulate a mock stewardship campaign created to improve sites of the local environment

TARGETED INTELLIGENCE: Logical/Mathematical, Intrapersonal, and Naturalistic

CONTENT/STANDARD FOCUS: Mathematics—Mathematical Connections; Computation and Estimation & Science— Science in Personal and Social Perspectives

PRODUCT/PERFORMANCE/STUDENT OUTCOME: Budget/Ledger Sheet

"PARTICIPATING IN AN ENVIRONMENTAL STEWARDSHIP CAMPAIGN" (page 257)

Discuss the processes of both environmental stewardship efforts and conservation projects that take place in most communities to protect natural resources and wildlife, and even campaign for the aesthetics of architectural buildings that are visually pleasing. Ask students to pretend that they have $100,000.00 to spend on improvement projects for their local community that fall into the categories listed on the student activity sheet. Provide time for discussion of the needs of their own community in these categories before deciding how much to spend on each project and recording their allocations in the chart provided for that purpose.

©2004 Incentive Publications, Inc.
Nashville, TN

STAMP OUT POLLUTED THINKING

PURPOSE: To rank those things that can pollute a student's thinking or negatively affect his or her relationships with others

TARGETED INTELLIGENCE: Logical/Mathematical

CONTENT/STANDARD FOCUS: Social Studies—Individual Development and Identity; Individuals, Groups, and Institutions

PRODUCT/PERFORMANCE/STUDENT OUTCOME: Self-Check Rating Scale

"STAMP OUT POLLUTED THINKING" (page 258)

Point out the multiple applications of the concept of "pollution or pollutants" to students as one can pollute the environment, the body, or the learning process. Ask students to complete the rating scale on the student activity sheet that rates things/activities that can and do pollute a person's thinking ability.

A DIFFERENT KIND OF POLLUTION: IS HAIKU WHAT IT USED TO BE?

PURPOSE: To review the traditional Japanese haiku pattern and its humorous or "tongue in cheek" application to the world of technology

TARGETED INTELLIGENCE: Verbal/Linguistic and Naturalistic

CONTENT/STANDARD FOCUS: Language Arts—Standards 6, 11, and 12

PRODUCT/PERFORMANCE/STUDENT OUTCOME: Original Haiku

"A DIFFERENT KIND OF POLLUTION: IS HAIKU WHAT IT USED TO BE?" (page 259)

Review the pattern for creating Japanese haiku poetry with students. Emphasize the fact that this genre or type of poetry has traditionally focused on nature and the environment. Now, one finds many traditional poetry forms, like haiku, focusing on the world of technology rather than the world of Mother Nature. Ask students to read through the computer-generated haikus on the student activity sheet, and then to have fun creating some of their own.

WAYS THAT THE WEB CAN POLLUTE STUDENT LEARNING

PURPOSE: To explore ways that the Web and the Internet have contributed to the problem of cheating in the schools

TARGETED INTELLIGENCE: Logical/Mathematical and Intrapersonal

CONTENT/STANDARD FOCUS: All Subject Areas

PRODUCT/PERFORMANCE/STUDENT OUTCOME: Personal Inventory

"WAYS THAT THE WEB CAN POLLUTE STUDENT LEARNING" (page 260)

Begin this activity by discussing the many advantages that students have today because of advanced technology. In contrast, encourage students to comment on problems that have occurred because of technology innovations—everything from pornography to viruses and lack of privacy issues. Instruct students to complete the personal inventory on the student activity page, and then use their responses as a springboard for further discussion on the topic of "cheating" through Web and Internet access opportunities.

A WORD ABOUT BODY POLLUTANTS

PURPOSE: To discuss the special medical problems faced by many adolescents today, especially those that involve polluting the body with undesirable substances

TARGETED INTELLIGENCE: Bodily/Kinesthetic

CONTENT/STANDARD FOCUS: Health & Science—Life Science; Science in Personal and Social Perspectives

PRODUCT/PERFORMANCE/STUDENT OUTCOME: Guided Group Discussion

"A WORD ABOUT BODY POLLUTANTS" (page 261)

Use the student activity sheet as the basis for leading a large group discussion on the special medical problems faced by young adolescents today. Focus on those medical conditions that involve the use of "body pollutants" such as drugs, alcohol, tobacco, steroids, and poor eating habits.

©2004 Incentive Publications, Inc.
Nashville, TN

CAN BOOKS REALLY UPSET THE ECOLOGY OF THE MIND?

PURPOSE: To study the issue of banning books from libraries because they "endanger, pollute, or upset" the ecology of the minds of children and young adults

TARGETED INTELLIGENCE: Verbal/Linguistic

CONTENT/STANDARD FOCUS: Language Arts—Standards 2 and 3

PRODUCT/PERFORMANCE/STUDENT OUTCOME: Large Group Discussion

"CAN BOOKS REALLY UPSET THE ECOLOGY OF THE MIND?" (page 262)

Ask students to complete the questions and tasks on the student activity sheet in preparation for a group discussion on the overall topic of "banning books" by selected groups and target populations. Encourage students to use their responses as notes during a group discussion on the topic. You may want to pick individual students to lead the discussion, rather than the teacher, so that they have the experience of facilitating a discussion among their peers.

SEEKING THE IDEAL ENVIRONMENT

PURPOSE: To invent an ideal environmental area for the future

TARGETED INTELLIGENCE: Logical/Mathematical, Visual/Spatial, Interpersonal, and Naturalistic

CONTENT/STANDARD FOCUS: Social Studies—People, Places, and Environments

PRODUCT/PERFORMANCE/STUDENT OUTCOME: Map/Legend

"SEEKING THE IDEAL ENVIRONMENT" (page 263)

Divide students into small cooperative learning groups and ask each group to imagine an environmental utopia for themselves anywhere in the world. Provide students with large sheets of drawing paper and crayons/markers with which to develop a simple map and legend of their special place. Provide time for students to share their completed maps with one another, and to explain the features they considered important to creating the perfect environmental area.

ARBOR DAY ANY DAY

PURPOSE: To plan an Arbor Day celebration for the class or school that could be held on any day of the year to enhance the environment and encourage planting trees

TARGETED INTELLIGENCE: Bodily/Kinesthetic, Interpersonal, and Naturalistic

CONTENT/STANDARD FOCUS: Science—Science in Personal and Social Perspectives

PRODUCT/PERFORMANCE/STUDENT OUTCOME: Arbor Day Celebration Plan

"ARBOR DAY ANY DAY" (page 264)

Discuss the reasons for having an Arbor Day celebration as a national focus during each calendar year. Determine reasons why Arbor Day could be celebrated at almost any time of year, depending upon your geographic location and climate conditions. Divide students into small cooperative learning groups to plan such a celebration for their class or school. Choose the best plan to implement, or combine various elements of several plans.

ENERGY CONSERVATION BRINGS CHAOS!

PURPOSE: To create an original comic strip depicting one humorous solution to the energy crisis that threatens many modern societies

TARGETED INTELLIGENCE: Visual/Spatial and Bodily/Kinesthetic

CONTENT/STANDARD FOCUS: Language Arts—Standards 11 and 12 & Science—Science in Personal and Social Perspectives

PRODUCT/PERFORMANCE/STUDENT OUTCOME: Comic Strip

"ENERGY CONSERVATION BRINGS CHAOS!" (page 265)

Ask students to complete the student activity sheet as directed. Display and discuss completed student work. Lead a discussion about the world's energy crisis and the resulting effect on lifestyles today.

ROLE-PLAYING AN ECOLOGY COUNCIL FOR YOUR CLASS

PURPOSE: To role-play the creation and operation of an environmental council for the classroom

TARGETED INTELLIGENCE: Bodily/Kinesthetic and Interpersonal

CONTENT/STANDARD FOCUS: Social Studies—People, Places, and Environments; Power, Authority, and Governance

PRODUCT/PERFORMANCE/STUDENT OUTCOME: Council Session

"ROLE-PLAYING AN ECOLOGY COUNCIL FOR YOUR CLASS" (page 266)

Discuss the concept of "the classroom as an ecological environment" by definition. Consider the physical space itself, as well as the relationships between the students and the culture (beliefs, expectations, traditions, rituals, routines etc.) of the classroom setting. Next, discuss the purpose and organizational structure of an ecology council and its application to the individual classroom and the total school environment. Finally, place students into small cooperative learning groups, and have each group outline a proposal for creating their own ecology council. As time permits, synthesize the best ideas from each group and discuss implementation of the council concept into the school program. Conclude some of the effects of such an addition.

CHOOSE A CONSERVATION MINI-ACTIVITY TO DO

PURPOSE: To select and complete a conservation-related mini activity

TARGETED INTELLIGENCE: All Intelligences

CONTENT/STANDARD FOCUS: All Content Areas

PRODUCT/PERFORMANCE/STUDENT OUTCOME: Conservation Mini-Activity

"CHOOSE A CONSERVATION MINI-ACTIVITY TO DO" (page 267)

Read and discuss the list of optional mini-activities on the student activity page with students. Ask each student to select one of the cumulative tasks to complete as the conclusion of their study of the environment and conservation of natural resources.

THEME: ENVIRONMENT   VALUE: STEWARDSHIP

STEWARDSHIP: WHAT DOES IT MEAN?

Directions: Read through each of the dictionary definitions of "steward" written below, and then infer what it would mean in this context: "It is important that all world citizens share in the stewardship of our natural resources and environment." Express your thoughts in a comprehensive paragraph, and then create a symbol to represent the idea of "environmental stewardship."

DICTIONARY DEFINITIONS OF "STEWARD":

1. A person who manages another's property, finances, or other affairs.

2. A person in charge of the household affairs of a large estate, club, hotel, or resort.

3. An officer on a ship in charge of provisions and dining arrangements.

4. An attendant on a ship or airplane.

I THINK "STEWARD" and "STEWARDSHIP" OF THE ENVIRONMENT MEANS THAT WE:

_____

_____

_____

_____

_____

NEXT, CREATE A SYMBOL TO REPRESENT THE CONCEPT OF "ENVIRONMENTAL STEWARDSHIP."

Name: _____

THE INTERCONNECTEDNESS OF MAN AND BEAST

Directions: A famous Indian Chief in the mid-1800's once wrote a letter to the President of the United States expressing his concern about the white man's inhumane and unfair treatment of animals. Indians, unlike the white man, never killed any living creature unless it was necessary for their survival. It was never done for sport, money, or personal gain. Today, many birds, animals, and other wildlife creatures are endangered and becoming extinct because people have failed to protect them from destruction, and because many people do not really value the "interconnectedness" of man and beast. In the space below, create a simple drawing, poem, song, or essay to show what you think Chief Seattle of the Duwamish tribe meant when he wrote: "If all the beasts were gone, men would die from a great loneliness of spirit, for whatever happens to the beast happens also to man."

MY CREATIVE INTERPRETATION OF CHIEF SEATTLE'S CONCERN FOR ANIMALS

Name:

TYPES OF ENVIRONMENTAL POLLUTION

Directions: Pollution is defined as "the damage done to the environment by harmful substances." Pollution comes in many forms and affects the air, land, and water all over the world. Work with a partner to test your own knowledge and awareness of environmental and pollution issues as they exist in your world today. Fill in the chart below with your ideas and opinions. Finally, construct a Venn Diagram that shows the common causes and/or effects of air, water, and noise pollution as you see them. Use the other side of this paper for your Venn Diagram.

AIR POLLUTION	WATER POLLUTION	SOUND POLLUTION
List Causes	List Causes	List Causes
List Effects	List Effects	List Effects
Possible Solutions	Possible Solutions	Possible Solutions

Name:

CONSERVATION AND RECYCLING

Directions: Although most individuals are knowledgeable about basic conservation and recycling efforts in their community, very few people take an active part in protecting our natural resources. Use the Opposing Forces Chart below to determine potential causes of and solutions for this conservation/recycling dilemma. At the top of the chart, write the problem statement: "Learning how to conserve and recycle at home." In the arrows under the DRIVING FORCES heading, record as many forces as you can that you think would help you do a better job of conserving/recycling, and under the OPPOSING FORCES heading, record as many obstacles as you can think of that are keeping you from doing a better job of conserving/recycling. Use this as a tool for eliminating the problem areas and capitalizing on the positive areas.

Opposing Forces Chart

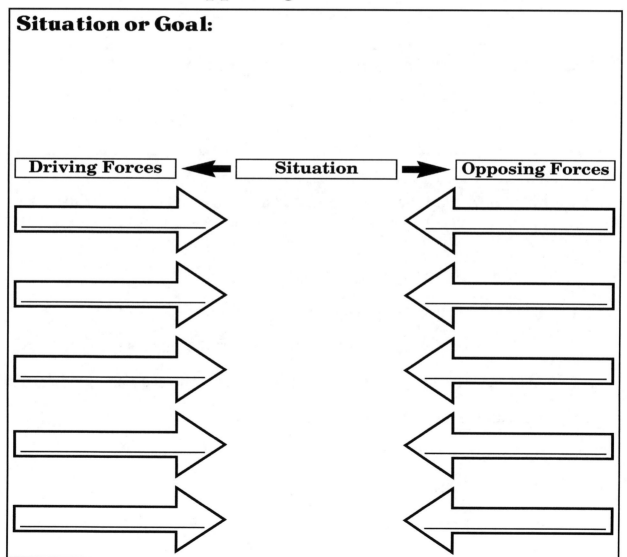

Name:

TECHNOLOGICAL ADVANCES HINDER STEWARDSHIP EFFORTS

Directions: Read through the quotation taken from Alvin Toffler's book, *Future Shock*, published in 1970, and complete the tasks outlined below.

> "Industrial vomit . . . fills our skies and seas. Pesticides and herbicides filter into our foods. Twisted automobile carcasses, aluminum cans, non-returnable glass bottles and synthetic plastics form immense kitchen middens in our midst as more and more of our detritus resists decay. We do not even begin to know what to do with our radioactive wastes—whether to pump them into the earth, shoot them into outer space, or pour them into the oceans. Our technological powers increase, but the side effects and potential hazards also escalate."

1. Look up the these words in the dictionary and write their definitions:

    Middens _____

    Detritus _____

2. Explain what you think the author means by "industrial vomit." _____

    _____

3. Describe the image created by the author's words: "twisted automobile carcasses."

    _____

    _____

4. Work with members of your cooperative learning group to complete one of the following sections of a classroom mural that reflects each of these images created by Toffler in the excerpt from his book, *Future Shock*:

    . . . . . Industrial vomit filling skies and seas

    . . . . . Pesticides and herbicides filtering into our foods

    . . . . . Twisted automobile carcasses in dumps, junkyards, or graveyards

    . . . . . Aluminum cans, non-returnable glass bottles and synthetic plastics in local dumps

    . . . . . Radioactive wastes pumped into the earth

    . . . . . Radioactive wastes shot into outer space

    . . . . . Radioactive wastes poured into the ocean

Name: _____

©2004 Incentive Publications, Inc.
Nashville, TN

CREATING "I URGE YOU" TELEGRAMS

Directions: Use the blank rectangles below to create a series of mock telegrams that express your primary concerns about pollution, the destruction of the environment, and the deterioration of the quality of life for today and future generations as you see it. Begin each telegram with the words: "I URGE . . . " and end each telegram with completion of the word "BECAUSE . . . " For example, you might write something like this: "I URGE people to recycle their paper products BECAUSE it saves millions of trees from being cut down unnecessarily." When all students in your cooperative learning group have completed their telegram cards as individuals, cut them out and spread them out on a table. Next, cooperatively classify or categorize the telegrams into similar groups or topics. Finally, study the telegrams and together draw some conclusions as to what types of destruction and pollution are of most concern to members of your group.

═══ **TELEGRAM** ═══

I urge _____

_____

_____

_____

Because _____

_____

_____

_____

★ ★ ★ **TELEGRAM** ★ ★ ★

I urge _____

_____

_____

_____

Because _____

_____

_____

_____

Name:

AMERICA THE BEAUTIFUL

Directions: Listen to a recording of "America the Beautiful" or locate the lyrics and music of all verses in a music book. List all of the land forms or special places that are named in this famous and patriotic composition. Try writing each word so that the word itself graphically reflects the meaning of the word. (Example: He mentions "mountains." Can you write the word "mountain" in the shape of one?) If time permits, try adding other verses to the song, and include some lines about other land forms such as deserts, lakes, rivers, and islands.

Fill these shapes with corresponding words from the song.

Name:

THE SOLID WASTE DILEMMA

Directions: Garbage is solid waste. It includes candy wrappers, old newspapers, soda cans, milk cartons, juice bottles, plastic detergent bottles, cereal boxes, used straws, styrofoam cups, aluminum foil, plastic bags, empty toothpaste tubes, and broken pencils—just to name a few. Solid waste often winds up in landfills at the dump, although it becomes litter when it is dumped carelessly where it doesn't belong. Use a variety of solid waste items to create a simple sculpture that shows the viewer what kinds of things are considered garbage when they are discarded after use. Sketch a plan of your sculpture in the space below.

Name:

Advisory Plus!

BEAUTY IS ABOVE AND BELOW ME

Directions: Think about all the places of beauty in your neighborhood, community, state, or country. Consider such beautiful surroundings as one finds in parks, gardens, beaches, mountains, deserts, forests, countrysides, and landscapes. Then, browse through a number of magazines and travel brochures and cut out pictures of beautiful places. Paste them on a large piece of oak tag, poster board, or newsprint to make a collage, montage, or poster display. In the middle of the collage, montage, or poster display print these words from a popular Navajo Indian chant.

Beauty is before me and beauty is behind me.

Above and below me hovers the beautiful.

I am surrounded by it . . .

Name:

PARTICIPATING IN AN ENVIRONMENTAL STEWARDSHIP CAMPAIGN

Directions: Many environmental and conservation organizations plan and carry out local, regional, and national stewardship campaigns to generate funds for improving the environment or promoting conservation to protect the earth's plants, animals, habitats, and natural resources. These campaigns encourage the public to give personal donations for many different programs or purposes, ranging from recycling and beautification projects to eliminating litter and oil spills. Pretend you are the student representative on a local environmental stewardship committee that is raising and allocating $100,000.00 for purposes of improving and/or beautifying the environment in your area. The projects that are being considered by the committee for funding are listed below. Decide which projects you would want to fund, and how much you would want to allocate for each project. Be sure you write down a specific place or location in each general category that actually exists in your community before completing the budget. Be able to defend and give reasons for each of your special project sites and the amount to be allocated from the $100,000 fund.

MY BUDGET/LEDGER SHEET FOR PROPOSED EXPENDITURES

TYPE OF SITE SPECIFIED	PLACE/LOCATION OF SITE IN MY COMMUNITY	PROPOSED AMOUNT TO BE ALLOCATED
1. Public Garden	_____	_____
2. Zoo	_____	_____
3. Park/Picnic Area	_____	_____
4. Beach/Lake/River	_____	_____
5. Boulevard/Street	_____	_____
6. Cultural Center	_____	_____
7. Civic Building	_____	_____
8. Tourist Attraction	_____	_____
9. Urban Area	_____	_____
10. Recreation Site	_____	_____
11. Shopping Center	_____	_____
12. Other	_____	_____

Name: _____

STAMP OUT POLLUTED THINKING

Directions: Rank each of the things below according to how they would negatively affect your self-respect or your positive relationships with others. List them in order of their potential harm and influence on you, with 1 being most harmful and 10 being least harmful.

_____Gambling

_____R-Rated movies

_____Music with inappropriate lyrics

_____Violent video games

_____MTV

_____Tabloid television shows

_____Pornographic websites

_____Off-color jokes

_____Tabloid magazines and newspapers

_____Pin-up pictures, posters, or magazines

Now . . . Justify your first and last choices on the lines below.

_____

_____

_____

_____

Finally, comment on who has the most influence on you when it comes to eliminating polluted thinking—parents, friends, teachers, church leaders, others, or yourself?

_____

_____

_____

Name: _____

A DIFFERENT KIND OF POLLUTION: IS HAIKU WHAT IT USED TO BE?

Directions: The Japanese are the masters of haiku, a poetry pattern that consists of three lines of five syllables, seven syllables, and five syllables respectively. The beauty of the haiku is that, when written correctly, it communicates a timeless message about the natural wonders and beauty of the world, using an extreme economy of words to achieve a wistful and/or powerful insight.

Now, one can find the Japanese haikus (which used to deal with cherry blossoms, sunshine and shadows, and snow-covered peaks) focused on the technological world of computers. Read through the haikus about the computer age written here, and then create a few of your own. Note how these haikus poke fun at the computer age.

EXAMPLE ONE	EXAMPLE TWO	EXAMPLE THREE
Computer virus,	Internet access.	Computers are here
So contagious as can be	Helps big and little kids when	Taking time and so much fun
Makes me mad and sick	There's no book to read	Away from my friends

HERE IS ONE OF MY OWN COMPUTER-ORIENTED HAIKUS AND ONE TRADITIONAL HAIKU HONORING THE BEAUTY OF NATURE!

_____   _____

_____   _____

_____   _____

Name: _____

WAYS THAT THE WEB CAN POLLUTE STUDENT LEARNING

Directions: Think about how you use the Web and the Internet to help you with your work, both at home and at school. Then, take a few minutes to complete this personal inventory on your learning habits and how technology may have helped make cheating an integral part of school life. Try to be as specific as possible in each of your responses.

MY PERSONAL WEB/INTERNET VIEWS AND ACTIVITIES

1. How often do you use the Web or the Internet to help you with your assignments at home and at school? _____

2. What types of websites do you find most helpful in completing your assignments?

   _____

3. How might students in your class or school misuse or cheat while using the Web or Internet when doing their schoolwork? How often does this occur? _____

   _____

4. It has been said that "cheating is part of the schooling process." Do you agree or disagree and why? _____

   _____

5. Do you know the meaning of "plagiarizing" as it relates to doing research on the Web or Internet? Explain. _____

   _____

6. How do you acknowledge the words, ideas, illustrations, or quotations taken from the Web or Internet in your assignments? _____

   _____

7. How has the Web or Internet made cheating so easy? _____

   _____

8. Are parents today putting too much pressure on kids to succeed in school, leading to more cheating as a survival effort by their children? Why do you feel as you do?

   _____

   _____

Name: _____

A WORD ABOUT BODY POLLUTANTS

Directions: Did you know that teens might have the worst health care of any age group in the United States today? This is partly because teens see doctors less than any other age group, partly because of poverty (poor teens have less access to health care) and partly because parents and doctors do not always take their symptoms seriously. Teens are in greater danger today, it seems, because they are experimenting with risky behavior at younger and younger ages. Take a few minutes to review the tasks and information below, and then use these thoughts as a tool to prepare for a group discussion on the topic of teenage health care.

1. Some common health care problems facing many teens are: drug, tobacco, and alcohol abuse; sexually transmitted diseases and unwanted pregnancies; automobile accidents; physical and mental abuse; poor nutrition, lack of exercise, and obesity problems; sports-related injuries and steroid use. Which of these do you think poses the greatest threat to you and your friends?

2. It has been said that the risky behaviors kids have always experimented with now happen at younger ages, and that even though children mature sooner physically, there has been no parallel emotional maturity. Do you agree with the statement that "we have too many adolescents—especially the ones 12 to 14—in mature bodies with immature minds." Explain.

3. Most kids don't make healthy food choices, and eating disorders can be a serious problem for teenagers. Is this true for you and your friends? Give reasons for your answer.

4. The warning signs of teen medical problems are: fatigue, being withdrawn or isolated, chronic cough, declining school performance or a change in interests, a change in eating and sleep habits, weight loss or gain, and headaches or abdominal pain. What things might cause these warning signs for you and others in your class?

5. Parents or guardians can do much to help their children. Five things for them to consider are: developing good communication, avoiding power struggles, setting a good example, planning regularly scheduled meals, and getting a doctor both they and their teen like and trust. Which one of these do you consider most important?

6. Consultations between teens and their doctors generally are protected by confidentiality laws, especially those involving sexual matters and abortion. Do you agree with this practice? Why or why not?

Name:

CAN BOOKS REALLY UPSET THE ECOLOGY OF THE MIND?

Directions: Did you know that the week of September 22nd is "Banned Books Week" in the United States, which is a time set aside to celebrate the expression of ideas and to ensure that even unpopular and controversial ideas are available to anyone who wishes to read them. It should also be a time when parents and educators talk with kids about books and the power of language. In fact, representatives of the Office for Intellectual Freedom, which traces book challenges in schools and libraries around the country, urge parents and kids to have those conversations all year long. Take a few minutes to record your thoughts on this topic, and then use your notes as a basis for participating in a large group discussion.

1. What do you think is the role of the Office for Intellectual Freedom? _____

    _____

2. Why do you think that selected groups of people use the right of censorship to advocate banning certain books in school libraries? _____

    _____

    _____

3. What book have you read that some parents, educators, and censors might consider to be a viable candidate for banning from school and public libraries? Explain why others might not approve of it for their children. _____

    _____

    _____

4. When classroom teachers recommend a book for a classroom assignment that some parents find offensive for their children to read, the teacher is often required to offer an alternative assignment. Do you agree with this practice? Why or why not?

    _____

    _____

    _____

5. Explain what you think this statement implies: "You can tell a lot about a person by what he or she chooses to read."_____

    _____

    _____

6. To learn more about the subject of banned and challenged books, as well as the history of censorship, check out these websites: www.ala.org/bbooks, the site of the American Library Association and www.title.forbiddenlibrary.com, a website listing recent and historical cases of literary censorship.

Name: _____

SEEKING THE IDEAL ENVIRONMENT

Directions: Imagine that you were going to select and settle in a newly discovered and uninhabited area anywhere in the world. Think about what you would need to know in order to survive, and the climate and natural resources you would seek as a priority.

Draw a simple map of the ideal environmental area you would choose, complete with a legend that depicts the natural resources, animal/plant life, and climate variables that would be important to you. Do this in the space below.

Name:

ARBOR DAY ANY DAY

Directions: On Arbor Day, people in many parts of the world plant trees. In fact, the United States has actually "exported" Arbor Day to many countries as a conservation effort, and in many places Arbor Day is celebrated throughout the entire year. As you know, trees are important because they clean carbon dioxide from the air, produce and release oxygen in the air, and provide roots to hold the topsoil in place. Some trees, of course, even produce food such as fruit or nuts. Plan an Arbor Day celebration for your school that could take place any month during the year. Record your thoughts below.

MY PLAN FOR AN ARBOR DAY CELEBRATION _____

_____

DATE, TIME, AND PLACE OF CELEBRATION _____

_____

MEMBERS/ROLES OF ARBOR DAY PLANNING COMMITTEE _____

_____

ACTIVITIES TO BE HELD DURING THE ARBOR DAY CELEBRATION _____

_____

_____

MARKETING/PUBLICITY STRATEGIES TO PROMOTE ARBOR DAY IN OUR SCHOOL

_____

_____

_____

MATERIALS/RESOURCES NEEDED TO IMPLEMENT CELEBRATION SUCCESSFULLY

_____

_____

POSSIBLE PROBLEMS/OBSTACLES TO OVERCOME IN PLANNING CELEBRATION

_____

_____

_____

_____

Name: _____

ENERGY CONSERVATION BRINGS CHAOS!

Directions: There has been an ongoing energy crisis of some sort for many years, and with technology and the demand for higher-priced and gas-guzzling cars, trucks, SUVs, busses, trailers, and motor homes, things are not likely to change. Humor is sometimes used in the newspaper to exaggerate an environmental issue or problem such as those caused by depletion of energy supplies. Try the same tactic to answer the question, "What would happen if all motor vehicles suddenly turned into non-motorized go-carts, scooters, bicycles, or skateboards?"

Create a cartoon that shows the scene of parents, kids, and/or families arriving at a destination such as an airport to catch a plane, a supermarket to purchase groceries, a middle school to pick up children, a football stadium to see a game, or a restaurant to eat dinner on their non-motorized vehicles. What would parking lots look like? What kinds of traffic jams might occur? What type of rules would need to be followed? What kinds of complications might surface?

Name: _____

ROLE-PLAYING AN ECOLOGY COUNCIL FOR YOUR CLASS

Directions: The dictionary defines "ecology" as "the relationship between organisms and their environment," and "ecosystems" as "an ecological community, together with its physical environment, considered as a unit." In fact, by these definitions, the classroom itself is considered to be an ecological community. Think of some reasons why this might be true. Then, work with members of your class to organize an ecology council that meets as needed to address ecology issues that surface during the school year. For example, is litter in the halls and on the school grounds a problem? Is waste of paper in your classroom a problem? Is graffiti in bathrooms a problem? Is vandalism of school property a problem? To draft a proposal for such an ecology council, complete the outline below.

OUR PROPOSAL FOR AN ECOLOGY COUNCIL _____

_____

PURPOSE OF COUNCIL: _____

_____

NUMBER AND ROLES OF MEMBERS TO SERVE ON COUNCIL: _____

_____

_____

HOW MEMBERS ARE TO BE SELECTED FOR COUNCIL: _____

_____

SUGGESTED MEETING DATES/TIMES/PLACE FOR COUNCIL: _____

_____

POSSIBLE ECOLOGICAL ISSUES/PROBLEMS TO BE ADDRESSED BY COUNCIL: _____

_____

_____

METHODS FOR DISTRIBUTING INFORMATION/OUTCOMES OF COUNCIL SESSIONS: _____

_____

_____

Name: _____

CHOOSE A CONSERVATION MINI-ACTIVITY TO DO

Directions: Choose one of these mini-activities to complete as you think about different ways to conserve resources at home, at school, or in the community.

MINI-ACTIVITY ONE: List one creative way to reuse each of the following items at home when they are no longer good for their original use: computer, clock, radio or television set, typewriter, bicycle or tricycle.

MINI-ACTIVITY TWO: Create a display ad for a newspaper, one-minute commercial for television, home-page for website, or advertisement for a kid's magazine that promotes conservation at home, at school, or in the community.

MINI-ACTIVITY THREE: Most people have times when they must deal with scarcity of resources such as time or money to meet their wants and needs. Describe a time when you or someone you know experienced a scarcity of time or money. How was the situation dealt with?

MINI-ACTIVITY FOUR: Plan a short demonstration or chalk talk to show others the importance of recycling paper, plastic containers, glass jars/bottles, and metal cans from the home.

MINI-ACTIVITY FIVE: Prepare a one-page flyer that shows the reader how conservation begins at home.

MINI-ACTIVITY SIX: You have been asked to compose a want ad for the perfect conservationist to join the staff of the science department for a new school. Be sure to include all the important qualities you seek.

MINI-ACTIVITY SEVEN: Organize an oral group story about conservation using the lines here as the first lines and then having others add a line or two to the story until it is finished.

To "conserve" means to "protect" or "take care of." In ecology, conservation means to protect the Earth's plants, animals, habitats, and natural resources. But from what does the Earth need to be protected?

MINI-ACTIVITY EIGHT: Authors of children's books use many descriptive words to create visual images in a reader's mind. Design a page for small children that is filled with these "word pictures" on the topic of conservation.

MINI-ACTIVITY NINE: Think of two very different items, such as a glass bottle and a waste basket, and write a three paragraph conservation story that includes both of them.

MINI-ACTIVITY TEN: Picture the cover of a new magazine that has just come out to teach teenagers about conservation. Describe the cover in detail and tell what the magazine is about.

Name:

THEME: ENVIRONMENT   VALUE: STEWARDSHIP

MARCH

	MY BEST WORK	MY SO-SO WORK	MY NOT SO GOOD WORK?
	☺	☺	☹

1. Quality of my paragraph and symbol of environmental stewardship . . . . ☐
2. Quality of my drawing representing interconnectedness . . . . ☐
3. Quality of my Venn Diagram about environmental pollution . . . . ☐
4. Quality of my conservation graphic organizer . . . . ☐
5. Quality of my quotation interpretation . . . . ☐
6. Quality of my "I Urge You" telegram . . . . ☐
7. Quality of my musical interpretation . . . . ☐
8. Quality of my solid waste sculpture sketch . . . . ☐
9. Quality of my collage/montage/poster . . . . ☐
10. Quality of my budget/ledger sheet . . . . ☐
11. Quality of my rating scale about polluted thinking . . . . ☐
12. Quality of my computer-generated haiku . . . . ☐
13. Quality of my personal inventory about web and Internet use . . . . ☐
14. Quality of my notes and discussion about body pollutants . . . . ☐
15. Quality of my notes and discussion about the Banning of Books . . . . ☐
16. Quality of my map . . . . ☐
17. Quality of my Arbor Day plan of celebration . . . . ☐
18. Quality of my cartoon . . . . ☐
19. Quality of my conservation mini-activity . . . . ☐
20. Quality of my proposal for an ecology council . . . . ☐

Name: _____

THEME: BOOKS AND MEDIA   VALUE: HUMOR

It has been said that a good book either informs, inspires, or entertains, and an occasional great book does all three. Could the same thing be said for television and radio, or newspaper, magazine, and Internet articles?

- **HOW DO YOU FEEL ABOUT READING?—PURPOSE:** To respond to questions in a personal, self-check reading inventory

- **LET'S MEASURE YOUR HUMOR QUOTIENT!—PURPOSE:** To rate a student's "sense of humor" using an inventory with a rating scale

- **ARE YOU A TELEVISION ADDICT?—PURPOSE:** To determine how dependent a student is on watching television for entertainment during his/her leisure time

- **THE GENRES OF LITERATURE—PURPOSE:** To introduce and explain the major genres of literature to students

- **INTRODUCING THE ELEMENTS OF LITERATURE—PURPOSE:** To identify and describe the key elements of most literary works

- **A SURVEY OF YOUR HUMOR HISTORY—PURPOSE:** To complete a set of humor-related starter statements that focus on one's personal humor history

- **TYPES OF WRITING FOUND IN BOOKS, NEWSPAPERS, MAGAZINES, AND WEBSITES—PURPOSE:** To introduce and discuss the four basic types of writing most commonly found in books, newspapers, magazines, and informative websites

- **A LAUGH A DAY KEEPS THE DOCTOR AWAY—PURPOSE:** To explore the advantages of using humor in the workplace or the classroom

- **THE GREAT TELEVISION DEBATE—PURPOSE:** To take a position on the positive or negative effects of television and selected television shows on their viewers

- **THE RADIO AS A FORM OF MEDIA—PURPOSE:** To discuss the advantages and limitations of the radio as compared to other popular sources of media

- **PUBLISHING A CLASSROOM/ADVISORY NEWSPAPER—PURPOSE:** To summarize the major parts of a newspaper and apply these concepts to the creation of a classroom/advisory newspaper

- **MAGAZINE MAGIC—PURPOSE:** To examine many different magazines and relate them to one's reading preferences and means of self-interest and self-expression

- **SOME INTERESTING TELEVISION-RELATED PROJECTS—PURPOSE:** To complete a television-related independent project

- **SMUGGLING MORE HUMOR INTO THE CLASSROOM—PURPOSE:** To implement one or more strategies that make humor work effectively in the classroom as an instructional tool

- **THE ART AND SCIENCE OF PERSUASION—PURPOSE:** To investigate the different value-laden techniques of advertising in the media

- **CENSORSHIP IN THE MEDIA—PURPOSE:** To examine the role of censorship in these situations: banning of books in the library, ratings of films in the movies, and freedom of speech in newspapers

- **LEARNING TO WRITE A MEDIA REVIEW—PURPOSE:** To write a review of a multimedia source or program

- **YOU, TOO, CAN BE A COMEDIAN!—PURPOSE:** To use a series of humorous springboards as the basis for creating original student adaptations

- **HOLD A CLASSROOM JOKE MARATHON—PURPOSE:** To organize a classroom Joke-A-Thon and measure the stages of laughter generated for each student's joke using Kuhn's model

- **CREATING A HUMOR PORTFOLIO FOR FUN AND LAUGHS—PURPOSE:** To create a student portfolio of humorous anecdotes and artifacts

©2004 Incentive Publications, Inc.
Nashville, TN

THEME: BOOKS AND MEDIA   VALUE: HUMOR

"The fun of reading is not that something is told to you, but that you stretch your mind. Your own imagination walks along with the author's, or even goes beyond his. Your experience, compared with his, yields the same or different conditions and your ideas develop as you understand his."

—Bennet Cerf

Read and react to Mr. Cerf's remark by writing about a book you have read recently that caused you to stretch your mind and use your imagination to develop new ideas or to change or expand ideas you had already.

_____

_____

_____

_____

_____

"Laugh and the world laughs with you, weep and you weep alone."

—Ella Wheeler Wilcox

Most of us have heard this saying used so many times that we never stop to think of who said it first or why. We have to wonder what the circumstances were that caused the early twentieth-century poet, Ella Wheeler Wilcox, to create these lines that have become a much quoted proverb. Write about your personal interpretation of the proverb and why you think it has remained a timeless saying.

_____

_____

_____

_____

_____

APRIL CALENDAR

WEEK ONE

DAY ONE	**"How Do You Feel About Reading?"** Responding to questions in a personal, self-check reading inventory
DAY TWO	**"Let's Measure Your Humor Quotient!"** Rating a student's "sense of humor" using an inventory with a rating scale
DAY THREE	**"Are You a Television Addict?"** Determining how dependent a student is on watching television for entertainment during his/her leisure time
DAY FOUR	**"The Genres of Literature"** Understanding the major genres of literature
DAY FIVE	**"Introducing the Elements of Literature"** Identifying and describing the key elements of most literary works

WEEK TWO

DAY ONE	**"A Survey of Your Humor History"** Completing a set of humor-related starter statements that focus on one's own personal humor history
DAY TWO	**"Types of Writing Found in Books, Newspapers, Magazines, and Websites"** Introducing and discussing the four basic types of writing most commonly found in books, newspapers, magazines, and informative websites
DAY THREE	**"A Laugh a Day Keeps the Doctor Away"** Exploring the advantages of using humor in the workplace or the classroom
DAY FOUR	**"The Great Television Debate"** Taking a position on the positive or negative effects of television and selected television shows on their viewers
DAY FIVE	**"The Radio as a Form of Media"** Discussing the advantages and limitations of the radio as compared to other popular sources of media

THEME: BOOKS AND MEDIA   VALUE: HUMOR

WEEK THREE

DAY ONE	**"Publishing a Classroom/Advisory Newspaper"** Summarizing the major parts of a newspaper and applying these concepts to the creation of a classroom/advisory newspaper
DAY TWO	**"Magazine Magic"** Examining many different magazines and relating them to students' reading preferences and means of self-interest and self-expression
DAY THREE	**"Some Interesting Television-Related Projects"** Completing a television-related independent project
DAY FOUR	**"Smuggling More Humor into the Classroom"** Implementing one or more strategies that makes humor work effectively in the classroom as an instructional tool
DAY FIVE	**"The Art and Science of Persuasion"** Investigating the different value-laden techniques of advertising in the media

WEEK FOUR

DAY ONE	**"Censorship in the Media"** Examining the role of censorship in the situations of: banning books in the library; rating movies; and freedom of speech in the newspapers
DAY TWO	**"Learning to Write a Media Review"** Writing a review of a multimedia source or program
DAY THREE	**"You, Too, Can Be a Comedian!"** Using a series of humorous springboards as the basis for creating original student adaptations
DAY FOUR	**"Hold a Classroom Joke Marathon"** Organizing a classroom Joke-A-Thon and measuring the stages of laughter generated by each student's joke using Kuhn's model
DAY FIVE	**"Creating a Humor Portfolio for Fun and Laughs"** Creating a student portfolio of humorous anecdotes and artifacts

THEME: BOOKS AND MEDIA   VALUE: HUMOR

HOW DO YOU FEEL ABOUT READING?

PURPOSE: To respond to questions in a personal, self-check reading inventory

TARGETED INTELLIGENCE: Verbal/Linguistic and Intrapersonal

CONTENT/STANDARD FOCUS: Language Arts—Standards 1, 2 & 6

PRODUCT/PERFORMANCE/STUDENT OUTCOME: Reading Inventory

"HOW DO YOU FEEL ABOUT READING?" (page 284)

Instruct students to complete the end-of-the-year Reading Inventory on the student activity sheet, according to directions given. Allow time for students to share their responses orally in small peer groups or in a large group discussion. Ask students to compare their responses to this inventory with a similar one they took at the beginning of the school year as part of the September module. Provide time for pondering the question, "Have my reading feelings and habits changed any over the course of the year?"

LET'S MEASURE YOUR HUMOR QUOTIENT!

PURPOSE: To rate a student's "sense of humor" using an inventory with a rating scale

TARGETED INTELLIGENCE: Logical/Mathematical and Intrapersonal

CONTENT/STANDARD FOCUS: Social Studies—Individual Development and Identity & Mathematics—Computation and Estimation

PRODUCT/PERFORMANCE/STUDENT OUTCOME: Humor Inventory

"LET'S MEASURE YOUR HUMOR QUOTIENT" (page 285)

Instruct students to complete the Humor Inventory on the student activity sheet according to directions given. Then, ask them to compute their scores and compare their humor quotient with others in the classroom. Lead a discussion of ways that students can develop a better sense of humor and how humor can relieve both stress and boredom.

ARE YOU A TELEVISION ADDICT?

PURPOSE: To determine how dependent a student is on watching television for entertainment during his/her leisure time

TARGETED INTELLIGENCE: Visual/Spatial and Intrapersonal

CONTENT/STANDARD FOCUS: Social Studies—Individual Development and Identity

PRODUCT/PERFORMANCE/STUDENT OUTCOME: Television Self-Checklist

"ARE YOU A TELEVISION ADDICT?" (page 286)

Introduce this topic by having each student estimate the number of hours he/she spends watching television every week. Then, total the minutes for the entire class. Ask students to complete the Television Self-Checklist on the student activity sheet, and use this to confirm or negate any television addiction behaviors they might exhibit.

THE GENRES OF LITERATURE

PURPOSE: To introduce and explain the major genres of literature to students

TARGETED INTELLIGENCE: Verbal/Linguistic and Intrapersonal

CONTENT/STANDARD FOCUS: Language Arts—Standards 2 and 6

PRODUCT/PERFORMANCE/STUDENT OUTCOME: Top Ten List of Favorite Books

"THE GENRES OF LITERATURE" (page 287)

Review the major genres of literature with students so that they understand these important classifications of literature. Then, ask students to recall favorite books they have read recently in each of these categories and to record them on the student activity sheet.

INTRODUCING THE ELEMENTS OF LITERATURE

PURPOSE: To identify and describe the key elements found in literary works

TARGETED INTELLIGENCE: Verbal/Linguistic

CONTENT/STANDARD FOCUS: Language Arts—Standards 2 and 6

PRODUCT/PERFORMANCE/STUDENT OUTCOME: Chart of Literary Elements

"INTRODUCING THE ELEMENTS OF LITERATURE" (page 288)

Review the elements of literature with students and explain how they are common to all types of fictional writing. Instruct students to construct a chart of two columns and to put each literary term in the first column, with its application to a novel they are currently reading (or have recently read) in the second column.

A SURVEY OF YOUR HUMOR HISTORY

PURPOSE: To relate to a set of humor-related starter statements that focus on one's personal humor history

TARGETED INTELLIGENCE: Verbal/Linguistic and Intrapersonal

CONTENT/STANDARD FOCUS: Language Arts—Standards 11 and 12 & Social Studies—Individual Development and Identity

PRODUCT/PERFORMANCE/STUDENT OUTCOME: Responses to Set of Starter Statements

"A SURVEY OF YOUR HUMOR HISTORY" (page 289)

Introduce this topic by relating some of your own personal history as it pertains to humor. Consider sharing your funniest movies, television shows, books, jokes, personal incidents, etc. Then, instruct students to complete the student activity sheet as directed. Allow time for students to share their responses in small groups, or in a large group session.

TYPES OF WRITING FOUND IN BOOKS, NEWSPAPERS, MAGAZINES, AND WEBSITES

PURPOSE: To introduce and discuss the four basic types of writing most commonly found in books, newspapers, magazines, and informative websites

TARGETED INTELLIGENCE: Verbal/Linguistic and Intrapersonal

CONTENT/STANDARD FOCUS: Language Arts— Standards 5, 6, 11, and 12

PRODUCT/PERFORMANCE/STUDENT OUTCOME: Original Piece of Writing

"TYPES OF WRITING FOUND IN BOOKS, NEWSPAPERS, MAGAZINES, AND WEBSITES" (page 290)

If possible, share excerpts from books, newspapers, magazines, or websites that represent each of these types of writing: descriptive, analytical, narrative, and persuasive. Then, ask students to experiment with one or more of these styles of writing by following the directions on the student activity sheet.

A LAUGH A DAY KEEPS THE DOCTOR AWAY

PURPOSE: To explore the advantages of using humor in the workplace or the classroom

TARGETED INTELLIGENCE: Verbal/Linguistic, Bodily/Kinesthetic, and Intrapersonal

CONTENT/STANDARD FOCUS: Language Arts—Standards 1 and 12 & Science—Science in Personal and Social Perspectives

PRODUCT/PERFORMANCE/STUDENT OUTCOME: Personal Anecdotes

"A LAUGH A DAY KEEPS THE DOCTOR AWAY" (page 291)

Review each of the identified benefits of humor and laughter on the student activity sheet. Then ask students to think of personal anecdotes that can be related to one or more of these potential benefits.

THE GREAT TELEVISION DEBATE

PURPOSE: To take a position on the positive or negative effects of television and selected television shows on their viewers

TARGETED INTELLIGENCE: Verbal/Linguistic, Logical/Mathematical, and Intrapersonal

CONTENT/STANDARD FOCUS: Language Arts—Standards 4, 11, and 12 & Social Studies—Individuals, Groups, and Institutions

PRODUCT/PERFORMANCE/STUDENT OUTCOME: Position Paper

"THE GREAT TELEVISION DEBATE" (page 292)

Ask students to think about the positive and negative effects of television on their lives. Encourage them to reflect on what they like about television and what they don't like about it. Then, ask students to take one of the two positions about the positive or negative impact of television on its viewers, defending their position in a short paper.

THE RADIO AS A FORM OF MEDIA

PURPOSE: To discuss the advantages and limitations of the radio as compared to other popular sources and uses of media

TARGETED INTELLIGENCE: Verbal/Linguistic and Logical/Mathematical

CONTENT/STANDARD FOCUS: Language Arts—Standards 4, 11, and 12 & Social Studies—Individuals, Groups, and Institutions

PRODUCT/PERFORMANCE/STUDENT OUTCOME: Original Radio Announcement, Advertisement, or News Item

"THE RADIO AS A FORM OF MEDIA" (page 293)

If time permits, provide a few minutes for students to listen to a short radio broadcast—a talk show or news summary, advertisements, commentaries, etc. Ask students to think about the advantages of the radio over other forms of media, such as television or the Internet. Then, guide students through the student activity sheet and ask them to try writing a simple radio announcement, advertisement, or news broadcast according to directions given.

PUBLISHING A CLASSROOM/ADVISORY NEWSPAPER

PURPOSE: To summarize the major parts of a newspaper and apply these concepts to the publishing of a classroom/advisory newspaper

TARGETED INTELLIGENCE: Verbal/Linguistic, Visual/Spatial, Bodily/Kinesthetic, and Interpersonal

CONTENT/STANDARD FOCUS: Language Arts—Standards 1, 3, 5, and 12

PRODUCT/PERFORMANCE/STUDENT OUTCOME: Classroom Advisory Newspaper

"PUBLISHING A CLASSROOM/ADVISORY NEWSPAPER" (page 294)

Share copies of the local newspaper with students, and have them locate examples of a lead story, news story, feature story, editorial, editorial cartoon, book/play/movie review, display ad, classified ad, comic strip, sports article, business section, advice column, and entertainment section. Next, ask students to work in small groups and brainstorm various topics for each of these categories that might work for a school or classroom advisory newspaper issue. Finally, encourage each student to write at least one piece for the newspaper and publish it as a source of information for parents so they can find out what is going on with their middle schoolers.

MAGAZINE MAGIC

PURPOSE: To examine many different magazines and relate them to one's reading preferences and means of self-interest and self-expression

TARGETED INTELLIGENCE: Verbal/Linguistic, Visual/Spatial, and Intrapersonal

CONTENT/STANDARD FOCUS: Language Arts—Standards 1, 3, 11, and 12

PRODUCT/PERFORMANCE/STUDENT OUTCOME: Mock Magazine Cover Page Design

"MAGAZINE MAGIC" (page 295)

Ask students to bring in several magazine samples from home that members of their family subscribe to or purchase on a regular basis. Also, plan to bring in many magazine samples from the school's media center. Display these magazines and allow students to take some time browsing through them, looking for those titles that appeal to special interests they or others in the class might have. Next, instruct students to complete the tasks outlined on the student activity sheet, according to directions given.

SOME INTERESTING TELEVISION-RELATED PROJECTS

PURPOSE: To complete a television-related independent project

TARGETED INTELLIGENCE: Verbal/Linguistic, Bodily/Kinesthetic, and Musical/Rhythmic

CONTENT/STANDARD FOCUS: Language Arts— Standards 4, 5, 8, 11, and 12

PRODUCT/PERFORMANCE/STUDENT OUTCOME: Television Project

"SOME INTERESTING TELEVISION-RELATED PROJECTS" (page 296)

Review the project options with students on the student activity sheet. Instruct students to select one of the tasks to complete, and provide time for students to share their finished products with one another, if possible.

SMUGGLING MORE HUMOR INTO THE CLASSROOM

PURPOSE: To implement one or more strategies that make humor work effectively in the classroom as an instructional tool

TARGETED INTELLIGENCE: All Intelligences

CONTENT/STANDARD FOCUS: All Subject Areas

PRODUCT/PERFORMANCE/STUDENT OUTCOME: Series of Humorous Events/Tasks

"SMUGGLING MORE HUMOR INTO THE CLASSROOM" (page 297)

Divide students into small cooperative learning groups, and ask each group to review the list of strategies for "smuggling" more humor into the classroom. Ask each group to select one of the suggested tasks/events from the list to implement collaboratively with their peers. Develop a Classroom Humor Implementation Plan to help students "pull off" their ideas.

©2004 Incentive Publications, Inc.
Nashville, TN

THE ART AND SCIENCE OF PERSUASION

PURPOSE: To investigate the different value-laden techniques of advertising in the media

TARGETED INTELLIGENCE: Verbal/Linguistic, Logical/Mathematical, Visual/Spatial, and Intrapersonal

CONTENT/STANDARD FOCUS: Language Arts—Standards 4, 5, 8, and 11 & Social Studies—Production, Consumption, and Distribution; Individual Development and Identity; Science, Technology, and Society

PRODUCT/PERFORMANCE/STUDENT OUTCOME: Discussion and Piece of Advertising

"THE ART AND SCIENCE OF PERSUASION" (page 298)

Discuss the multiple values of different populations in our society and how advertisers cater to these values. Spend time with students discussing many of the television, radio, and magazine promotional gimmicks that are used by sponsors in their advertising to influence consumer spending. Use the questions on the student activity sheet to guide the discussion. Finally, instruct students to use one of the value-oriented advertising strategies to create an original ad, as suggested on the student activity sheet.

CENSORSHIP IN THE MEDIA

PURPOSE: To examine the role of censorship in these situations: banning of books in the library, rating of films in the movie industry, and freedom of speech in newspapers

TARGETED INTELLIGENCE: Logical/Mathematical and Intrapersonal

CONTENT/STANDARD FOCUS: Social Studies—Individual Development and Identity; Individuals, Groups, and Institutions; Culture; Science, Technology, and Society

PRODUCT/PERFORMANCE/STUDENT OUTCOME: Set of Reaction Paragraphs

"CENSORSHIP IN THE MEDIA" (page 299)

Briefly define the concept of "censorship" as it relates to these three enterprises: banning of books in the public/school library, rating of films in the movie industry, and freedom of speech in newspapers. Ask students to complete a series of reaction paragraphs to each of these censorship issues, expressing their personal thoughts and convictions.

LEARNING TO WRITE A MEDIA REVIEW

PURPOSE: To write a review of a multimedia source or program

TARGETED INTELLIGENCE: Verbal/Linguistic, Visual/Spatial, and Intrapersonal

CONTENT/STANDARD FOCUS: Language Arts—Standards 1, 3, 6, 8, 11, and 12

PRODUCT/PERFORMANCE/STUDENT OUTCOME: Book, Film, Magazine, Television, or Website Review

"LEARNING TO WRITE A MEDIA REVIEW" (page 300)

Share various types of reviews with students on a current book, film, magazine, television show, or Internet website. Discuss both the purpose and structure of a review, using specific examples whenever possible. Require students to select a current and/or popular book, film, magazine, television show, or website to use as a basis for writing an original review. Encourage students to write a review that is appropriate for the age of their peer group and that uses both facts and opinions to make salient points.

YOU, TOO, CAN BE A COMEDIAN!

PURPOSE: To use a series of humorous springboards as the basis for creating original student adaptations

TARGETED INTELLIGENCE: Verbal/Linguistic and Visual/Spatial

CONTENT/STANDARD FOCUS: Language Arts—Standards 4, 5, 6, 11, and 12

PRODUCT/PERFORMANCE/STUDENT OUTCOME: Samples of Original Humor

"YOU, TOO, CAN BE A COMEDIAN!" (page 301)

Review the examples of different types of humor on the student activity sheet. Discuss the unique springboards for: Daffy Definitions, Puns, Hink Pinks, Paraphrased Proverbs, and Hidden Meanings. Then, have students create humorous examples of their own, using one or more of the humor springboard models.

©2004 INCENTIVE PUBLICATIONS, Inc.
Nashville, TN

HOLD A CLASSROOM JOKE MARATHON

PURPOSE: To organize a classroom Joke-A-Thon and measure the laughter generated for each student's joke using Kuhn's Six Stages of Laughter

TARGETED INTELLIGENCE: Verbal/Linguistic, Bodily/Kinesthetic, and Interpersonal

CONTENT/STANDARD FOCUS: Language Arts—Standards 4, 5, 11, and 12

PRODUCT/PERFORMANCE/STUDENT OUTCOME: Participation in a Joke-A-Thon

"HOLD A CLASSROOM JOKE MARATHON" (page 302)

Review each of Kuhn's Six Stages of Laughter on the student activity sheet and for fun, allow time for students to practice each level. Next, have students browse through a number of joke and riddle books or publications until they each find one or more that they want to share in a classroom joke marathon setting. Hold the marathon and have each student record on their sheets both the joke teller's name and the stage of laughter each was able to achieve from the reactions of the audience.

CREATING A HUMOR PORTFOLIO FOR FUN AND LAUGHS

PURPOSE: To create a student portfolio of humorous anecdotes and artifacts

TARGETED INTELLIGENCE: Verbal/Linguistic, Logical/Mathematical, Visual/Spatial, Bodily/Kinesthetic, and Intrapersonal

CONTENT/STANDARD FOCUS: Language Arts—Standards 1, 4, 6, 11, and 12

PRODUCT/PERFORMANCE/STUDENT OUTCOME: Portfolio of Humorous Artifacts

"CREATING A HUMOR PORTFOLIO FOR FUN AND LAUGHS" (page 303)

Introduce students to the concept of a "humor portfolio" as a collection of humorous items, anecdotes, or artifacts from a variety of sources, including books, magazines, newspapers, and websites. Allow time for students to browse through many of these resources until they are able to find an example of each type of humor listed on the student activity sheet. Instruct students to put their collection of humor in a folder complete with a table of contents and the source from which each item was selected.

THEME: BOOKS AND MEDIA   VALUE: HUMOR

HOW DO YOU FEEL ABOUT READING?

Directions: Write a response to each of these "How Do You Feel About Reading?" questions. Review your responses, and based on your own self-analysis, rate your comfort level about reading on a 1 to 5 point scale with 1 = "I don't like to read very much" and 5 = "I would rather read than do most anything."

1. How do you feel about having free time to do anything you want, with one of your choices being to read a book without interruption?

   MY RESPONSE: _____

2. How do you feel when finishing a book that you have enjoyed? Do you look back over the pages, read the review on the cover, or take a few minutes to reflect on the story line?

   MY RESPONSE: _____

3. How do you feel about going to the school or public library to select a book to read? Do you take your time to find something or are you likely to make a choice and leave quickly?

   MY RESPONSE: _____

4. How do you feel about being required to read books of many different authors and genres?

   MY RESPONSE: _____

5. How do you feel about reading and taking notes from a textbook as an out-of-class homework assignment versus doing your reading for information from websites on the Internet?

   MY RESPONSE: _____

6. How do you feel when others inquire about what you are reading? Do you agree with the idea that "a book is only half read until you talk about it?"

   MY RESPONSE: _____

7. When waiting for appointments in a doctor or dentist office, do you find yourself reading books or magazine articles, or just flipping through pages of magazines to fill up the time?

   MY RESPONSE: _____

8. How do you feel about the way you were taught to read in school? Was learning to read easy or hard for you?

   MY RESPONSE: _____

   CONCLUSION: On a 1 to 5 point scale, I would rate myself a _____ because _____

   _____

   _____

Name: _____

LET'S MEASURE YOUR HUMOR QUOTIENT!

Directions: Rate yourself on a scale of 1 to 5 (with 1 being untypical of you and 5 being very typical of you) when it comes to your sense of humor and your ability to laugh at yourself.

1. _____My peers in school think I am funny and consider me a delight to have in the classroom.

2. _____My friends and family outside of school consider my sense of humor to be one of my greatest personality traits.

3. _____I do not depend on off-color or unkind types of humor to be funny.

4. _____I often laugh at my own mistakes and stupidity.

5. _____I often find myself laughing at any time of day or under varied circumstances.

6. _____I get much pleasure from laughing at funny jokes and stories shared by others.

7. _____I am always on the lookout for humorous material such as cartoons, sit-coms, comic strips, or anecdotes as stimulants for my own sense of humor.

8. _____I collect humorous material just for the fun of it.

9. _____My sense of humor often reduces stress for me at home, school, or at play.

10. _____I am usually upbeat and see the glass as half full rather than half empty.

11. _____I regularly send funny notes and greeting cards to friends and family on special days.

12. _____My sense of humor often keeps me out of trouble.

13. _____I love to use humor in my classroom assignments/projects whenever I can.

14. _____I find myself acting silly when people least expect it or to relieve tension in others.

15. _____I love to laugh out loud when appropriate to do so as it makes me feel good.

16. _____I use humor as a memory device in school whenever I can.

_____SCORE: A perfect score of 80 means that you have not been honest with yourself. A score of 70 or above means you have been to humor school. A score of 60 or above means you are able to tickle the funny bones of others. A score of 50 or above means you need a remedial course in humor. A score of below 50 means you had better learn how to change a frown into a smile.

Name:

Advisory Plus!

ARE YOU A TELEVISION ADDICT?

Directions: Complete this simple Yes/No self-checklist to determine how dependent (or addicted) you are to television as a major source of entertainment in your life today.

1. _____ Do you spend more time watching TV than you do with your family and/or friends?

2. _____ Do you spend more time watching TV than you do on your computer and the Internet?

3. _____ Do you spent more time watching TV than you do playing sports or pursuing your special interests?

4. _____ Do you automatically turn on the TV when you get home from school or when you have nothing to do?

5. _____ Do you have the TV on in the background when you are doing other things such as homework, talking on the telephone, or working on a hobby?

6. _____ Do you ever read any TV magazines, guides, or program reviews?

7. _____ Do you ever pay attention to TV advertising and sometimes buy things (or ask your parents to buy things) you see advertised?

8. _____ Do you ever discuss TV programs or stars with your family members or friends?

9. _____ Do you ever imitate the speech, dress, hairstyles, or mannerisms of TV characters you admire?

10. _____ Do you ever play any games that are based on television shows such as: "Password," "Jeopardy," "Tic Tac Toe," or "Who Wants To Be A Millionaire?"

11. _____ Do you ever get excited, angry, depressed, or upset when you watch TV shows or programs?

12. _____ Do you ever think about the ways TV can influence you and your family?

13. _____ Do you think people in the real world generally act and behave like people do on TV?

14. _____ Do you ever learn anything meaningful or important from watching TV?

Name: _____

THE GENRES OF LITERATURE

Directions: A genre is a type or category of literature. Novels, poems, dramas, and short stories are all genres of fiction. Interestingly, we can also classify a novel or poem according to its own special type or genre. For example, novels might be classified as historical, adventure, realistic, fantasy, or science fiction genres. To review these important classifications of literature, read each of the definitions below and list the author and title of a book that you have read and enjoyed (or would like to read) for each genre listed here.

MY FAVORITE BOOK IN EACH GENRE

1. ADVENTURE: A book that has lots of physical action and movement and whose heroes are engaged in dangerous and exciting situations.
    TITLE and AUTHOR: _____

2. ANIMAL: A book that features animals as characters and has a plot that revolves around animal lifestyles, habits, characteristics, or concerns, often mimicking those of human beings.
    TITLE and AUTHOR: _____

3. BIOGRAPHY: A book written about the history of a person's life, using factual information from letters, diaries, documents, and eyewitness accounts.
    TITLE and AUTHOR: _____

4. FANTASY or FAIRY TALES: A book that is set in an unreal or imaginary world and which deals with the concerns and events of unreal characters.
    TITLE and AUTHOR: _____

5. HISTORICAL FICTION: A book that is based on real times, places, events, and people, but features imaginary or fictional characters in the action of the story.
    TITLE and AUTHOR: _____

6. MYSTERY: A book that offers clues to solve a crime or discover the truth. Full of suspense and plot twists, these books take the reader and the characters on a wild ride.
    TITLE and AUTHOR: _____

7. NONFICTION: A book that is factual and informative in presenting its subject matter.
    TITLE and AUTHOR: _____

8. POETRY: A book of varied and colorful poetic styles and forms that uses descriptive words, phrases, and images to convey a visual picture, message, or story.
    TITLE and AUTHOR: _____

9. REALISTIC: A book that deals with people, places, and events that are familiar to us because they focus on our own everyday experiences and circumstances.
    TITLE and AUTHOR: _____

10. SCIENCE FICTION: A book that transports students through time and also to different places and realms, often taking place in a reality unlike our own.
    TITLE and AUTHOR: _____

Name: _____

INTRODUCING THE ELEMENTS OF LITERATURE

Directions: All novels and short stories have a set of key elements that readers should be able to recognize and describe when sharing the details of a story or book they have read. Choose a favorite story or book you have enjoyed recently and construct a chart of two columns on the other side of this paper. In the first column, list the ten literary terms listed below, and in the second column, describe these elements as they apply to your chosen story.

LITERARY ELEMENTS TO USE

1. SETTING: the time and place in which a story takes place

2. PROTAGONIST: the main character in a story; the hero or heroine

3. ANTAGONIST: the most prominent character who opposes the protagonist; the villain

4. CONFLICT: the primary battle or problem faced by the protagonist
   INTERNAL CONFLICT: the struggle within a character
   EXTERNAL CONFLICT: the character's struggle with an outside force

5. CLIMAX: the turning point of the plot or story action, usually characterized by great intensity

6. FALLING ACTION: the plot events immediately following the climax that lead to the resolution

7. POINT OF VIEW: the perspective from which a story is told

8. THEME: the author's message or the main idea of the story

9. MOOD: the general feeling evoked in a reader through the author's use of words

10. PLOT: the sequence of major story events

Name: _____

                    ©2004 Incentive Publications, Inc.
Nashville, TN

A SURVEY OF YOUR HUMOR HISTORY

Directions: Complete each of these humor-related starter statements using your best thinking and writing.

1. Some things that are done at home, school, or play that encourage my sense of humor are: _____

   _____

2. Some things that are done at home, school, or play to discourage my sense of humor are:

   _____

3. Some inappropriate uses of humor I have encountered at home, school, or play are:

   _____

4. A funny thing that happened to me recently at home, school, or play was: _____

   _____

5. People I have considered to be funniest in my life are those who: _____

   _____

6. A time I really had to laugh at myself was when: _____

   _____

7. The average child laughs 400 times a day, while the average adult laughs only 15 times a day, which leads me to think that: _____

   _____

8. As I look back over the past few weeks/months, I would have to say that these are my funniest choices to date:

   Funniest Movie: _____

   Funniest Television Show: _____

   Funniest Book: _____

   Funniest Classmate: _____

   Funniest Adult: _____

   Funniest Comic Strip: _____

Name: _____

TYPES OF WRITING FOUND IN BOOKS, NEWSPAPERS, MAGAZINES, AND WEBSITES

Directions: Learn the four different types or styles of writing that are most commonly found in media today. Try your hand at writing a short paragraph for each style, using the suggested springboard given, or making up one of your own.

1. DESCRIPTIVE WRITING: This type of writing employs details to tell about a given subject. Describe a video game, sport, or other activity that you enjoy doing. Describe a person or hero that you have always admired.

_____

_____

_____

_____

2. ANALYTICAL WRITING: This type of writing explains how to do something, and often makes inferences and draws conclusions about people, places, or things. Explain the causes and effects of pollution, prejudice, or terrorism. Tell why you favored a particular book, movie, or video game.

_____

_____

_____

_____

3. NARRATIVE WRITING: This type of writing tells what happened and shares both feelings and emotions in the process of doing so. Create your own tall tale, legend, poem, or fairy tale. Write about a time when you made a fool of yourself, or when you did someone a big favor.

_____

_____

_____

_____

4. PERSUASIVE WRITING: This type of writing urges others to understand and support your point of view on an issue or topic. Tell the pros and cons of running for office or trying out for a sports team. Explain why young people should not do drugs or smoke cigarettes.

_____

_____

_____

_____

Name: _____

A LAUGH A DAY KEEPS THE DOCTOR AWAY

Directions: Did you know that there are many physical, emotional, psychological, and intellectual benefits to be gained from using humor in the classroom or workplace? Review each of the benefits outlined below, and relate a personal time when you actually experienced this benefit from humor or laughter. Be ready to share your humor-related experiences or anecdotes with others in your group.

1. People who can laugh together can better learn together, because laughter helps to build social bonds and relationships among students.

2. The body releases certain chemicals and hormones called endorphins during laughter, which act as a stress reducers, thus making the learner more alert to what is going on around him or her.

3. Laughter can open up the minds of students because it is often associated with unusual, unique, novel, or non-traditional ideas that encourage creativity.

5. A good laugh aids in retention of material because it increases student-teacher rapport and makes learning more enjoyable.

6. Humor helps students feel less threatened or embarrassed and often engages students in lively discussions because it relieves monotony and helps students stay tuned in to the lesson or lecture.

7. Humor provides temporary relief from institutional regulations and restrictions because it causes us to laugh at ourselves and our rules from time to time.

8. Laughter, humor, and funny situations provide students with outlets for "thinking outside the box."

9. Humor makes learning fun because it can help us cope with our academic problems, and can be a safety valve for aggression.

10. Humor often brings successful results in communication between student and teacher or among students when other methods have failed.

11. Laughter stimulates a mild to moderate cardiovascular workout, and helps fight the chronic pain associated with muscle tension.

12. Laughter reduces self-consciousness and boosts self-confidence.

Name:

THE GREAT TELEVISION DEBATE

Directions: Choose one of the following positions about the positive or negative impact of television on its viewers, and defend your choice in a short position paper. Then, select the best television show (if you think television is a positive influence) or the worst television show (if you think television is a negative influence) for each type of program below.

POSITION ONE: Television is an effective and efficient source of information; a vehicle for accessing important people, places, and events from locations near and far; a smorgasbord or feast of creative ideas and ideals that contribute to a successful life and existence.

POSITION TWO: Television is a medium that fosters bad behaviors, unrealistic expectations, and untruths; a "pollutant of the mind," or a form of legalized lying when it comes to advertising. It has a detrimental effect on everything from family life to political issues.

TYPES OF PROGRAMS TO CONSIDER IN LIGHT OF POSITION ONE OR POSITION TWO

1. News Broadcast _____

2. Documentary _____

3. Drama _____

4. Adventure _____

5. Soap Opera _____

6. Talk Show _____

7. Cartoon _____

8. Situation Comedy _____

9. Game _____

10. Sports _____

11. Music Video _____

12. Wildlife _____

Name: _____

THE RADIO AS A FORM OF MEDIA

Directions: Have you ever thought about the many advantages of the radio over other types of media such as television, films, and books? People can listen to the radio while doing other types of things, such as driving a car, cooking a meal, or completing a homework assignment. Even though radio does not actually provide personal contact, it creates the illusion that the communicator is speaking only to the receiver, creating a special kind of intimacy between the communicator and the listener. Radio can only send sound images, and thus it forces the listener to create personal pictures in their imaginations about what they hear. Radio messages can reach extremely large audiences at a cost much less than those transmitted by television and print media. Finally, radio messages can be prepared and broadcast on very short notice, unlike other major types of media. The radio is also a very effective and easy way to design certain types of messages, such as announcements, advertisements, and news broadcasts. Try writing a simple announcement, advertisement, or news update in the spaces below that could be used to promote your classroom or advisory program over the school's PA system and will simulate the radio broadcast process.

MY ANNOUNCEMENT:

MY ADVERTISEMENT:

MY NEWS ITEM:

Name:

Advisory Plus!

PUBLISHING A CLASSROOM ADVISORY NEWSPAPER

Directions: Review each of these main parts of a typical community newspaper, and then work with other members of your class to collaboratively publish a newspaper that focuses on your advisory program. Make it interesting, informative, entertaining, and interpretive. Create the newspaper as a tool to share information about the advisory and classroom program with parents. To begin this process, read the description of each newspaper concept in the first column, think of two or three possible topics for the concept in the second column, and then write the name(s) of individuals who are going to write an article/item related to the concept in the third column. Once this planning process is completed, all members of the class should develop their piece for the newspaper itself.

NEWSPAPER CONCEPT:	POSSIBLE TOPIC:	PERSON(S) RESPONSIBLE:
1. Lead Story—Most important news story of the day		
2. News Story—Article of factual information		
3. Feature Story—Article that is person-oriented rather than news-oriented in content		
4. Editorial—Material stating viewpoint of newspaper		
5. Editorial Cartoon—Cartoon that illustrates newspaper's opinion on an issue		
6. Book/Play/Movie Review—Review of a current event or book		
7. Display Ad—Large advertisement with bold typeface and illustrations		
8. Classified Ad—Small advertisement offering a service or item for sale		
9. Comic Strip—A humorous set of frames/balloons depicting a comical character and situation		
10. Sports/Business/Advice Column/Entertainment Sections—These are special parts of the newspaper that cater to unique interests of readers		

Name: _____

©2004 INCENTIVE Publications, Inc.
Nashville, TN

MAGAZINE MAGIC

Directions: Review the list of magazine titles below, and add some titles of your own that you enjoy reading. Then, complete each of the tasks according to directions given.

MAGAZINE TITLES TO CONSIDER FOR THIS ACTIVITY ARE ...

TV Guide, American Girl, Sports Illustrated, Ladies' Home Journal, Psychology Today, Family Circle, Time, Seventeen, Reader's Digest, Mountain Biking, Runner's World, Natural Health, Outdoor Life, Yoga, U.S. News & World Report, Parents, Consumer Reports, Life, New Yorker, Business Week, Money, Glamour, Better Homes and Gardens, Southern Living, National Geographic, Wrestling, People, Motorcycle, National Health, Vogue, Shape, Taste of Cooking

1. Pick any five magazines that you would want to subscribe to, and explain how they relate to special hobbies, interests, skills, or personality traits that you possess.

    YOUR CHOICES: _____

    _____

    _____

    _____

    _____

2. If you could choose a magazine for each of the following people in you life, which one would you select for your (a) best friend; (b) father or mother; (c) favorite teacher; (d) favorite adult. Give reasons for each choice.

    YOUR CHOICES: _____

    _____

    _____

    _____

3. Design a cover for the next issue of any of the magazines listed above.

    Draw your design on the back of this sheet. If time permits, try designing an interesting layout for a page in the magazine as well.

Name: _____

SOME INTERESTING TELEVISION-RELATED PROJECTS

Directions: Choose one of these television-related projects to complete. Have fun and be sure to stretch your imagination and tease your mind when coming up with ideas.

OPTION 1: Design a simple set of exercises for a "couch potato" to do while watching television. Be sure to describe your exercises, and sketch the body actions required to do them correctly.

OPTION 2: Create a "Well-Balanced" TV diet for your family and friends. Make certain the diet is a seven-day diet and is varied in terms of time and programs to be viewed.

OPTION 3: Compose a rhythm pattern or series of musical notes that could be used by a television station as: (1) background for a talk show; (2) notification of a bad weather alert; or (3) precedent for announcing an earthshaking news event.

OPTION 4: Think of as many uses as you can for a broken television set. Consider recycling its parts and components.

OPTION 5: Write a short story about how the television got its nickname of the "boob tube" or its reputation as nothing better than "chewing gum for the eyes."

OPTION 6: Imagine that you are a television set. Describe how you are feeling on a certain day under a special set of circumstances such as: (1) You are in a playroom of preschoolers; (2) You are in a classroom of teenagers; (3) You are in the waiting room of a doctor's office; (4) You are in the limousine of an important government official on election day; (5) You are in a TV repair shop with many other broken television sets; or (6) You are mistakenly left on while the family who owns you has gone on a ten day vacation during hurricane season.

OPTION 7: Write an acrostic poem about television. Remember that an acrostic is a poem in which the first letter, word, or phrase of each line begins with a letter in the word "television."

OPTION 8: Pretend you are an eyewitness to a significant event that is occurring at this very moment. Think of a special historic, scientific, political, sporting, earthshaking or disaster-related event and record what you see and feel as you watch it unfolding again through a live television broadcast.

OPTION 9: Draw a series of cartoon bubbles and write down what your television would say if it could talk to each of the following: a computer, a radio, a CD player, a videotape, a digital camera, and a walkie-talkie.

OPTION 10: Pretend your television station is on trial for corrupting the morals, values, and ethics of the younger generation today due to the violence, sexual scenarios, and foul language often viewed during its programs. Prepare a series of remarks that could be used by attorneys for either the defense or the prosecution. Think about persons or roles you might call to testify for either side, and what position a jury might take.

Name:

SMUGGLING MORE HUMOR INTO THE CLASSROOM

Directions: Work with members of your cooperative learning group and discuss each of the suggestions below for infusing humor into your classroom setting. Then, working together in your group, prioritize the list, with 1 being your group's first choice of a humorous activity/event to implement in the classroom and 10 being your last choice. Compile the results and share them with other groups working on this project to reach a consensus as to what would be the most fun things to do in order to make humor work in the classroom. Present a "Classroom Humor Implementation Plan" to the teacher.

_____ Open up each class session with something humorous to start the period off right. Rotate students on a daily basis and have them take turns reading aloud the selection for the day. Use a search engine such as www.google.com to locate several Internet joke lists or go to www.humormatters.com/jokeof.htm on the Web.

_____ Organize a "humor day" for the school. Encourage students to dress up in silly costumes, share funny jokes and riddles, write funny plays and skits, and read funny stories, comic books or magazines. Share "Mad Libs" or write some of your own.

_____ Keep a toy box in the classroom full of fun games and props that students can use whenever things get tense, or whenever students need a change of pace.

_____ Stage a joke telling contest or marathon. Compile a classroom joke/riddle book to pass on to another class or grade.

_____ Create humor collages of funny facial expressions, cartoons, situations, advertisements, headlines, or anecdotes.

_____ Plan a silly hat, tie, or tee shirt day or a clever badge or button day. Bring funny bumper stickers to class, and display them on the bulletin board.

_____ Publish a classroom newsletter that is on the lighter side.

_____ Listen to humorous audiotapes, or watch humorous videotapes.

_____ Ask students to bring cameras to school and pose for funny pictures throughout the day. Put best photos into a "Class Clown" photo album.

_____ Force yourself to laugh. Look into mirrors and vow to make the person looking back at you laugh.

Name:

Advisory Plus!

THE ART AND SCIENCE OF PERSUASION

Directions: Have you noticed that television commercials and magazine ads use promotional strategies that are varied and that to the differing values of many populations, ranging from the very young to the very old in our culture? Some of these values are: wealth or luxury, security with little or no worries, physical attractiveness, justice or concern for others, power or strength, ego or pride, guilt or feelings of inadequacy, status or being looked up to, ease or comfort, and conformity. Browse through some different magazines, or recall some television commercials that appeal to each of these values, and write down the product and its sponsor for each one. Then, select one of these persuasive strategies to convince your teacher, parent, or guardian to give you something or allow you to do something. Consider each of the situations suggested at the bottom of the page for this purpose. Finally, take a few minutes to discuss and comment on each of these questions:

1. Why do advertisers appeal to values such as those given here? What do they hope to accomplish?

2. What sells you on a given product? When have you been disappointed in a product?

3. Why are most commercials aimed at a fifth-grade reading, listening, and comprehension level?

4. How much of advertising is truth, and how much is lies? How can you tell the difference?

5. What can you do when products don't live up their advertisements?

<u>USE ONE OF THESE VALUE-ORIENTED STRATEGIES TO. . . .</u>

1. Persuade your teachers to give you less homework.

   _____

   _____

2. Convince your principal to give you a day off from school.

   _____

   _____

3. Argue that kids should get paid for going to school.

   _____

   _____

Name: _____

CENSORSHIP IN THE MEDIA

Directions: Share your thoughts about each of these forms of censorship that exist in our world today.

- Who would want to ban books in libraries, and why? _____

  _____

- How do you feel about a person or group's right to ban books in your school or public library? _____

  _____

- Who rates films in movie theaters, and how do these affect the average moviegoer?

  _____

  _____

- How do you feel about the current movie rating system and its application or relevance to your life? _____

  _____

- Who has the ultimate responsibility for freedom of speech and the censorship of classified information in the news media? How does this work?

  _____

  _____

  _____

- How do you feel about the news media and its right to publish and say whatever it wants to emphasize on given issues? Who keeps them honest?

  _____

  _____

  _____

Name: _____

LEARNING TO WRITE A MEDIA REVIEW

Directions: Choose a current and/or popular book, film, magazine, television show, or website to review and recommend to others in your class. Use the outline below for creating your review.

NAME AND DATE_____

MY REVIEW OF _____

BOOK _____   FILM _____   MAGAZINE _____   TV SHOW _____   WEBSITE _____

1. THREE THINGS I LIKED BEST ABOUT THIS ITEM WERE _____

    _____

2. SOME THINGS I LIKED LEAST ABOUT THIS ITEM WERE _____

    _____

3. I WOULD RECOMMEND THIS ITEM TO OTHERS WHO _____

    _____

4. I WOULD NOT RECOMMEND THIS ITEM TO OTHERS WHO _____

    _____

5. SOME SUGGESTIONS I HAVE FOR IMPROVING THIS ITEM ARE _____

    _____

MY OVERALL EVALUATION OF THIS ITEM IS: _____

_____

_____

_____

_____

Name: _____

YOU, TOO, CAN BE A COMEDIAN!

Directions: Read through each of the humor samples below, and create an original one of your own following the suggested pattern or format. Do your work on the back of this sheet.

HUMOR SPRINGBOARD ONE: **Daffy Definition**

1. What is a good definition of archeology? *Answer: Digging up the past.*

2. What is justice? *Answer: What we get when the decision is in our favor.*

HUMOR SPRINGBOARD TWO: **Pun**

1. A bicycle can't stand on its own because it is too tired.

2. For a while, she had a boyfriend with a wooden leg, but then she broke it off.

HUMOR SPRINGBOARD THREE: **Hink Pink**

1. What do we call a lawful bird? *Answer: A legal eagle*

2. What do you call an imaginary pal?

   Answer: A pretend friend

HUMOR SPRINGBOARD FOUR: **Paraphrased Proverb**

1. The early bird catches the worm. "The prompt feathered friend overtakes the creepy crawler."

2. Where there's a will, there's a way. "Where there's a will, there's sure to be a won't."

HUMOR SPRINGBOARD FIVE **Hidden Meaning**

1. How is a coward like a leaky faucet? *Answer: They both run.*

2. Why did a fight break out on the train? *Answer: The conductor punched the ticket.*

Name:

HOLD A CLASSROOM JOKE MARATHON

Directions: Make certain that everyone in the class finds a joke and practices telling their joke before an audience in less than one minute. Ask students to rate one another's jokes as they are shared, using Kuhn's Six Stages of Laughter:

SMILE: Silent, voluntary, and controllable upturning of the corners of the mouth

GRIN: Silent, controllable, but uses more facial muscles and wider than smile

GIGGLE: Emergence of sound with facial muscles leading up to a full laugh

LAUGH: Involves facial and chest muscles as well as abdomen and has sound of barking or snorting

HOWL: Volume and pitch rise higher and higher and body becomes more animated

ROAR: Lose individuality as whole audience roars

RECORD EACH JOKE TELLER'S NAME IN THE FIRST COLUMN AND THE CLASS'S STAGE OF LAUGHTER IN THE SECOND COLUMN.

JOKE TELLER'S NAME	STAGE OF LAUGHTER ACHIEVED
_____	_____
_____	_____
_____	_____
_____	_____
_____	_____
_____	_____

Name: _____

CREATING A HUMOR PORTFOLIO FOR FUN AND LAUGHS

Directions: Search the Internet, school or public library, bookstores, magazines, newspapers, and other reference sources to collect and organize a sample for each of the types of humor listed below. Record the specific reference (book, website, magazine, newspaper, library book, etc.) for each item selected so that you have a bibliographic entry that is accurate and complete. Organize your collected items into a "Humor Portfolio," making certain to have a table of contents for the finished product.

CONTENTS OF MY HUMOR PORTFOLIO

1. A FAVORITE JOKE: _____

    Bibliographic Entry _____

2. A FAVORITE COMIC STRIP: _____

    Bibliographic Entry _____

3. A FAVORITE QUOTATION: _____

    Bibliographic Entry _____

4. A FAVORITE EDITORIAL CARTOON: _____

    Bibliographic Entry _____

5. A FAVORITE POEM OR LIMERICK: _____

    Bibliographic Entry _____

6. A FAVORITE PERSONAL ANECDOTE: _____

    Bibliographic Entry _____

7. A FAVORITE NEWSPAPER/MAGAZINE STORY OR ADVERTISEMENT: _____

    _____

    Bibliographic Entry _____

8. A FAVORITE ILLUSTRATION/PICTURE/PHOTOGRAPH: _____

    Bibliographic Entry _____

9. A FAVORITE MAXIM OR PROVERB: _____

    Bibliographic Entry _____

10. A FAVORITE TONGUE TWISTER OR PUN: _____

    Bibliographic Entry _____

11. A FAVORITE TYPE OF HUMOR NOT INCLUDED HERE: _____

    Bibliographic Entry _____

Name: _____

THEME: BOOKS AND MEDIA   VALUE: HUMOR

APRIL
_____

RATING SCALE: **1** – I think so   **2** – I hope so   **3** – I don't know for sure!

_____1   I learned more about myself when it comes to my reading likes, dislikes, and habits.

_____2.   I learned more about the benefits of humor for me and others at home, at school, and at play.

_____3.   I learned more about censorship in the media as it relates to banning books in the library, ratings of films in the movies, and freedom of speech in the newspapers.

_____4.   I learned how to both value and create humor in my life.

_____5.   I learned more about the positive and negative impact of television on its viewers and on my television viewing habits.

_____6.   I learned more about the four styles of writing most commonly found in today's media: descriptive, analytical, narrative, and persuasive.

_____7.   I learned how to recognize these genres of literature: adventure, animal, biography, fantasy/fairy tales, historical fiction, mysteries, poetry, realistic fiction, science fiction, and nonfiction.

_____8.   I learned how to identify these elements of good literature: setting, protagonist, antagonist, conflict, climax, falling action, point of view, theme, mood, and plot.

_____9.   I learned how to write a media review.

_____10.   I learned more about propaganda and advertising techniques used to persuade consumers.

_____11.   I learned about the major sections of the newspaper.

_____12.   I learned how various magazines are written to appeal to a person's reading preferences.

_____14.   I learned more about radio, television, and the press as a form of media.

_____15.   I learned how to compile a humor portfolio for fun and laughs.

Name: _____

MODULE NINE
MAY
✳

THEME: FUTURE   VALUE: VISION

It has been said that, "The only thing we know for sure about the future is that it will be different, that change is inevitable, and unpredictable." Is it not a certainty then, that with the evolution of modern technology, the differences are sure to be vast and far-reaching? Looking to the future, how can students of today prepare themselves for the greatest freedom of all, freedom from the fear of change?

- **LEARNING TO BE THE ME I WANT TO BE—PURPOSE:** To explore a personal vision of future life from eight different viewpoints

- **NO ONE IS AN ISLAND!—PURPOSE:** To discover ways that technology has influenced the globalization of the world

- **PREPARING A PICTURE DISPLAY OF LIFE IN YOUR SCHOOL TODAY (FOR STUDENTS OF TOMORROW)—PURPOSE:** To create a set of mock photographs that convey information about the student's school life today for prospective students of tomorrow

- **UNDERSTANDING THE PAST IN ORDER TO PREDICT THE FUTURE— PURPOSE:** To consider events of the past and the present in order to determine how these events will shape the curriculum for students of the future

- **A DILLER, A DOLLAR, A SAILOR, A SCHOLAR: WHAT WILL I BE?— PURPOSE:** To rank, in terms of importance, ten factors influencing career choices in order to summarize and better understand personal preferences related to the work world of the future

- **FREE TO BE YOU AND ME—PURPOSE:** To contemplate the future and what it may hold

- **LEARNING TO THINK CREATIVELY ABOUT THE FUTURE—PURPOSE:** To view the future in highly creative terms

- **GOVERNMENT OF THE PEOPLE, FOR THE PEOPLE, AND BY THE PEOPLE— PURPOSE:** To explore ways that different governments around the world perceive problems related to the needs of young people

- **ENVISIONING A PERFECT COMMUNITY FOR LIFE IN THE FUTURE— PURPOSE:** To describe the features essential to building a place for future generations

- **DEVELOPING A COMMON LANGUAGE TO BETTER COMBAT INTOLERANCE— PURPOSE:** To define those terms most commonly associated with prejudice, discrimination, and stereotypes

- **BREAKING THE CYCLE OF PREJUDICE TO MAKE A BETTER WORLD FOR TOMORROW—PURPOSE:** To think of ways to combat prejudice and to break the cycle of hate through knowledge and mini-projects

- **PICTURING THE FUTURE—PURPOSE:** To complete a futuristic drawing exercise

- **EVALUATING YOUR SCHOOL CLIMATE AS RELATED TO PREPARATION FOR STUDENT SUCCESS IN THE WORK WORLD OF TOMORROW—PURPOSE:** To determine and offer improvements for student preparation for the world of work

- **THINGS THAT MIGHT MAKE THE FUTURE BRIGHTER—PURPOSE:** To complete a simple task that positively impacts one's perception of the future

- **DESIGNING A BILLBOARD TO PROMOTE CONSERVATION—PURPOSE:** To create a lifelike billboard to advertise the natural resources of the United States

- **TO RECYCLE OR NOT TO RECYCLE—PURPOSE:** To examine the concept of recycling and its implications for society

- **CONSUMERISM AND CAREERS OF THE FUTURE—PURPOSE:** To determine potential products, services, and careers relevant to the future

- **SYMBOLS SAY A LOT—PURPOSE:** To create a series of symbols to serve as reminders of values important to freedom, peace, tolerance, and hope for future generations

- **SOLVING SERIOUS PROBLEMS TODAY FOR A BETTER TOMORROW— PURPOSE:** To generate possible solutions to ten world problems that exist today and influence tomorrow

- **WHAT DOES THE FUTURE HOLD FOR YOU?—PURPOSE:** To plan and conduct a poll about student attitudes and perceptions of the future and what it holds for them

---

©2004 Incentive Publications, Inc.
Nashville, TN

THEME: **FUTURE**   VALUE: **VISION**

A famous artist once said: "Map out your future, but do it in pencil." Think about what he meant by this statement. Then, use a pencil to sketch out a visual map or timeline of the major milestones that you expect to achieve throughout your life span. Consider highlights such as high school graduation, entry into the job market, career goals, family aspirations, and other important highlights you hope your future will hold.

One of America's greatest statesmen and presidents said, "Those who desire to give up freedom in order to gain security will never have, nor do they deserve, either one." Ponder this statement as it relates to the future of your country and agree or disagree with President Jefferson's statement. Write a short essay expressing your views.

_____

_____

_____

_____

_____

_____

_____

THEME: FUTURE   VALUE: VISION

WEEK ONE

DAY ONE	**"Learning to Be the Me I Want to Be"** Exploring a personal vision of future life from eight different viewpoints
DAY TWO	**"No One Is an Island!"** Discovering ways that technology has influenced the globalization of the world
DAY THREE	**"Preparing a Picture Display of Life in Your School Today (For Students of Tomorrow)"** Creating a set of mock photographs that convey information about the student's school life today for prospective students of tomorrow
DAY FOUR	**"Understanding the Past In Order to Predict the Future"** Considering events of the past and the present in order to determine how these events will shape the curriculum for students of the future
DAY FIVE	**"A Diller, A Dollar, A Sailor, a Scholar: What Will I Be?"** Ranking, in terms of importance, ten factors influencing career choices of the future in order to summarize and better understand personal preferences related to the work world of the future

WEEK TWO

DAY ONE	**"Free to Be You and Me"** Contemplating the future and what it may hold
DAY TWO	**"Learning to Think Creatively About the Future"** Viewing the future in highly creative terms
DAY THREE	**"Government Of the People, By the People, and For the People"** Exploring ways that different governments around the world perceive problems related to the needs of young people
DAY FOUR	**"Envisioning a Perfect Community for Life in the Future"** Describing the essential features of a place for future generations
DAY FIVE	**"Developing a Common Language to Better Combat Intolerance"** Defining those terms most commonly associated with prejudice, discrimination, and stereotypes

©2004 Incentive Publications, Inc.
Nashville, TN

THEME: FUTURE   VALUE: VISION

WEEK THREE

DAY ONE	**"Breaking the Cycle of Prejudice to Make a Better World for Tomorrow"** Thinking of ways to combat prejudice and to break the cycle of hate through knowledge and activities
DAY TWO	**"Picturing the Future"** Completing a futuristic drawing exercise
DAY THREE	**"Evaluating Your School Climate as Related To Preparation for Student Success in the Work World of Tomorrow"** Determining and offering improvements for student preparation for the world of work
DAY FOUR	**"Things that Might Make the Future Brighter"** Completing a simple task that positively impacts one's perception of the future
DAY FIVE	**"Designing a Billboard to Promote Conservation"** Creating a lifelike billboard to advertise the natural resources of the United States

WEEK FOUR

DAY ONE	**"To Recycle or Not to Recycle"** Examining the concept of recycling and its implications for society
DAY TWO	**"Consumerism and Careers of the Future"** Determining potential products, services, and careers relevant to the future
DAY THREE	**"Symbols Say a Lot"** Creating a series of symbols to serve as reminders of values important to freedom, peace, tolerance, and hope for future generations
DAY FOUR	**"Solving Serious Problems Today for a Better Tomorrow"** Generating possible solutions to ten world problems that exist today and influence tomorrow
DAY FIVE	**"What Does the Future Hold for You?"** Planning and conducting a poll about student attitudes and perceptions of the future and what it holds for them

LEARNING TO BE THE ME I WANT TO BE

PURPOSE: To explore a personal vision of future life from eight different viewpoints

TARGETED INTELLIGENCE: Intrapersonal, Interpersonal, and Verbal/Linguistic

CONTENT/STANDARD FOCUS: Language Arts—Standards 3, 5, 12 & Social Studies— Individuals, Groups, and Institutions; Culture; Time, Continuity, and Change; Individual Development and Identity

PRODUCT/PERFORMANCE/STUDENT OUTCOME: Completion of the eight part graphic organizer, "Learning to Be the Me I Want to Be"

"LEARNING TO BE THE ME I WANT TO BE" (page 320)

Discuss the circles on the activity sheet in a total group setting. Then, ask the students to think carefully about each one before writing a very personal response. Ask them to review the completed diagram, beginning with one and moving around the center circle through eight to get a composite look at their vision of life as an adult.

NO ONE IS AN ISLAND!

PURPOSE: To discover ways that technology has influenced the globalization of the world

TARGETED INTELLIGENCE: Logical/Mathematical, Visual/Spatial, and Intrapersonal

CONTENT/STANDARD FOCUS: Social Studies—Global Connections; Science, Technology, and Society & Science— Science and Technology; Science in Personal and Social Perspectives

PRODUCT/PERFORMANCE/STUDENT OUTCOME: Reaction Paragraphs

"NO ONE IS AN ISLAND!" (page 321)

Introduce the concepts of "globalization" and "global village" to students. Ask students to reflect on reasons why the world has "gotten smaller," leading to the notion that "No man is an island." Then, instruct students to complete the reaction paragraphs on the student activity sheet according to directions given.

PREPARING A PICTURE DISPLAY OF LIFE IN YOUR SCHOOL TODAY (FOR STUDENTS OF TOMORROW)

PURPOSE: To create a set of mock photographs that conveys information about a student's school life today for prospective students of tomorrow

TARGETED INTELLIGENCE: Verbal/Linguistic, Visual/Spatial, and Interpersonal

CONTENT/STANDARD FOCUS: Language Arts—Standards 5, 11, and 12 & Social Studies—Individuals, Groups, and Institutions

PRODUCT/PERFORMANCE/STUDENT OUTCOME: Set of Descriptive Photos

"PREPARING A PICTURE DISPLAY OF LIFE IN YOUR SCHOOL TODAY (FOR STUDENTS OF TOMORROW)" (page 322) Encourage students to think of the things that would be of most interest to future students who will be attending their school decades down the road. Ask students to write six different descriptive paragraphs in each photo square on the student activity sheet that would best describe "life in their school" at this point in time. Then, if possible, provide students with a camera and film to translate their photo descriptions into real photographic images.

UNDERSTANDING THE PAST IN ORDER TO PREDICT THE FUTURE

PURPOSE: To consider events of the past and the present in order to determine how these events will shape the curriculum for students of the future

TARGETED INTELLIGENCE: Verbal/Linguistic, Intrapersonal, and Interpersonal

CONTENT/STANDARD FOCUS: Language Arts—Standards 2, 5, and 7 & Social Studies—Time, Continuity, and Change; Global Connections & Science—Science in Personal and Social Perspectives; History and Nature of Science.

PRODUCT/PERFORMANCE/STUDENT OUTCOME: Science or Social Studies unit topics and outline.

"UNDERSTANDING THE PAST IN ORDER TO PREDICT THE FUTURE" (page 323) Distribute and discuss the activity sheets. Then, ask students to work in small groups to complete the activities according to the directions given. Ask each group to appoint a spokesperson to verbally share the group's titles and outline with the total group. Provide time for discussion of unit topics, and the reasons for their selection.

A DILLER, A DOLLAR, A SAILOR, A SCHOLAR: WHAT WILL I BE?

PURPOSE: To rank order, in terms of importance, ten factors influencing career choices of the future, in order to summarize and better understand personal preferences related to the work-world of the future

TARGETED INTELLIGENCE: Verbal/Linguistic, Intrapersonal

CONTENT/STANDARD FOCUS: Language Arts—Standards 4, 5, 7, & Social Studies—Time, Continuity, and Change; Individual Development and Identity

PRODUCT/PERFORMANCE/STUDENT OUTCOME: Summary statement of a personal vision of a future career

"A DILLER, A DOLLAR, A SAILOR, A SCHOLAR: WHAT WILL I BE?" (page 324)

Present the activity sheet to students and provide time for completion and class discussion.

FREE TO BE YOU AND ME

PURPOSE: To contemplate the future and what it may hold

TARGETED INTELLIGENCE: Verbal/Linguistic, Logical/Mathematical, and Intrapersonal

CONTENT/STANDARD FOCUS: Language Arts—Standards 3, 4, 6, 11, and 12

PRODUCT/PERFORMANCE/STUDENT OUTCOME: Piece of Original Writing

"FREE TO BE YOU AND ME" (page 325)

Review each of the ten options available to students on the student activity sheet. Discuss the many writing formats that are available to the students when selecting a task to complete. Collect finished work and display for others in the class to enjoy.

©2004 Incentive Publications, Inc. Nashville, TN

LEARNING TO THINK CREATIVELY ABOUT THE FUTURE

PURPOSE: To view the future in highly creative terms

TARGETED INTELLIGENCE: Verbal/Linguistic, Logical/Mathematical, and Visual/Spatial

CONTENT/STANDARD FOCUS: Language Arts—Standards 4, 11, and 12 & Social Studies—Science, Technology, and Society

PRODUCT/PERFORMANCE/STUDENT OUTCOME: Series of Creative Responses

"LEARNING TO THINK CREATIVELY ABOUT THE FUTURE" (page 326)

Review each of the creative tasks listed on the student activity sheet. Discuss what is involved in each task, and encourage students to select one they would like to complete.

A GOVERNMENT OF THE PEOPLE, BY THE PEOPLE, AND FOR THE PEOPLE

PURPOSE: To explore ways that different governments around the world perceive problems related to the needs of young people

TARGETED INTELLIGENCE: Verbal/Linguistic, Logical/Mathematical, Interpersonal, and Intrapersonal

CONTENT/STANDARD FOCUS: Language Arts—Standards 1, 3, 5, 7, 8, and 11 & Social Studies—Culture; Individuals, Groups, and Institutions; Power, Authority, and Governance; Science, Technology, and Society; Global Connections

PRODUCT/PERFORMANCE/STUDENT OUTCOME: Research and Group Discussion

"A GOVERNMENT OF THE PEOPLE, BY THE PEOPLE, AND FOR THE PEOPLE"

(page 327) Provide time and resources for students to research the basic structures of several different types of governments around the world. Then, instruct students to complete the questions on the student activity sheet based on their research findings. Finally, lead students in a group discussion on ways that different governments around the world do or do not handle problems related to the needs of young people.

ENVISIONING A PERFECT COMMUNITY FOR LIFE IN THE FUTURE

PURPOSE: To describe the features essential to building a place for future generations

TARGETED INTELLIGENCE: Logical/Mathematical, Visual/Spatial, and Naturalistic

CONTENT/STANDARD FOCUS: Social Studies—People, Places, and Environments; Individuals, Groups, and Institutions; Production, Distribution, and Consumption; Science, Technology, and Society & Science—Life Science; Earth and Space Science; Science and Technology; Science in Personal and Social Perspectives

PRODUCT/PERFORMANCE/STUDENT OUTCOME: Creative Description

"ENVISIONING A PERFECT COMMUNITY FOR LIFE IN THE FUTURE" (page 328)

Spend a few minutes asking students to think about a special community, other than their own, that they know something about. Encourage students to think about this location from several perspectives including its demographics, topography, natural resources, educational and career opportunities, industries, and amenities. Knowledge of the community could be gained from reading, study, or personal experience. Have the students imagine a utopian location that would be a perfect place in which to live and work as adults, and write a brief description of its unique characteristics.

DEVELOPING A COMMON LANGUAGE TO BETTER COMBAT INTOLERANCE

PURPOSE: To define those terms most commonly associated with prejudice, discrimination, and stereotypes

TARGETED INTELLIGENCE: Verbal/Linguistic, Visual/Spatial, and Bodily/Kinesthetic

CONTENT/STANDARD FOCUS: Language Arts—Standards 3 and 9 & Social Studies—Culture, Individuals, Groups, and Institutions

PRODUCT/PERFORMANCE/STUDENT OUTCOME: Set of Flash Cards or Game Cards

"DEVELOPING A COMMON LANGUAGE TO BETTER COMBAT INTOLERANCE"

(page 329) Review the terms and definitions described on the student activity sheet. Then, provide students with a supply of blank file cards and either magic markers, crayons, or colored pencils, and instruct them to make a set of flash or game cards according to directions given. Allow time for students to learn the vocabulary terms by using the flash cards or game cards in an informal setting.

BREAKING THE CYCLE OF PREJUDICE TO MAKE A BETTER WORLD FOR TOMORROW

PURPOSE: To think of ways to combat prejudice and to break the cycle of hate through knowledge and activities

TARGETED INTELLIGENCE: All Intelligences

CONTENT/STANDARD FOCUS: Language Arts—Standards 4, 5, 7, 9, and 11 & Social Studies—Culture; People, Places, and Environments; Global Connections

PRODUCT/PERFORMANCE/STUDENT OUTCOME: Mini-Project

"BREAKING THE CYCLE OF PREJUDICE TO MAKE A BETTER WORLD" (page 330)

Ask students to elaborate on these questions: What causes prejudice in our society? How does prejudice lead to feelings of hate and hate crimes in our country? What does one have to do to break these cycles of prejudice and hate throughout the world? Next, review each of the activities on the student activity sheet and have students select one of the mini-projects to complete.

PICTURING THE FUTURE

PURPOSE: To complete a futuristic drawing exercise

TARGETED INTELLIGENCE: Visual/Spatial, Bodily/Kinesthetic, and Intrapersonal

CONTENT/STANDARD FOCUS: Science—Physical Science; Life Science; Earth and Space Science; Science and Technology; Science in Personal and Social Perspectives

PRODUCT/PERFORMANCE/STUDENT OUTCOME: Original Drawing

"PICTURING THE FUTURE" (page 331)

Provide students with supplies of drawing paper and drawing utensils such as crayons, magic markers, colored pencils, colored chalk, or even watercolors, if available. Then, instruct students to select one of the springboards on the student activity sheet as the subject for a personal drawing or sketch.

EVALUATING YOUR SCHOOL CLIMATE AS RELATED TO PREPARATION FOR STUDENT SUCCESS IN THE WORK WORLD OF TOMORROW

PURPOSE: To determine and offer improvements for student preparation for the world of work

TARGETED INTELLIGENCE: Interpersonal, Logical/Mathematical

CONTENT/STANDARD FOCUS: Social Studies—Culture; People, Places, and Environments; Individuals, Groups, and Institutions; Civic Ideals and Practices & Language Arts—Standards 5, 6, and 12

PRODUCT/PERFORMANCE/STUDENT OUTCOME: Completion of the student activity sheet in accordance with Williams' Taxonomy

"EVALUATING YOUR SCHOOL CLIMATE AS RELATED TO PREPARATION FOR STUDENT SUCCESS IN THE WORK WORLD OF TOMORROW" (page 332)

Present the activity sheet to students and ask them to review each of the seven tasks, reflecting on how they would respond to each one. Instruct them to then select one task to complete.

THINGS THAT MIGHT MAKE THE FUTURE BRIGHTER

PURPOSE: To complete a simple task that could positively affect the future from an imaginative and hypothetical point of view

TARGETED INTELLIGENCE: All Intelligences

CONTENT/STANDARD FOCUS: Social Studies—Time, Continuity, and Change; People, Places, and Environments; Individual Development and Identity; Individuals, Groups, and Institutions; Science, Technology, and Society & Science—Science and Technology; Science in Personal and Social Perspectives

PRODUCT/PERFORMANCE/STUDENT OUTCOME: Mini-Task

"THINGS THAT MIGHT MAKE THE FUTURE BRIGHTER" (page 333)

Review each of the mini-tasks outlined on the student activity sheet, and have each student select one or more to complete and share with one another.

DESIGNING A BILLBOARD TO PROMOTE CONSERVATION

PURPOSE: To create a lifelike billboard to advertise the natural resources of the United States

TARGETED INTELLIGENCE: Visual/Spatial, Bodily/Kinesthetic, and Intrapersonal

CONTENT/STANDARD FOCUS: Social Studies—Individual Development and Identity; Individuals, Groups, and Institutions; Civic Ideals and Practices

PRODUCT/PERFORMANCE/STUDENT OUTCOME: A king-sized billboard

"DESIGNING A BILLBOARD TO PROMOTE CONSERVATION" (page 334)

Discuss the concept of the "billboard" as a form of advertising in today's society. Think about both the sources and topics of these billboards that one sees while traveling throughout a given area. How many of them do you think advertise products that are detrimental to or wasteful of our country's natural resources? How many encourage wise use or conservation of these same or comparable resources? Finally, ask students to create a mock billboard design that would remind motorists and tourists to care for the earth and preserve its resources.

TO RECYCLE OR NOT TO RECYCLE

PURPOSE: To reflect upon the concept of recycling goods and products as a means of conserving the world's natural resources.

TARGETED INTELLIGENCE: Verbal/Linguistic, Logical/Mathematical, Interpersonal, Intrapersonal, and Naturalistic

CONTENT/STANDARD FOCUS: Language Arts—Standards 5, 11, and 12 & Social Studies—Science, Technology, and Society & Science—Science in Personal and Social Perspectives

PRODUCT/PERFORMANCE/STUDENT OUTCOME: Letter to the Editor

"TO RECYCLE OR NOT TO RECYCLE" (page 335)

Introduce to students the subject of recycling goods and products in order to protect the earth's resources, and ask them to think about the recycling process from a scientific as well as social point of view. Next, encourage the students to discuss each of the four questions on the student activity sheet. Finally, instruct each student to write a letter to the editor of their local newspaper, commenting on their perceptions and feelings about recycling as it relates to the future.

CONSUMERISM AND CAREERS OF THE FUTURE

PURPOSE: To determine potential products, services, and careers relevant to the future

TARGETED INTELLIGENCE: Verbal/Linguistic, Visual/Spatial, and Bodily/Kinesthetic

CONTENT/STANDARD FOCUS: Language Arts—Standards 5, 11, and 12 & Social Studies—Production, Distribution, and Consumption; Science, Technology, and Society & Science—Science in Personal and Social Perspectives

PRODUCT/PERFORMANCE/STUDENT OUTCOME: Yellow Page Ad and Classified Ad

"CONSUMERISM AND CAREERS OF THE FUTURE" (page 336)

Share examples of both Yellow Page ads from the local telephone directory and classified ads from the local newspaper. Discuss their purpose, format, and use in the local area. Next, instruct students to select one of the futuristic jobs on the student activity sheet and use it as the basis for constructing either a future-oriented Yellow Page ad, a classified ad, or both. Finally, ask students to think about what products and services these jobs would offer to future citizens.

SYMBOLS SAY A LOT

PURPOSE: To create a series of symbols to serve as reminders of values important to freedom, peace, tolerance, and hope for future generations

TARGETED INTELLIGENCE: Verbal/Linguistic, Visual/Spatial

CONTENT/STANDARD FOCUS: Language Arts—Standards 1, 4, and 7 & Social Studies—Culture; Civic Ideals and Practices

PRODUCT/PERFORMANCE/STUDENT OUTCOME: Completion of the symbols for peace, hope, freedom, and tolerance

"SYMBOLS SAY A LOT" (page 337)

Distribute the student activity sheet and ask students to complete the symbols as directed. Provide space for displaying the completed work, and time for students to view and discuss individual interpretations of the symbols.

©2004 Incentive Publications, Inc.
Nashville, TN

SOLVING SERIOUS PROBLEMS TODAY FOR A BETTER TOMORROW

PURPOSE: To generate possible solutions to ten world problems that exist today and influence tomorrow

TARGETED INTELLIGENCE: Logical/Mathematical and Naturalistic

CONTENT/STANDARD FOCUS: Social Studies—People, Places, and Environments; Culture; Global Connections & Science—Science in Personal and Social Perspectives & Mathematics—Mathematics as Communication

PRODUCT/PERFORMANCE/STUDENT OUTCOME: Problem/Solution Chart

"SOLVING SERIOUS PROBLEMS TODAY FOR A BETTER TOMORROW" (page 338)

Review the ten world problems listed on the student activity sheet, and encourage students to rank order them as a group from the most important or pressing problem to the least important or pressing problem. Then, divide students into small cooperative learning groups, and have each group offer a possible solution or suggestion for dealing with each of the ten problems.

WHAT DOES THE FUTURE HOLD FOR YOU?

PURPOSE: To plan and conduct a poll about student attitudes and perceptions of the future and what it holds for them

TARGETED INTELLIGENCE: Logical/Mathematical, Bodily/Kinesthetic, and Interpersonal

CONTENT/STANDARD FOCUS: Mathematics—Mathematics as Reasoning; Computation and Estimation; Statistics

PRODUCT/PERFORMANCE/STUDENT OUTCOME: Conducting a Poll

"WHAT DOES THE FUTURE HOLD FOR YOU" (page 339)

Review the purposes and procedures for conducting a poll. Give examples of how polls are used to get information about candidates running for election, about viewers' reactions to new television show debuts, or even readers' attitudes towards economic issues. Review the six steps for conducting a poll on the student activity sheet. Finally, plan and implement a poll for the students in your classroom to carry out on their views or feelings about the future.

THEME: FUTURE   VALUE: VISION

LEARNING TO BE THE ME I WANT TO BE

Fill in each circle below to get a better picture of your vision of the future from a very personal standpoint.

Center circle: Learning to Be the Me I Want to Be
Circle #1: My Top Three Values Are:
Circle #2: My Top Three Goals for the Future Are:
Circle #3: My Top Three Career Choices Are:
Circle #4: One place I especially want to go as an adult is:
Circle #5: One thing I especially want to discover as an adult is:
Circle #6: Three talents and abilities I want to develop as an adult are:
Circle #7: Three things I especially want to own as an adult are:
Circle #8: The main thing I hope people will say about me as an adult is:

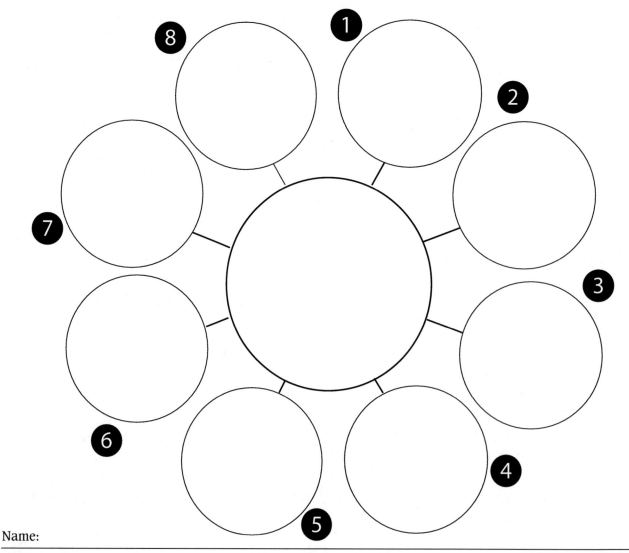

Name:

NO ONE IS AN ISLAND!

Directions: British poet John Donne once wrote: "No man is an island." Little did he realize it at the time, but in the future, our world would actually become a "global village." Think about these concepts, and record your reactions to the ideas below.

1. React to Donne's statement: "No man is an island." Do you agree or disagree that this will be more true in the near future than it is now? Why? _____

_____

_____

2. React to this idea: The concept of the world as a global village is becoming more fact than fiction with every passing day—thanks, in large part, to the evolution of technology.

_____

_____

_____

3. React to this idea: "Television has been a major influence in making the world smaller. It has even been suggested that the United Nations should establish a number of television channels that would allow all types of governments and groups to broadcast whatever messages they wished to send out to the world without cost or censor." What do you think the consequence of this suggestion becoming a reality would be?

_____

_____

_____

4. React to this idea: "The computer and the Internet have only just begun to eliminate world borders and bring cultures, countries, and continents closer together." Do you agree or disagree? Be specific.

_____

_____

_____

5. React to this idea: "The future success of the space program is important when it comes to global interdependence." Do you agree or disagree? Be specific.

_____

_____

_____

Name:

Advisory Plus!

PREPARING A PICTURE DISPLAY OF LIFE IN YOUR SCHOOL TODAY (FOR STUDENTS OF TOMORROW)

Directions: Have you ever thought about how much information a picture can really convey to others about a given person, place, or thing? Your task is to think of at least six very different but informative pictures that could portray life in your school today and could be stored away as valuable references for future generations. In each of the squares below, describe in detail what each particular picture would convey to the viewer.

Name:

UNDERSTANDING THE PAST IN ORDER TO PREDICT THE FUTURE

Directions: Understanding the past and being aware of the influence of current events on one's thinking and value development provides the foundation upon which a vision of the future is built. As we study the lessons to be learned from history, we see the future begin to unfold before us.

Work in small groups of three or four to discuss the influence of the past on your present school curriculum. Then, consider the big events of life in the world today and determine how these events will shape the curriculum of students of your age in the future. Brainstorm titles of five social studies units that might be required in the future for students at your grade level. Develop an outline for one of the units.

Social Studies Units for the Future:

1. _____

2. _____

3. _____

4. _____

5. _____

Discussion Notes:

_____

_____

_____

_____

_____

_____

_____

_____

Name: _____

A DILLER, A DOLLAR, A SAILOR, A SCHOLAR: WHAT WILL I BE?

Directions: Visualizing allows one to reach beyond the realities of today to imagine and dream about the future. Visualizing the future will enable you to think clearly of places you want to go and things you want to do as an adult. As you wonder about and ponder the life you hope to be leading fifteen or twenty years from now, there are some things you can think about today to help you set realistic goals for the life you hope to be leading tomorrow.

To help you set these goals, rank the following from 1 (highest) to 10 (lowest) in order of their importance to you when think of an adult career.

_____1. Teamwork

_____2. Excitement

_____3. Fame

_____4. Money

_____5. Low stress

_____6. Challenging tasks

_____7. Learning new things

_____8. Free and/or flexible time

_____9. Service and/or community involvement

_____10. Pleasant environment

When you have completed your ranking, use this space to summarize your vision of a career for the future, as indicated by your order.

Name: _____

FREE TO BE YOU AND ME

Directions: Choose one of these writing options to put your thoughts down on paper as you contemplate what the future might bring to you in the years ahead. Use the back of this sheet to complete your chosen task.

WRITING OPTION ONE: You have started a new fad that will live on long after your death. Describe it in a newspaper article, and complete it with an exciting headline!

WRITING OPTION TWO: You have served your country well and been elected to serve in public office. Compose an acceptance speech that you will give during your formal inauguration ceremony.

WRITING OPTION THREE: As president or CEO of a large, worldwide company, you are about to write a letter to your employees reminding them of the company's success. What will you say?

WRITING OPTION FOUR: You have been recruited to create a bumper sticker for the Department of Transportation that conveys positive images about the world of tomorrow. List at least six short pieces of advice or words of wisdom that would make good copy for a set of bumper stickers.

WRITING OPTION FIVE: Special visitors from around the world are coming to visit your community and experience your lifestyle as you become a distinguished senior citizen. Plan an agenda for the day that outlines what they would do and see.

WRITING OPTION SIX: Pretend you are living in a space colony. Write a diary entry that tells what life is like in the colony.

WRITING OPTION SEVEN: You have been asked to make a list of the top ten things you have accomplished in your lifetime. Compile this list of accolades.

WRITING OPTION EIGHT: You have just been internationally recognized for your expertise in robotics. Write a postcard to your favorite robot telling him/her about this award.

WRITING OPTION NINE: Construct a Venn Diagram that compares the events of your life with that of someone from history you admire.

Name:

LEARNING TO THINK CREATIVELY ABOUT THE FUTURE

Directions: Read through these tasks with a look toward the future. Select one to complete, and do so on the back of this sheet.

CHALLENGE ONE: Pretend you have been assigned the task of creating a set of rules as master of a new and emerging universe. Based on past history and experiences, what would be on your list of things to do and things not to do?

CHALLENGE TWO: Express your feelings about the future using these language patterns:

I used to think _____ — but now I know _____

_____

The important thing about _____ is _____

_____

But the most important thing is _____

_____

CHALLENGE THREE: Explain how you would program a robot to do an important job for you using these eight commands, and one of your own choosing: move forward _____ steps; move backward _____ steps; pick up _____ (object); put down _____ (object); turn left; turn right; open up_____; close_____.
Then, design a personal robot, giving it a name and explaining all of its functions.

CHALLENGE FOUR: To improve the world and make it better for the future, what would you make larger? What would you make smaller? What would you make disappear? What would you make reappear? What would you make better? What would you make stronger?

CHALLENGE FIVE: Describe the colors, tastes, sounds, textures, and smells of the future.

CHALLENGE SIX: List as many "-ing" words as you can think of to describe the past, the present, and the future.

CHALLENGE SEVEN: Make a list of some things that are hard to envision about the future.

Name: _____

©2004 Incentive Publications, Inc.
Nashville, TN

A GOVERNMENT OF THE PEOPLE, BY THE PEOPLE, AND FOR THE PEOPLE

Directions: Compare and contrast the basic structures of several different types of governments from around the world. Consider everything from monarchies and socialism to democracies and communism. Then, draw some conclusions about how different governments are likely to respond to the concerns and needs young people of today will face as adults of tomorrow. Write your individual thoughts for each of the questions below, and use these notes as preparation for a large group discussion on the topic.

QUESTION ONE: Generally speaking, how do you think technology available for use by government officials around the world has influenced concern for the needs of kids and youth in their respective cultures? _____

_____

_____

QUESTION TWO: Do you think students in other parts of the world have the same basic concerns for the future as you do? Are students in other countries better informed about challenges the future may hold than you are? In what countries do you think they may be less informed? Explain. _____

_____

_____

QUESTION THREE: If you were going to cite a major law, mandate, or decision recently acted upon by your government that indicates a real concern for the future good of young people in today's society, which one would it be, and why? _____

_____

_____

QUESTION FOUR: If the government established a group of powerful representatives to protect the interests of young people in your culture today and to prepare them for life as adults, which priority areas would you like to see them focus on, and why? Consider health care, education, drug and substance abuse, poverty, family structure, or crime and violence.

_____

_____

_____

_____

Name: _____

ENVISIONING A PERFECT COMMUNITY FOR LIFE IN THE FUTURE

Directions: Think about a community (other than your own) that you know enough about to think it could be the place you would like to live and work in as an adult. Think about all the things that make it special. Consider demographics (size and location), topography (lay of the land), natural resources (vegetation, farmland, minerals, oil, water, and food sources), and educational and career opportunities as well as industry (factories and businesses), and amenities (parks, recreation areas, and cultural activities). Next, in the space below, list and describe the unique features of the community that would make it the perfect place in which to live and work in the future.

Name:

©2004 Incentive Publications, Inc.
Nashville, TN

DEVELOPING A COMMON LANGUAGE TO BETTER COMBAT INTOLERANCE

It is not difficult for people who look to the future optimistically to envision a world with tolerance and respect for racial and cultural differences. One way to combat intolerance and build respect for people from all backgrounds is by trying to better understand the meanings and consequences of terms related to intolerance.

Directions: Use blank file cards to create a set of flash cards or game cards for the terms listed below. If constructing flash cards, put the term on one side of the card and the definition on the other side of the card. If constructing game cards to play a memory game, make a set of cards with only the term on one side of each card and a corresponding set of cards with the definition only on one side of each card. Use these flash cards or game cards to learn the concepts related to prejudices, stereotypes, and discriminatory acts.

Anti-Semitism: A prejudice or discrimination against Jews because of their religious beliefs or their group membership

Bias: A preference either for or against an individual or group that interferes with impartial judgment

Bigotry: An irrational attachment to negative stereotypes and prejudices

Culture: A set of patterns of daily life practiced by a given group of people that includes patterns related to their language, arts, customs, celebrations, food, religion, clothing, dating rituals, and governing practices, etc.

Discrimination: A denial of justice and fair treatment by both individuals and institutions in such areas as employment, education, housing, banking, and political rights

Diversity: A reference to people from different races, cultures, and places

Hate Crime: An act by any person against another individual or group that in any way constitutes hostility toward the victim because of his/her race, religion, sexual orientation, national origin, disability, gender, or ethnicity

Multicultural: A community population of people from many different cultures

Prejudice: A pre-judging or the making of a decision about a person or group without sufficient knowledge

Racism: A type of prejudice or discrimination based on the social construction of "race," with an emphasis on differences in physical characteristics

Scapegoating: An act of blaming an individual or group for something when, in reality, there is no one person or group responsible for the problem

Sexism: A prejudice or discrimination based on gender

Stereotype: An oversimplified generalization about a person or group of people without regard for individual differences

Name:

BREAKING THE CYCLE OF PREJUDICE TO MAKE A BETTER WORLD FOR TOMORROW

Directions: Students of today can be powerful forces in breaking the cycle of prejudice and hate that exists among people. Choose one or more of these activities or projects to implement in your middle school setting to fight prejudice.

1. Create a simple flag, poster, or banner that symbolizes your school's position on diversity and multicultural issues and display it at all school events such as open houses, concerts, assemblies, and sports events.

2. Plan a student-run Speaker's Bureau of students with varied ethnic backgrounds, and encourage them to speak about their unique heritage.

3. Create a "Diversity Quilt" (paper squares will do), with each patch representing an individual's special heritage. Hang it in the school office area.

4. Write an original song/chant/rap that expresses and celebrates your school's ideal of multiculturalism, and perform it whenever you get a chance.

5. Prepare ethnic foods and cuisines to share with one another on special days.

6. Collect children's books representing the experiences of different ethnic groups, and display them in a special place in the library or media center for others to read and enjoy.

7. Display a poster size version (or print up wallet-size versions) of a campaign slogan that combats prejudice and reads something like this: "I pledge from this day onward to do my best to interrupt prejudice and to stop those who, because of hate, would hurt, harass, or violate the civil rights of another."

Name:

©2004 INCENTIVE Publications, Inc.
Nashville, TN

PICTURING THE FUTURE

Directions: Pretend you have been invited to submit a futuristic drawing to be hung in a space gallery. Choose one of these subjects for your drawing, and sketch it on the other side of this sheet.

1. Draw a picture of a spaceship traveling to another galaxy.

2. Draw a picture of your family celebrating a birthday together in outer space.

3. Draw a picture of a cultural event on the moon such as an art show, a concert, or a play on stage.

4. Draw a picture of a space station.

5. Draw a picture of a space warrior.

6. Draw a picture of children at play on the moon.

7. Draw a picture of a space settlement inhabited by people from planet Earth.

8. Draw a picture of a moonbeam.

9. Draw a picture of yourself orbiting around the earth in a spaceship.

10. Draw a picture of a space suit a visitor to the moon might wear ten years from now.

Name:

EVALUATING YOUR SCHOOL CLIMATE AS RELATED TO PREPARATION FOR STUDENT SUCCESS IN THE WORK WORLD OF TOMORROW

FLUENCY
List as many ways as you can think of that your present school climate prepares students for success in the work world of tomorrow.

FLEXIBILITY
Classify the ways listed in your fluency list, and explain your classification system.

ORIGINALITY
Think of something that you could suggest to your teachers to improve the climate in your school as it relates to student success in the work world of tomorrow.

ELABORATION
Decide which fact below contributes most to a positive climate for promoting student success in the work world of tomorrow, and be able to explain the basis of your decisions:

1. The curriculum
2. Teacher attitudes and interaction with students
3. Student behavior and interactions
4. Community/school relationships
5. Parent support and involvement
6. Facilities: plant, equipment, supplies
7. High expectations

RISK TAKING
If you could change any one thing about your school to make the climate more supportive of student success in the work world of tomorrow, what would it be?

COMPLEXITY
On a scale of one to twelve (one being the lowest, twelve the highest), rate your school climate as to its contribution to student success in the work world of tomorrow.

CURIOSITY
Formalize a good question to ask your classmates to determine the personal opinions of your peers concerning the positive or negative influence of your school climate on student success in the work world of tomorrow.

IMAGINATION
Visualize the ultimate school climate for providing a positive influence on student success in tomorrow's work world. Write a brief essay, taking into account: facilities, administrators, teachers, community support, curriculum, extracurricular activities, and school and classroom management, including scheduling, rules, and student assessment.

Name:

THINGS THAT MIGHT MAKE THE FUTURE BRIGHTER

Directions: Choose one or more of these future-related tasks to complete and share with others in your class.

TASK OPTION ONE: What would you most want to invent that would improve the future if you were given the unlimited funds, expertise, and technology to do so?

TASK OPTION TWO: If you were asked to identify the five most desirable places in the world that could serve as model communities for the future, what particular criterion or characteristics would be most important to you?

TASK OPTION THREE: How would you design a family fun park for the future that would be radically different from the amusement parks of today?

TASK OPTION FOUR: If you were backed by a group of global investors to create a collaborative rather than competitive sport throughout the world, what would it look like?

TASK OPTION FIVE: If you had the intelligence and power to solve one major problem in the world today that would never return in the future, what problem would you eradicate, and why?

TASK OPTION SIX: What addition would you make to the existing list of the Seven Wonders of the World?

TASK OPTION SEVEN: If you could proclaim a new international holiday, which could make the world a better place to live, what would it be, and how would it be celebrated?

TASK OPTION EIGHT: If you could resurrect one of the all-time greatest world leaders to serve as a model for future generations, whom would you choose, and why?

TASK OPTION NINE: If this generation could somehow give one of the following intangible gifts to every person born in the future, which one would you choose—freedom, peace, hope, or faith? Give reasons for your answer.

TASK OPTION TEN: What suggestions would you give to future generations for settling international differences?

Name: _____

DESIGNING A BILLBOARD TO PROMOTE CONSERVATION

Directions: One of the greatest challenges facing citizens of the world today is that of stewardship of the world's natural resources. It is our responsibility to care for these resources in order to pass them on to the next generation. Imagine that the United States government has authorized you to create and place a gigantic billboard somewhere in the United States that would attract the attention of motorists and convey the importance of conserving our natural resources. What would this billboard look like? Sketch your ideas below.

Name: _____

TO RECYCLE OR NOT TO RECYCLE

Directions: Although we are not often affected by this reality, the earth's natural resources are limited. It is the duty of responsible citizens to protect and preserve these resources for the generations of the future by consuming less and recycling more. To get you started thinking about recycling, discuss the following questions with a classmate:

(1) Even though recycling household goods does require time and patience, many people make a commitment to doing so on a regular basis, while others say the limited amount of actual reusable materials rendered make it a waste of time, and not worth the effort involved. Which point of view do you agree with? Give reasons for your answer.

(2) List at least five products that are recyclable, along with the natural material that each is derived from. Which of these products do you think is most in danger of being exhausted by consumers of your generation?

(3) In your opinion, are schools doing a good job of teaching today's students the importance of conserving natural resources, and are teachers and administrators providing good role models for students? What are some ways that "conservation education" could improve?

Society today has been labeled as "a throwaway society." What do you think this term means, and is it a fair label? Is today's society more wasteful of natural resources than the society of a hundred years ago? Why? Incorporating all that you have discussed about recycling, write a letter to the editor of your local newspaper, reminding him of the importance of actively preserving resources for future generations and the methods available to do this, including recycling.

DEAR EDITOR:

_____

_____

_____

_____

_____

_____

_____

_____

_____

Regards,

Name: _____

CONSUMERISM AND CAREERS OF THE FUTURE

Directions: The world of work and the world of consumerism twenty years from now will feature innovative products, services, and jobs that are likely to be very different from those we have available in our world today.

Speculate as to what each of the future-oriented jobs listed below will entail, and create a classified ad for one or more of them. Then, think about possible related products that will have to be manufactured and services that will have to be created for this new future of ours. Design an advertisement showing some of these products and services of the future. Do this on the back side of this sheet.

JOBS TO CONSIDER

1. Geriatric social worker
2. Genetic engineer
3. Robot technician
4. Space shuttle pilot
5. Space colony architect
6. Laser expert
7. Astrogeologist
8. Biotechnologist
9. Weather machinist
10. Food pill nutritionist
11. Planetary health physician
12. Space security agent
13. Time zone adjustor
14. Space historian
15. Traveling space physician
16. Artificial intelligence worker

Name: _____

SYMBOLS SAY A LOT

Directions: Flags, banners, icons, logos, letterheads, seals, and other graphics that symbolize values, beliefs, missions, covenants, and vows of importance are reminders of history and commitment, and often serve as rallying points for service and action. Think carefully about each term below before designing a symbol for each that could be recognized and respected by people around the world.

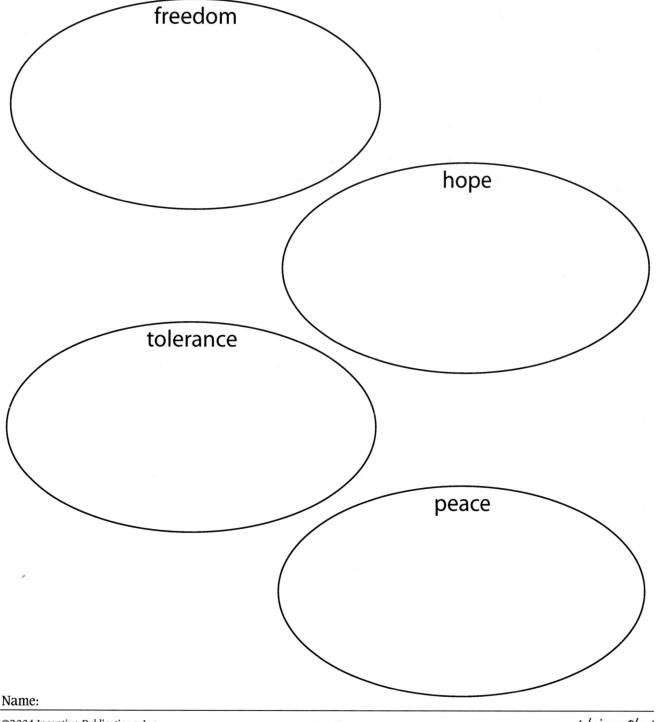

Name:

SOLVING SERIOUS PROBLEMS TODAY FOR A BETTER TOMORROW

Directions: Listed below, you will find nine problems that have reached crisis proportions in our country and world today. If solutions are not found, these problems will only become greater in the years ahead. Work with members of your group to suggest one possible solution to each problem. Write a summary statement of the group's suggestion in the spaces provided.

WORLD PROBLEM

OUR SOLUTION TO THE PROBLEM

1. Pollution _____

2. Terrorism _____

3. Crime and Violence _____

4. Prejudice & Hate _____

5. Poverty & Homelessness _____

6. Overpopulation _____

7. AIDS _____

8. Hunger _____

9. Health Care _____

Name: _____

©2004 Incentive Publications, Inc.
Nashville, TN

WHAT DOES THE FUTURE HOLD FOR YOU?

Directions: Polling is a method used by a group or an individual to find out about a target population's likes and dislikes, fears and feelings, or positions and perspectives on a certain issue. When one conducts a poll, these steps should be followed carefully: (1) State the purpose of your poll in specific terms. What are you trying to find out? (2) Identify the audience or target population you want to survey. (3) Design a questionnaire that you can give to a group of people who represent a sample of your larger target population. (4) Choose your sample or a small part of the population you want to survey. (5) Conduct your survey using the questionnaire. (6) Assess your results and draw your conclusions. In this activity, you are to design a questionnaire and conduct a poll to determine how students in your classroom or school feel about the future and what it has in store for them.

COMPLETE THIS OUTLINE TO HELP YOU PLAN AND CONDUCT YOUR POLL.

1. What is the specific purpose of your poll? State this goal in your own words.

    _____

    _____

2. What target population or audience are you trying to reach? State the ages and grades of the audience to be surveyed. _____

    _____

3. What questions do you want to ask in your survey? State these questions clearly and concisely. _____

    _____

    _____

4. How many people do you plan to survey in your sample? State the exact number.

    _____

5. When and where will you conduct the survey? State the time and location.

    _____

6. What are your results, and what conclusions can you make from these results? State the results for each question on the survey, and then try to draw some conclusions about what they mean as a whole.

    _____

    _____

    _____

    _____

Name:

©2004 INCENTIVE Publications, Inc.
Nashville, TN

Advisory Plus!

THEME: FUTURE   VALUE: VISION

MAY

RATING SCALE:

MY BEST WORK	MY SO-SO WORK	MY NOT SO GOOD WORK
☺	☺	☹

Draw the appropriate rating for your work in this module at the end of each statement.

1. Quality of my future-oriented graphic organizer .... ☐
2. Quality of my globalization reaction paragraphs .... ☐
3. Quality of my photo squares depicting life at school .... ☐
4. Quality of my multiple intelligence activity .... ☐
5. Quality of my summary statement about careers .... ☐
6. Quality of my piece of original writing .... ☐
7. Quality of my set of creative responses .... ☐
8. Quality of my group discussion skills .... ☐
9. Quality of my vision for the perfect community .... ☐
10. Quality of my set of flash cards to combat intolerance................... ☐
11. Quality of my mini-project about prejudice .... ☐
12. Quality of my original picture of the future .... ☐
13. Quality of my evaluation of the school climate .... ☐
14. Quality of my mini-task to make the future brighter .... ☐
15. Quality of my conservation billboard .... ☐
16. Quality of my letter to the editor .... ☐
17. Quality of my career advertisement .... ☐
18. Quality of my symbols .... ☐
19. Quality of my problem/solution chart .... ☐
20. Quality of my poll .... ☐

Name:

APPENDIX

ENGLISH LANGUAGE ARTS STANDARDS

GRADES K-8, INTERNATIONAL READING ASSOCIATION/ NATIONAL COUNCIL OF TEACHERS OF ENGLISH

Standard 1:

Students read a wide range of print and nonprint text to build an understanding of texts, of themselves, and of the cultures of the United States and the world, to acquire new information, to respond to the needs and demands of society and the workplace, and for personal fulfillment. Among these texts are fiction and nonfiction, classic and contemporary works.

Standard 2:

Students read a wide range of literature from many periods in many genres to build an understanding of the many dimensions (e.g. philosophical, ethical, aesthetic) of human experience.

Standard 3:

Students apply a wide range of strategies to comprehend, interpret, evaluate, and appreciate texts. They draw on their prior experience, their interactions with other readers and writers, their knowledge of word meaning and of other texts, their identification strategies, and their understanding of textual features (e.g., sound-letter correspondence, sentence structure, context, graphics).

Standard 4:

Students adjust their use of spoken, written, and visual language (e.g., conventions, style, vocabulary) to communicate effectively with a variety of audiences for a variety of purposes.

Standard 5:

Students employ a wide range of strategies as they write and use different writing process elements appropriately to communicate with different audiences for a variety of purposes.

Standard 6:

Students apply knowledge of language structure, language conventions (e.g., spelling and punctuation), media techniques, figurative language, and genre to create, critique, and discuss print and nonprint texts.

©2004 Incentive Publications, Inc.
Nashville, TN

Standard 7:

Students conduct research on issues and interests by generating ideas and questions, and by posing problems. They gather, evaluate, and synthesize data from a variety of sources (e.g., print and nonprint texts, artifacts, people) to communicate their discoveries in ways that suit their purpose and audience.

Standard 8:

Students use a variety of technological and informational resources (e.g., libraries, databases, computer networks, video) to gather and synthesize information and to create and to communicate knowledge.

Standard 9:

Students develop an understanding of and respect for diversity in language use, patterns, and dialects across cultures, ethnic groups, geographic regions, and social roles.

Standard 10:

Students whose first language is not English make use of their first language to develop competency in the English language arts and to develop understanding of content across the curriculum.

Standard 11:

Students participate as knowledgeable, reflective, creative, and critical members of a variety of literacy communities.

Standard 12:

Students use spoken, written, and visual language to accomplish their own purposes (e.g., for learning, enjoyment, persuasion, and the exchange of information).

Standards for the English Language Arts, by the International Reading Association and the National Council of Teachers of English, Copyright 1996 by the International Reading Association and the National Council of Teachers of English. Reprinted with permission.

NATIONAL COUNCIL OF TEACHERS OF MATHEMATICS STANDARDS AND DEFINITIONS

Mathematics as Problem Solving

In grades 5-8, the mathematics curriculum should include numerous and varied experiences with problem solving as a method of inquiry and application so that students can: use problem solving approaches to investigate and understand mathematical content; formulate problems from situations within and outside mathematics; develop and apply a variety of strategies to solve problems; with emphasis on multistep and nonroutine problems; verify and interpret results with respect to the original problem situations; and acquire confidence in using mathematics meaningfully.

Mathematics as Communication

In grades 5-8, the study of mathematics should include opportunities to communicate so that students can: model situations using oral, written, concrete, pictorial, graphical, and algebraic methods; reflect on and clarify their own thinking about mathematical ideas, including the role of definitions; use the skills of reading, listening, and viewing to interpret and evaluate mathematical ideas; discuss the mathematical ideas and make conjectures and convincing arguments; appreciate the value of mathematical notation and its role in the development of mathematical ideas.

Mathematics as Reasoning

In grades 5-8, reasoning shall permeate the mathematics curriculum so that students can: recognize and apply deductive reasoning processes, with special attention to spatial reasoning and reasoning with proportions and graphs; make and evaluate mathematical conjectures and arguments; validate their own thinking; appreciate the pervasive use and power of reasoning as a part of mathematics.

Mathematical Connections

In grades 5-8, the mathematics curriculum should include the investigation of mathematical connections so that students can: see mathematics as an integrated whole; explore problems and describe results using graphical, numerical, physical, algebraic, and verbal mathematical models or representations; use a mathematical idea to further their understanding of other mathematical ideas; apply mathematical thinking and modeling to solve problems that arise in other disciplines, such as art, music, psychology, science, and business; value the role of mathematics in our culture and society.

Number and Number Relationships

In grades 5-8, the mathematics curriculum should include the investigation of mathematical connections so that students can: understand and use numbers in a variety of equivalent forms in real-world problem situations; develop number sense for whole

©2004 Incentive Publications, Inc.
Nashville, TN

numbers, fractions, decimals, integers, and rational numbers; apply ratios, proportions, and percents in a variety of situations; investigate relationships among fractions, decimals, and percents in a variety of situations; represent numerical relationships in 1- and 2-dimensional graphs.

Number Systems and Number Theory

In grades 5-8, the mathematics curriculum should include the study of number systems and number theory so that students can; understand and appreciate the need for numbers beyond the whole numbers; develop and use order relations for whole numbers, fractions, decimals, integers, and rational numbers; extend their understanding of whole number operations to fractions, decimals, integers, and rational numbers; understand how the basic arithmetic operations are related to one another; develop and apply number theory concepts (e.g., primes, factors, and multiples) in real-world and mathematical problem situations.

Computation and Estimation

In grades 5-8, the mathematics curriculum should develop the concepts underlying computation and estimation in various contexts so that students can: compute with whole numbers, fractions, decimals, integers, and rational numbers; develop, analyze, and explain procedures for computation and techniques for estimation; develop, analyze, and explain methods for solving proportions; select and use an appropriate method for computing from among mental arithmetic, paper-and-pencil, calculator, and computer methods, use computation, estimation, and proportions to solve problems; and use estimation to check the reasonableness of results.

Patterns and Functions

In grades 5-8, the mathematics curriculum should include explorations of patterns and functions so that students can: describe, extend, analyze, and create a wide variety of patterns; describe and represent relationships with tables, graphs, and rules; analyze functional relationships to explain how a change in one quantity results in change in another; use patterns and functions to represent and solve problems.

Algebra

In grades 5-8, the mathematics curriculum should include explorations of algebraic concepts and processes so that students can: understand the concepts of variable, expression, and equation; represent situations and number patterns with tables, graphs, verbal rules, and equations and explore the interrelationships of these representations; analyze tables and graphs to identify properties and relationships; develop confidence in solving linear equations using concrete, informal, and formal methods; investigate inequalities and nonlinear equations informally; apply algebraic methods to solve a variety of real-world and mathematical problems.

Statistics

In grades 5-8, the mathematics curriculum should include exploration of statistics in real-world situations so that students can: systematically collect, organize, and describe date; construct, read, and interpret tables, charts, and graphs; make inferences and convincing arguments that are based on data analysis; evaluate arguments that are based on data analysis; and develop an appreciation for statistical methods as powerful means for decision-making.

Probability

In grades 5-8, the mathematics curriculum should include explorations of probability in real-world situations so that students can: model situations by devising and carrying out experiments or simulations to determine probabilities; model situations by constructing a sample space to determine probabilities; appreciate the power of using a probability model by comparing experimental results with mathematical expectations; make predictions that are based on experimental or theoretical probabilities; develop an appreciation for the pervasive use of probability in the real world.

Geometry

In grades 5-8, the mathematics curriculum should include the study of the geometry of one, two, and three dimensions in a variety of situations so that students can: identify, describe, compare, and classify geometric figures; visualize and represent geometric figures with special attention to developing spatial sense; explore transformations of geometric figures; represent and solve problems using geometric models; understand and apply geometric properties and relationships; and develop an appreciation of geometry as a means of describing the physical world.

Measurement

In grades 5-8, the mathematics curriculum should include extensive concrete experiences using measurement so that students can: extend their understanding of the process of measurement; estimate, make, and use measurements to describe and compare phenomena; select appropriate units and tools to measure to the degree of accuracy required in a particular situation; understand the structure and use of systems of measurement; extend their understanding of the concepts of perimeter, area, volume, angle measure, capacity, and weight and mass; develop the concepts of rate and other derived and indirect measurements; and develop formulas and procedures for determining measures to solve problems.

Reprinted with permission from Standards for Mathematics for Grades 5–8, copyright 2001 by the National Council of Teachers of Mathematics.

NATIONAL ACADEMY OF SCIENCES STANDARDS

Unifying Concepts and Processes

As a result of activities in grades 5-8, all students should develop understanding and abilities aligned with the following concepts: systems, order, and organization; evidence, models, and explanation; constancy, change, and measurement; evolution and equilibrium; and form and function.

Science as Inquiry

As a result of activities in grades 5-8, all students should develop: abilities necessary to do scientific inquiry and understandings about scientific inquiry.

Physical Science

As a result of their activities in grades 5-8, all students should develop an understanding of: properties and changes of properties in matter, motions and force, and transfer of energy.

Life Science

As a result of their activities in grades 5-8, all students should develop an understanding of: structure and function in living systems; reproduction and heredity; regulations and behavior; populations and ecosystems; and diversity and adaptations of organisms.

Earth and Space Science

As a result of their activities in grades 5-8, all students should develop an understanding of: structure of the Earth system; Earth's history; and Earth in the solar system.

Science and Technology

As a result of their activities in grades 5-8, all students should develop: abilities of technological design and understandings about science and technology.

Science in Personal and Social Perspectives

As a result of their activities in grades 5-8, all students should develop understandings of: personal health; populations, resources, and environments; natural hazards, risks and benefits; and science and technology in society.

History and Nature of Science

As a result of activities in grades 5-8, all students should develop understanding of: science as human endeavor; nature of science; and history of science.

Reprinted with permission from National Science Education Standards.
Copyright 1996 by the National Academy of Sciences.
Courtesy of the National Academy Press, Washington, D.C.

CURRICULUM STANDARDS FOR SOCIAL STUDIES

Culture

Social studies programs should include experiences that provide for the study of culture and cultural diversity so that the middle grades learner can:

1. compare similarities and differences in the ways groups, societies, and cultures meet human needs and concerns.

2. explain how information and experiences may be interpreted by people from diverse cultural perspectives and frames of reference.

3. explain and give examples of how language, literature, the arts, architecture, other artifacts, traditions, beliefs, values, and behaviors contribute to the development and transmission of culture.

4. explain why individuals and groups respond differently to their physical and social environments and/or changes to them on the basis of shared assumptions, values, and beliefs.

5. articulate the implications of cultural diversity, as well as cohesion within and across groups.

Time, Continuity, and Change

Social studies programs should include experiences that provide for the study of the ways human beings view themselves in and over time, so that the middle grades learner can:

1. demonstrate an understanding that different scholars may describe the same event or situation in different ways but must provide reasons or evidence for their views.

2. identify and use key concepts such as chronology, causality, change, conflict, and complexity to explain, analyze, and show connections among patterns of historical change and continuity.

3. identify and describe selected historical periods and patterns of change within and across cultures, such as the rise of civilizations, the development of transportation systems, the growth and breakdown of colonial systems, and others.

4. identify and use processes important to reconstructing and reinterpreting the past, such as using a variety of sources, providing, validating, and weighing evidence for claims, checking credibility of sources, and searching for causality.

5. develop critical sensitivities such as empathy and skepticism regarding attitudes, values, and behaviors of people in different historical contexts.

6. use knowledge of facts and concepts drawn from history, along with methods of historical inquiry, to inform decision-making about and action-taking on public issues.

People, Places, and Environments

Social studies programs should include experiences that provide for the study of people, places, and environments, so that the middle grades learner can:

1. elaborate mental maps of locales, regions, and the world that demonstrate understanding of relative location, direction, size, and shape.

2. create, interpret, use, and distinguish various representations of the earth, such as maps, globes, and photographs.

©2004 Incentive Publications, Inc.
Nashville, TN

3. use appropriate resources, data sources, and geographic tools such as aerial photographs, satellite images, geographic information systems (GIS), map projections, and cartography to generate, manipulate, and interpret information such as atlases, data bases, grid systems, charts, graphs, and maps.

4. estimate distance, calculate scale, and distinguish other geographic relationships such as population density and spatial distribution patterns.

5. locate and describe varying landforms and geographic features, such as mountains, plateaus, islands, rain forests, deserts, and oceans, and explain their relationships within the ecosystem.

6. describe physical system changes such as seasons, climate and weather, and the water cycle and identify geographic patterns associated with them.

7. describe how people create places that reflect cultural values and ideals as they build neighborhoods, parks, shopping centers, and the like.

8. examine, interpret, and analyze physical and cultural patterns and their interactions, such as land use, settlement patterns, cultural transmission of customs and ideas, and ecosystem changes.

9. describe ways that historical events have been influenced by, and have influenced, physical and human geographic factors in local, regional, national, and global settings.

10. observe and speculate about social and economic effects of environmental changes and crises resulting from phenomena such as floods, storms, and drought.

11. propose, compare, and evaluate alternative uses of land and resources in communities, regions, nations, and the world.

Individual Development and Identity

Social studies programs should include experiences that provide for the study of individual development and identity, so that the middle grades learner can:

1. relate personal changes to social, cultural, and historical contexts.

2. describe personal connections to place—as associated with community, nation, and the world.

3. describe the ways family, gender, ethnicity, nationality, and institutional affiliations contribute to personal identity.

4. relate such factors as physical endowment and capabilities, learning, motivation, personality, perception, and behavior to individual development.

5. identify and describe ways regional, ethnic, and national cultures influence individuals' daily lives.

6. identify and describe the influence of perception, attitudes, values, and beliefs on personal identity.

7. identify and interpret examples of stereotyping, conformity, and altruism.

8. work independently and cooperatively to accomplish goals.

Individuals, Groups, and Institutions

Social studies programs should include experiences that provide for the study of interaction among individuals, groups, and institutions, so that the middle grades learner can:

1. demonstrate an understanding of concepts such as role, status, and social class in describing the interactions of individuals and social groups.

2. analyze group and institutional influences on people, events, and elements of culture.

3. describe the various forms institutions take and the interactions of people with institutions.

4. identify and analyze examples of tensions between expressions of individuality and group or institutional efforts to promote social conformity.

5. identify and describe examples of tensions between belief systems and government policies and laws.

6. describe the role of institutions in furthering both continuity and change.

7. apply knowledge of how groups and institutions work to meet individual needs and promote the common good.

Power, Authority, and Governance

Social studies programs should include experiences that provide for the study of how people create and change structures of power, authority, and governance, so that the middle grades learner can:

1. examine persistent issues involving the rights, roles, and status of the individual in relation to the general welfare.

2. describe the purpose of government and how its powers are acquired, used, and justified.

3. analyze and explain ideas and governmental mechanisms to meet needs and wants of citizens, regulate territory, manage conflict, and establish order and security.

4. describe the ways nations and organizations respond to forces of unity and diversity affecting order and security.

5. identify and describe the basic features of the political system in the United States, and identify representative leaders from various levels and branches of government.

6. explain conditions, actions, and motivations that contribute to conflict and cooperation within and among nations.

7. describe and analyze the role of technology in communications, transportation, information processing, weapons development, or other areas as they contribute to or help resolve conflicts.

8. explain and apply concepts such as power, role, status, justice, and influence to the examination of persistent issues and social problems.

9. give examples and explain how governments attempt to achieve their stated ideals at home and abroad.

Production, Distribution, and Consumption

Social studies programs should include experiences that provide for the study of how people organize for the production, distribution, and consumption of goods and services, so that the middle grades learner can:

1. give and explain examples of ways that economic systems structure choices about how goods and services are to be produced and distributed.

2. describe the role that supply and demand, prices, incentives, and profits play in determining what is produced and distributed in a competitive market system.

3. explain the difference between private and public goods and services.

4. describe a range of examples of the various institutions that make up economic systems such as households, business firms, banks, government agencies, labor unions, and corporations.

5. describe the role of specialization and exchange in the economic process.

6. explain and illustrate how values and beliefs influence different economic decisions.

7. differentiate among various forms of exchange and money.

8. compare basic economic systems according to who determined what is produced, distributed, and consumed.

9. use economic concepts to help explain historical and current developments and issues in local, national, or global contexts.

10. use economic reasoning to compare different proposals for dealing with a contemporary social issue such as unemployment, acid rain, or high quality education.

Science, Technology, and Society

Social studies programs should include experiences that provide for the study of relationships among science, technology, and society, so that the middle grades learner can:

1. examine and describe the influence of culture on scientific and technological choices and advancement, such as in transportation, medicine, and warfare.

2. show through specific examples how science and technology have changed people's perceptions of the social and natural world, such as in their relationship to the land, animal life, family life, and economic needs, wants, and security.

3. describe examples in which values, beliefs, and attitudes have been influenced by new scientific and technological knowledge, such as the invention of the printing press, conceptions of the universe, applications of atomic energy, and genetic discoveries.

4. explain the need for laws and policies to govern scientific and technological applications, such as in the safety and well-being of workers and consumers and the regulation of utilities, radio, and television.

5. seek reasonable and ethical solutions to problems that arise when scientific advancements and social norms or values come into conflict.

Global Connections

Social studies programs should include experiences that provide for the study of global connections and interdependence, so that the middle grades learner can:

1. describe instances in which language, art, music, belief systems, and other cultural elements can facilitate global understanding or cause misunderstanding.

2. analyze examples of conflict, cooperation, and interdependence among groups, societies, and nations.

3. describe and analyze the effects of changing technologies on the global community.

4. explore the causes, consequences, and possible solutions to persistent, contemporary, and emerging global issues, such as health, security, resource allocation, economic development, and environmental quality.

5. describe and explain the relationships and tensions between national sovereignty and global interests, in such matters as territory, natural resources, trade, use of technology, and welfare of people.

6. demonstrate understanding of concerns, standards, issues, and conflicts related to universal human rights.

7. identify and describe the roles of international and multinational organizations.

Civic Ideals and Practices

Social studies programs should include experiences that provide for the study of the ideals, principles, and practices of citizenship in a democratic republic, so that the middle grades learner can:

1. examine the origins and continuing influence of key ideals of the democratic republican form of government, such as individual human dignity, liberty, justice, equality, and the rule of law.

2. identify and interpret sources and examples of the rights and responsibilities of citizens.

3. locate, access, analyze, organize, and apply information about selected public issues—recognizing and explaining multiple points of view.

4. practice forms of civic discussion and participation consistent with the ideals of citizens in a democratic republic.

5. explain and analyze various forms of citizen action that influence public policy decisions.

6. identify and explain the roles of formal and informal political actors in influencing and shaping public policy and decision-making.

7. analyze the influence of diverse forms of public opinion on the development of public policy and decision-making.

8. analyze the effectiveness of selected public policies and citizen behaviors in realizing the stated ideals of a democratic republican form of government.

9. explain the relationship between policy statements and action plans used to address issues of public concern.

10. examine strategies designed to strengthen the "common good," which consider a range of options for citizen action.

Source: Curriculum Standards for Social Studies

GARDNER'S MULTIPLE INTELLIGENCES

Dr. Howard Gardner's Theory of Multiple Intelligences is an interesting way to teach a concept or skill in any subject area. Dr. Gardner has identified eight multiple intelligences. He defines these intelligences as eight different ways of knowing, perceiving, and understanding the world around us. Gardner also makes it clear that one or two intelligences are often stronger and more developed in a person, although everyone has the capacity for nurturing all eight. It is important that teachers design lesson plans with these multiple intelligences in mind and that students practice using all of these intelligences in their work.

INTELLIGENCE	DESCRIPTION	STRATEGIES	CAREERS
VERBAL/ LINGUISTIC	Involves ease in producing language, and sensitivity to the nuances, order, and rhythm of words	Journal writing, making speeches, storytelling, reading	Trial lawyers, poets, teachers, statesmen
LOGICAL/ MATHEMATICAL	Related to the ability to reason deductively or inductively, and to recognize and manipulate abstract relationships	Developing outlines, creating codes, calculating, problem solving	Engineers, scientists, military strategists, computer programmers
VISUAL/ SPATIAL	Includes the ability to create visual-spatial representations of the world and to transfer them mentally or concretely	Drawing, using guided imagery, making mind maps, making charts	Architects, astronomers, artists, map makers

Advisory Plus!

INTELLIGENCE	DESCRIPTION	STRATEGIES	CAREERS
BODY/ KINESTHETIC	Involves using one's physical body to solve problems, make things, and convey ideas and emotions	Role-playing, dancing, playing games, using manipulatives	Athletes, computer keyboarders, actresses, mechanics
MUSICAL/ RHYTHMIC	Encompasses sensitivity to the pitch, timbre, and rhythm of sounds as well as responsiveness to the emotional implication of these elements of music	Singing, performing, writing compositions, playing instruments, performing choral readings	Musicians, bandleaders, composers, singers
INTERPERSONAL	Refers to the ability to work effectively with other people and to understand them and recognize their goals, motivations, and intentions	Working with mentors and tutors, participating in interactive projects, using cooperative learning	Social workers, coaches, religious leaders, sales managers
INTRAPERSONAL	Entails the ability to understand one's own emotions, goals, and intentions	Using learning centers, participating in self-reflection tasks, using higher-order reasoning, taking personal inventories	Counselors, authors, philosophers, entrepreneurs
NATURALISTIC	Emphasizes the capacity to recognize flora and fauna, to make distinctions in the natural world, and to use the ability productively in activities such as farming and biological sciences	Observing, digging, planting, displaying, sorting, uncovering, and relating	Conservationists, forest rangers, farmers, biologists

OUTLINE FOR CREATING YOUR OWN RUBRIC

Directions: Use this outline and the criteria for creating your own rubric, project, or task. A holistic rubric assigns levels of performance with descriptors for each level. An analytic rubric assigns levels of performance with numerical points allocated for every descriptor at each level.

EXCELLENT LEVELS

DESCRIPTORS: POINTS AWARDED:

_____   _____

_____   _____

_____   _____

GOOD LEVELS

DESCRIPTORS: POINTS AWARDED:

_____   _____

_____   _____

_____   _____

NEEDS IMPROVEMENT

DESCRIPTORS: POINTS AWARDED:

_____   _____

_____   _____

_____   _____

Note: You can add additional levels and descriptors as needed. You can also create your own labels for the levels and use such categories as: Exemplary Achievement, Commendable Achievement, Limited Evidence of Achievement, and Minimal Achievement.

Comments by Student: _____

_____

Signed _____ Date _____

Comments by Teacher: _____

_____

Signed _____ Date _____

GUIDELINES FOR USING RUBRICS TO EVALUATE THE SUCCESS OF AN ADVISORY PROGRAM

1. Agree on a definition of a rubric and its importance to the evaluation process. The purpose of a rubric is to answer the question: "What are the conditions of success and to what degree are those conditions met by the student involved in a specific learning task?"

2. Effective rubrics reflect the most important elements of an assigned task, product, or performance, and they enable both student and teacher to accurately depict the level of competence or stage of development of that student.

3. Effective rubrics encourage student self-evaluations and, in fact, are shared with students prior to beginning the task, so students know exactly what represents quality work.

4. Rubrics are designed to explain more concretely what a child knows and can do and are less subjective than other means of student evaluation.

5. Every rubric must have two components, which are: (1) characteristics or criteria for quality work on a specific task, and (2) determination of the specific levels of proficiency or degrees of success for each part of a task.

6. A holistic rubric consists of paragraphs arranged in a hierarchy, so each level of proficiency has a paragraph describing factors that would result in that specific level.

7. An analytic rubric consists of a listing of criteria most characteristic of that task accompanied the degrees of success for each model listed separately beside or under each criterion.

8. Before implementing rubrics in a discipline, it is important to define and discuss the elements of a quality performance in that discipline and to collect samples of rubrics as models for scrutiny and potential application.

9. Before implementing rubrics in a discipline, study samples of student work to determine realistic attributes common to varied performances at different levels of proficiency. Translate these attributes into descriptors for the degrees of proficiency, and then establish a rating scale to delineate those degrees of proficiency.

©2004 Incentive Publications, Inc.
Nashville, TN

10. Avoid using generalities such as good, better, little, none, or somewhat in your rating scales; quantify and qualify in more specific terms. Construct analytical rubrics with four to six degrees of proficiency for each criterion. Then, weight each criterion to determine the percentage or number of points each is worth.

11. Distribute and discuss any rubric directly with the student before he or she embarks on the assigned product or performance task. Encourage the student to set personal goals for their desired level of accomplishment on each criterion. Insist that students revise their work if it does not meet minimum expectations on any criterion of the task.

12. When introducing rubrics to students, start out by collaboratively constructing a rubric for a fun class event such as planning a party, structuring a field trip, or designing a contest.

13. Remember that to be most effective as an important component of language arts programs, rubrics must be accompanied by carefully planned opportunities for meta-cognitive reflections throughout the assessment experience. While rubrics are comprised of checklists containing sets of criteria for measuring the elements of product, performance, or portfolio, the meta-cognitive reflections provide for self-assessment observations completely unique to the student's own learning goals, expectations, and experiences.

14. The use of rubrics can augment, reinforce, personalize, and strengthen, but not replace, the assessment program mandated by curriculum guidelines or system requirements. As with any well-balanced assessment program, the master teacher or teaching team will continue to take full advantage of all tools, strategies, and techniques available to construct and make use of a balanced assessment program to meet individual needs.

ALTERNATIVES FOR THE STANDARD ADVISORY SESSION

Procedural Suggestion: Examine each of the activities listed here as potential uses for a quality advisory period. Try to think of a particular task that you have done successfully in the classroom for each of the given categories. Be ready to share the task with others who might want to field test it with their own group of advisees.

1. Small and whole group discussion

2. Impromptu and mini-speeches or talks

3. Games or simulations

4. Book, movie, and television reviews

5. Role-plays and case studies

6. Study and test review sessions

7. Community field trips and experiences

8. Speaker's bureau of adults from the community at large

9. Virtual field trips to special websites using the Internet

10. Learning log or journal entries

11. Learning stations or portable desktop centers

12. Spelling bees, contests, and other academic competitions

13. Skits and plays

14. Silent sustained reading sessions with follow-up book dialogues

15. Demonstrations or exhibits

16. Experiments or investigations

17. Interviews, surveys, or questionnaires

18. Conflict resolution exercises

19. Panels, debates, and round table conversations

20. Current events

21. Films, movies, or videotapes

22. Holiday celebrations

23. Special club or activity days

24. Career and workplace explorations

25. Individual counseling and conference sessions

26. Service learning projects such as visits to nursing home, community beautification, cards and letters to shut-ins, etc.

27. Special art project related to advisory topic

28. Peer tutoring

29. Teacher appreciation project

30. Bonus library or media center period to pursue research related to advisory topic (to be arranged in advance with librarian or media center director)

31. Music or art appreciation session with parent or community resource person or concert of recorded music related to advisory topic

32. Debate to present two opposing views of an issue important to the advisory group

33. Free reading period, to be set aside in advance to allow both students and teachers to bring special reading material

CALENDAR FOR CREATING A MONTHLY ADVISORY PROGRAM

SUNDAY	MONDAY	TUESDAY	WEDNESDAY	THURSDAY	FRIDAY	SATURDAY
☐	☐	☐	☐	☐	☐	☐
☐	☐	☐	☐	☐	☐	☐
☐	☐	☐	☐	☐	☐	☐
☐	☐	☐	☐	☐	☐	☐
☐	☐	☐	☐	☐	☐	☐

CHECKLIST OF STUDENT NEEDS TO BE MET THROUGH ADVISORY

☐ 1. Need for movement and physical activity

☐ 2. Need for peer relationships and interactions

☐ 3. Need for active, over passive, learning experiences

☐ 4. Need for confronting moral and ethical questions directly

☐ 5. Need for diversity

☐ 6. Need for adult approval and affirmation of love

☐ 7. Need for opportunities for self-exploration and self-definition

☐ 8. Need for clear limits and structures that are fair and reasonable

☐ 9. Need for meaningful participation in school community

☐ 10. Need for confirmation of body changes and growth spurts as normal

☐ 11. Need for introspection and reflection in personal thoughts and feelings

☐ 12. Need for recognizing relevance of what is learned in school to real-world situations

☐ 13. Need for idealism and ambiguity when it comes to the meaning of life

☐ 14. Need for optimism and hope when it comes to the future

☐ 15. Need for competence and achievement in accomplishing tasks

☐ 16. Need for exploring options, making choices, and investigating alternatives as part of the schooling process

©2004 Incentive Publications, Inc.
Nashville, TN

Advisory Plus!

KEY ELEMENTS OF A SUCCESSFUL ADVISORY SESSION

1. Each advisor plays the role of a child advocate representing that student at team meetings, screening meetings, parent conferences, and other student/staff sessions as needed.

2. Each advisor initiates intervention procedures and referrals both within the advisory setting and, if necessary, in collaboration with counseling services.

3. Each advisor maintains a line of communication with the advisee's academic teachers and with the advisee's parents or guardians.

4. Each advisor engages in individual conferences with advisees on a predetermined and consistent basis.

5. Each advisor maintains accurate records on advisees, including such tools as an advisee information folder, advisee academic plan card, advisee attendance/behavior record, advisee report card and progress report, and advisee test scores, to name a few.

6. Each advisor supports the advisory concept and works to improve his/her performance in the advisory role and setting.

7. Each advisor is well informed on the unique needs and characteristics of the early adolescent and of the advisees assigned in his/her advisory class.

8. Each advisor becomes the single most important adult in the school for his/her advisees.

9. Each advisory class has a reasonable teacher-pupil ratio.

10. Each advisory class has a specific time and place to meet that is regularly scheduled.

11. Each advisory class meets a minimum of three times a week for an average of 20 to 30 minutes a day, or meets on an alternative predetermined plan.

12. Each advisory class provides advisees with activities that are varied, active, and student-centered.

13. Each advisory class has a common core curriculum with flexibility in its implementation.

14. Each advisory class represents a place where both advisors and advisees look forward to advisory time and tasks.

15. Each advisory class places a high emphasis on individual learning styles.

16. Each advisory class maintains a balance of individual, small group, and large group activities.

17. Each advisory class infuses higher-order creative and critical thinking skills whenever able to do so.

18. Each advisory class emphasizes an advisee's academic, social, emotional, physical, or psychological self-concept in its program.

ANNOTATED BIBLIOGRAPHY OF OTHER RESOURCES
FOR ADVISORY

Advisory & Affective Education By Imogene Forte and Sandra Schurr; 1997
   Research-based lessons and activities to help middle graders grow as students and
   as people

Challenges & Choices By Nancy Ullinskey and Lorri Hibbert; 1994
   Nine original stories highlight sensitive issues commonly faced by students.

Character Education: Grades 6-12, Years One and Two By John Heidel and
   Marion Lyman-Mersereau; 1999
   Complete program designed for a single classroom or an entire school. Values are taught
   in a monthly format through discussion questions, proverbs, activities, and stories from
   myriad cultures.

It Takes Character! By Cathy Griggs Newton; 2003
   Field guide for middle school youth to help their understanding of character and behavior
   to all the important aspects of life; such as relationships, school success, performance in
   sports/activities, having fun, etc.

I've Got Me & I'm Glad By Farnette, Forte, & Loss; 1989
   Self-awareness resource containing reproducible activities for students.

The Me I'm Learning to Be By Imogene Forte; 1991
   Self-awareness book filled with reproducible activity pages focused on feelings, attitudes,
   and self-esteem issues.

Partners in Learning and Growing By Jan and Ed Philpot; 1994
   Collection of original programs to foster community and parental involvement in the
   school and classroom

People Need Each Other By Farnette, Forte, and Loss; 1989
   Reproducible activity pages help students how to live, play, and work with others

Risk It! By Cathy Griggs Newton; 1996
   Shows teachers how to develop opportunities for positive risk in the classroom by directly
   addressing the risk-taking behaviors of young people.

INDEX

©2004 INCENTIVE Publications, Inc.
Nashville, TN

INDEX